DATE DUE

BUYographics

BUYographics

How Demographic and Economic Changes Will

Reinvent the Way Marketers Reach Consumers

Matt Carmichael

palgrave
macmillan

First published in 2013 by PALGRAVE MACMILLAN® in the United States—a division of St. Martin's Press LLC, 175 Fifth Avenue, New York, NY 10010.

Where this book is distributed in the UK, Europe and the rest of the world, this is by Palgrave Macmillan, a division of Macmillan Publishers Limited, registered in England, company number 785998, of Houndmills, Basingstoke, Hampshire RG21 6XS.

Palgrave Macmillan is the global academic imprint of the above companies and has companies and representatives throughout the world.

Palgrave® and Macmillan® are registered trademarks in the United States, the United Kingdom, Europe and other countries.

ISBN: 978-1-137-27863-0

Some material herein appeared in *Advertising Age* and on adage.com as part of the American Consumer Project. That material is reprinted here with permission of *Advertising Age,* copyright Crain Communications Inc.

Esri Tapestry data was provided courtesy of Esri and is used herein with permission. Copyright © 2013 Esri. All rights reserved.

Patchwork Nation data is reproduced courtesy of the Jefferson Institute, www.patchworknation.org.

Maps in Appendix II reproduced courtesy of Leo Burnett.

Library of Congress Cataloging-in-Publication Data

Carmichael, Matt.
  Buyographics : how demographic and economic changes will reinvent the way marketers reach consumers / Matt Carmichael.
    pages   cm
  ISBN 978-1-137-27863-0 (alk. paper)
  1. Consumer behavior—Social aspects. 2. Age. 3. Consumption (Economics) 4. Marketing. I. Title.
HF5415.32.C37   2013
658.8'34—dc23

2013014652

A catalogue record of the book is available from the British Library.

Design by Letra Libre Inc.

First edition: November 2013

10 9 8 7 6 5 4 3 2 1

Printed in the United States of America.

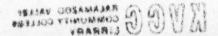

To my family for their inspiration, motivation, and unwavering support.

Contents

List of Figures

Acknowledgments

FIRST AND FOREMOST I WANT TO THANK ALFREDO, ANDREW, BASHA, CHRIS, Dale, Jay, Liz, Michael, Sandra, Rosemary, and their families. This book would never have been written if they hadn't been willing to open their lives and often their homes to a total stranger and, by extension, to all of you. Thanks for allowing me to tell your stories. Also to everyone along the way who helped connect me to you, especially the folks at Communispace, which used its online community-building skills to help me find some needles in haystacks.

My family deserve infinite thanks: my wife for her incredible support of this project and all it required of us and for picking up the slack when I was at the office more than at home; the twins for inspiring the project; and my elder daughter for her constant interest in the book after I explained that her daddy wouldn't have to go live in the library himself once he was an author. Also, to my very literary parents and sister for leaving me little choice but to be journalist/writer, and to Grandpa Ray and Grandma Darcy for their invaluable sitting services.

My editor at *Advertising Age,* Abbey Klaassen, not only listened with an open mind when I pitched her on the scope of the Consumer Project but gave it the resources it needed to happen. Further, the project would never have happened without David Klein, Allison Arden, and the rest of the *Ad Age* and Crain family. Particular thanks to Judann Pollack for editing many of the original stories, to Charlie Moran and Rahmin Pavlovic for helping make maps and databases, to Jesper Goransson and Jenn Chui for making it look good in print, and to Kevin Brown and Brad Johnson for being Kevin and Brad.

Three people in particular made the transition from magazine project to book happen. My patient and spot-on editor, Laurie Harting, who made this book much, much better than it ever would have been otherwise. And of course my fantastic agent, Cynthia Manson, and my lawyer, Thomas Levinson at Reed Smith. You should buy his book, too.

I also wish to thank the rest of the team at Palgrave Macmillan for stellar work in bringing this book to you and getting *Buyographics* into the world. Thanks to Lauren LoPinto, Alan Bradshaw, Elizabeth Tone, Lindsey Ruthen, Yasmin Mathew, and copy editor Georgia Maas who put the 'r' back in "throng."

Journal Communications was kind enough to accept this project as part of the deal when I joined, and I thank Bob Schwartzman and Casey Hester for letting me make room for it.

I was fortunate to have Stephen J. Serio shoot my author photo. He must have a good camera because his photos are always inspiring.

There's a lot of data in this book from a lot of great organizations. Thanks to the great people I worked with at each of them, including John Fetto at Experian Marketing Solutions, Julian Baim at GfK MRI, Andrew Lipsman at comScore, and Steve Krauss at Ipsos Mendelsohn. Also, to Andrea Bradner and David Shanker, who have since moved on from my survey partner, Ipsos Observer, and to Natalie Robuck there who oversaw the survey that was the backbone of chapter ten.

I'd also like to thank all the great people I met as I toured many of these counties, but especially Diane Travis, Ray San Fratello, Jamie Cox, Josephine Picerno, Kim Myers, and the fine folks in the Wednesday senior's league at the Clermont Bowling Center.

Very special thanks go to Donna Fancher at Esri who has been a prime enabler for this demographics junkie. Esri Tapestry data was provided courtesy of Esri and is used herein with permission. Copyright 2013 Esri. All rights reserved.

Dante Chinni's work with the Patchwork Nation was an inspiration for all of this. Thanks to Aaron Presnall at the Jefferson Institute for allowing me to use the framework.

Carol Foley's unending curiosity gives agency research a good name. She and the team at Leo Burnett who conducted the automotive research with me were a joy to work with.

Along the way I had great conversations with many amazing people about this book and related topics. Many are quoted on the record in the book. Some are not. Now that it's done, I owe each of you, especially George Scribner, Rose Cameron, Bill Frey, Dee Cohn, John Bracken, Bob Shullman, and Margaret Mueller, another beverage or two.

And finally the existence of *American Demographics* really set the stage for bringing this entire field of research into modern marketing. Its founder, Peter Francese, has been a great mentor throughout this process.

BUYographics

Introduction

PEOPLE SAY THAT WRITING A BOOK IS LIKE HAVING A CHILD. SO IT'S FITTING that this book started with an ultrasound.

It was early on and we were at the doctor's office awaiting confirmation that we were indeed pregnant. That thing on TV shows where the ultrasound tech tells you the gel will be cold is not true, or at least I've never heard an actual tech say those words. Instead, as she peered at the blurry image on her screen, she asked, "How do you feel about a large family?"

Twins!

We were skipping right from a three-person to a five-person household. I can give you all kinds of stats about five-person households. There aren't that many of them—they account for a mere 6 percent of households, but they're valuable consumers. Partially because of their size, these families spend 60 percent more than the average household.[1] I could tell you historical trends for twins and other "high-order" birthrates (short version: they are spiking). I could tell you about the Chicago-area fifth grade class that features a record twenty-two sets of twins.[2]

I was, at the end of the day, becoming just another demographic statistic. Granted, I was becoming not a trend-setter, but a trend-bucker. Peter Francese, the founder of *American Demographics* magazine and someone I would consider a mentor, is fond of pointing out that I have a way of defying all of the trends I write about.

In that way, the twins became an ongoing reminder that every number I write about is made up of individuals. Each number has a story. Including the number that is me.

What I didn't realize at that moment, shell-shocked as I was, is just how much all of our spending patterns would change. We weren't moving from one kid to two—we were adding that all-important third. Our car would no longer suffice because it could hold only *two* car seats. Hello, minivan. My wife and I thought we had all the stuff we needed, but now we had to buy it all again. Stroller, crib, bouncer, high chair—and a bigger kitchen table to put them at—the list went on. And so did the diapers.

My point is that demographics drive spending. My new demographic drives spending to Costco in a Honda Odyssey.

As a journalist, I have written a lot about the intersection of demographics and the economy. This all really made that research hit home. My situation also made me want to dig deeper. The trends taking place at both a macro level and an individual level—from cord-cutting consumers to aging Boomers—present challenges and opportunities for media and marketing alike.

Talk of "big data" is all the rage these days, especially in the fields of marketing and advertising. Marketers, media companies, and enterprising third parties are mining, extracting in the guise of games, and bartering for terabytes and petabytes of data each day from consumers bombarded with permission requests and privacy policies. All of this data gets algorithmed until the product seller knows what the buyers want before the buyers know it themselves.

At least, that's how it's promised to work.

But the truth is that even with all the data in the world, it's extremely difficult to find the insights buried within. For brands looking to impact an individual purchase decision—millions of times over—finding the stories in the data and translating them into something actionable is no easy task.

The more I loaded up my credit card at Amazon.com and various online and offline baby-related retailers, the more I thought about how obvious it was that something was going on with my spending. What if marketers could figure this out? I wondered.

Turns out, some of them can. How do they do it? With big data, coupled with demographic savvy.

I see the interplay of demographics and big data working like this: Big data lets marketers apply macro trends to individuals. Big data also makes it easier for marketers to aggregate what might otherwise be small disparate groups into an audience that's large enough to message and sell to.

It can then target that audience through direct mail, online, and by other means with a tailored message. It can also surface all kinds of other trends. There's the famous example of Walmart identifying beer and strawberry Pop-Tarts as staples of regions impacted by hurricanes.[3] The *New York Times* story from 2004 that first brought this crazy anecdote to light essentially introduced much of the world to the practice of consumer data mining. Even back then, the mega-marketer had 460 terabytes of consumer data stored on its servers. Data doesn't get much bigger than that.

This interplay of big data and demographic trends was a subject I found myself thinking more and more about. I needed to find some way to study this. Doing so would require some methodology. Big data is a ton of science, but still a lot of art. Conducting research on the big demographic trends that are driving consumer trends would need big data, for sure, but it would need more than that.

Part of the problem is summed up by Nobel Prize–winning economist Daniel Kahneman in his book on behavioral economics, *Thinking, Fast and Slow.*[4] "People who are taught surprising statistical facts about human behavior may be impressed to the point of telling their friends about what they have heard, but this does not mean that their understanding of the world has really changed. The test of learning psychology is whether your understanding of situations you encounter has changed, not whether you have learned a new fact."[5] His research suggests that the answer to building surprising new information into your consciousness—in other words, understanding and being able to act on this information—is to relate it to a more personal story. Examples of real people reacting in real ways to real situations help us learn.

I had received a surprising bit of data in a very personal way—TWINS!—and that made me look at my situation differently. My hope is that this book and the process it represents, which I'm calling Buyographics, will help you use data and demographics in a much more personal way, too.

Growing up, I used to think I was about as representative as you could get. After all, I was a white, Anglo-Saxon, Protestant, middle-class, Midwestern male. Except for being left-handed, I was about as typical as you could get. In today's America, that image of "typical" has gone out the window as we'll be discussing throughout this book. Finding "typical" can't be done in just one household. This introduction has been somewhat personal, but the rest of this book isn't about me.

Therefore, I have ten households to introduce to you. Each household is in a U.S. county that, based on two segmentation systems, the Jefferson Institute's Patchwork Nation and Esri's Tapestry Segmentation, is representative of the broader population.[6] The former breaks down each county based on its demographics, voting patterns, and religious beliefs. The latter is based on demographics and socioeconomic characteristics. Together they give us a very rich lens with which to examine the U.S.

Here's how Buyographics works.

I took one part big data from some of the best sources of insights into consumer behavior including Experian Marketing Services, comScore, GfK MRI, Ipsos, and Pew. I added government statistical data—an important distinction from behavioral data—from the U.S. Census Bureau and the Bureau of Labor Statistics among other sources. In addition, I did a lot of research in some obvious and some not-as-obvious fields. The lessons I'm rounding up come from demographics, of course, but also from neuroscience, sociology, and economics, with a dash of politics, urban planning, real estate and housing trends, and, of course, the lessons learned from talking with many, many marketers and agency researchers.

A numbers-heavy discussion of trends would be one way to tell the story of what's going on with the American consumer. It would just be a very boring way. I could easily fill this book with charts and data, except that you'd soon tire of reading it and, according to Dr. Kahneman, even the "aha" moments you had would quickly fade without some narrative foundation to help tie it in.

What I needed was people.

So I added an ethnography component to the data to provide a number-rich look at the changing American consumer that is anchored with stories on how these trends are shaped by and how they impact actual people.

This book began as a series of articles in *Advertising Age* under the banner "The American Consumer Project," which ran in 2011 and 2012. I conducted a lot of original research for this book. I'm also going to lean heavily on the reporting I did for the *Ad Age* stories. In this book, I'm going to tell you the stories of these families. They contain great examples and insights into how your customers are doing in this quasi-post-recession world. For the most part, they're still struggling. I'll explain, and let them explain, exactly how and what that means for them and for your brand.

Disregarding the data for a second, it's worth pointing out here that I somewhat randomly and somewhat very deliberately selected these families. Across generations, across race/ethnicity, across income levels, and just about any way you'd like to slice/dice the demographics of this—the recession hasn't really ended, and doesn't look as if it's going to for them. Whether we're working on Michigan Avenue or Madison Avenue, it's easy to forget sometimes just how many Americans are raising their families on not much money. As we'll discuss later, we're getting better and better at isolating ourselves.

In many ways, this book really centers on the changing middle class, which is the trend driving all the other trends.

Each chapter will focus on a key overarching trend that impacts the marketplace. Some of these are trends that have been building for a long time and are now reaching an important critical mass. Some are newer trends that will shape the coming decades. I'll start with a deep dive into the changes in the middle class, but you'll find that particular theme winding its way through the other chapters as it influences the shifts in household types, in parenting, in aging, and in more spending-related trends impacting industries such as health care. Each chapter will contain insights and best practices from marketers and agencies about how they are responding to these changes. I'll also include some analysis of the big data that ties into those trends. And of course I'll have the families discuss what it all means to them.

In the end, each of those numbers—in data sets big and small—is a person. Each of them has a story. As you read those stories, the trends will come to life and give you a greater understanding of how to reach your target. You might think your customer is a Baby Boomer farmer in Teton county, Montana, or a set of working parents in one of the most affluent counties in the U.S. But your customer is really Dale. Or Rosemary. Or Sandra. Or Alfredo. Getting to know their demographics, their consumer behaviors, and their stories—simply put, their Buyographics—will help you do your job better and smarter.

ONE

The Changing Middle Class

How the Income Gap Is Polarizing Markets and Marketers

WHEN YOU HEAR THE WORDS "MIDDLE CLASS," IT'S HARD NOT TO START picturing some idealized 1950s version of this scene: A blonde apron-wearing mom looks out the kitchen window of her ranch home at the yard where her adorable son and even more adorable daughter are playing. The neighborhood is safe. There might be an American-made Radio Flyer wagon in evidence. They live on a cul-de-sac. Dad's at work, and Mom is making meatloaf for dinner. She has a range oven and a counter full of new labor-saving devices. In your mind, this scene plays out in black and white, and that doesn't even strike you as odd.

As long as we're in fantasy flashback mode, think about ad agency jobs in that time. If *Mad Men* is to be believed, selling products to the middle class was easy and could be accomplished between cocktails and naps on the office couch. If you worked in this world, you knew everything about that middle-class mom. There were only a handful of shows she could and would watch and only a handful of places for her to buy the products she saw advertised there. You knew roughly what her husband's income was. In the driveway was an American-made car. She didn't have a credit card, and therefore she didn't really spend beyond her means.[1] She might have been worried about whether she needed a bomb shelter, but there was no chance she had ever thought about hormones in the milk her kids drank. If you had tried to explain a vegan to her, she would have thought you were talking about a communist.

More joined the middle class each year and those who aspired to join regarded that goal as achievable. In 1971, the middle class included 61 percent of Americans. Today we see only 51 percent in the middle income tiers.[2] In this chapter, we'll focus on the proportion of the population that could be called "middle class" which is:

- Shrinking—taking a lot of the "mass" out of the "mass-market" many products need;
- Financially drained on all fronts—leaving brands with fewer viable customers;
- Fundamentally impacted by the ever-increasing number of dual-income households.

In short, the middle class has changed. Many of these changes have been building for decades and have been hastened and exacerbated by the recession. Now the changes are reaching critical mass. The path of families who are struggling to get into the middle class has been made harder by the sudden removal of housing equity as a reliable road to get there. Those who are struggling to stay in the middle class are worried about what the loss of a job would do to their standing. They're being impacted by trends in income, in household structure, in credit and debt. Even the cul-de-sac suburban living they dreamed of makes it harder to sustain their lifestyle because they have to spend more on car ownership and more time in traffic than their younger, single, city-dwelling friends.

Throughout the rest of the book we'll talk about narrower segments like the aging, the affluent, the single-person households, and racial and ethnic groups and how changes in their demographics are impacting spending on such categories as health care and transportation.

First, though, let's start more broadly with a look at the changes in the middle class, which has long been the economic and spiritual heart of America. Many of the most well-known brands depend on the sheer bulk of this group and its discretionary spending prowess to fuel their growth and their very existence. The changes happening that are affecting this group of consumers are fundamental and therefore fundamentally important, so we'll start by getting a firm understanding of what's happening to them. I'll admit, the data doesn't paint a pretty picture. But in times of change there is also opportunity. Some brands are adapting to the changes successfully, and we'll take a look at those.

If the scenario at the start of the chapter is what you still think of as the middle class, you're increasingly thinking about someone like Rosemary.[3]

Rosemary, her husband, and their daughter live on a small residential street in a nearly rural area between Washington, D.C., and Baltimore. They have a four-bedroom home with a yard for their dog and a pair of Acuras parked in their two-car attached garage. They are the first occupants of the recent-construction home tricked out with the standard fare of granite countertops and stainless steel appliances. They recently finished the basement to add a play space for everyone—room for their daughter along with a workout room and a home office for the adults. For their daughter's first eighteen months, Rosemary worked, but she was able to work from home part of the week, and her mother came over to watch the little one. In what is increasingly a luxury move, she then decided to stay at home full-time, but she plans to return to work once her daughter gets a little older and starts school.

Your middle-class checklist looks pretty complete: two cars; nice house that's roomy but not a mansion by any means; nice non-flashy cars; established careers; educated parents.

Here's the problem with her as an example of middle-class living: Rosemary's income puts her well into the reaches of *upper* middle class. She's not rich, but neither is she anywhere near the median. Therefore, we'll talk more about Rosemary in the next chapter, which focuses on *her* bracket: the affluent.

I've spent years studying the impacts of demographic changes on consumers. I've analyzed the numbers and traveled through the U.S., sitting in living rooms and kitchens talking to real people about what's happening in their lives. As part of the research that led to this book, I tracked ten representative families who were as geographically and demographically diverse as you can imagine. But themes emerged. These days the middle class sounds a lot less like Rosemary and a lot more like these families:

"It seems like everything got more expensive. And for me, personally, I got the same pay rate that I've had for five, six years. So I'm being paid the same—and the gas prices aren't helping much, either."
—Alfredo, a married father with a son in middle school and a daughter in high school, Los Angeles County, California.

"We can't really help [our daughters in college.] We just can't afford to. So they've got a lot of student loans that they'll be paying off for a long time."
—Frankie, a married mother with three daughters— one in high school, one in college, and one recent college graduate, Teton County, Montana.

"I was living paycheck to paycheck with that job and so as much as a 5 percent pay cut sounds like, well, 'it's just 5 percent,' it was enough of a significant difference that I was like, 'Oh, my God.' So I actually started working part time for a radio station so that I could make up for it."
—Liz, an unmarried Millennial, Champaign County, Illinois.

"When my 18-year-old was growing up . . . there was concern about crime, but not to the extent that it is now. So I think I'm more protective of my [4-year-old]. Where we go, who she sees. Who I will let her stay with. Things like that. Just because of the way the world is changing."
—Sandra, a Gen-X single mother, East Baton Rouge Parish, Louisiana.

"All our homes here where we live, it's like, 'Wow, what happened to our . . . investments?'"
—Basha, a married empty nester, Lake County, Florida.[4]

If I had to sum up what separates the middle class from those classes above and below, I'd have to say it's about lifestyle and a word marketers love and fear: discretion.

The middle class has the economic flexibility to make choices, but its members understand that trade-offs must be made and are forced to consider the impacts. The affluent can make choices more freely. But more and more households have fewer and fewer options. That doesn't mean those households are "poor." In fact, many would be considered middle class by most definitions. They're struggling because they've been impacted on all sides of the financial equation: income, net worth, and debt.

Now try selling them something they *want*, rather than something they *need*.

The median household income in 1980 was $17,710 according to the U.S. Census Bureau's invaluable Current Population Survey. That rose to $50,054 in 2011. But in constant dollars, income grew only $4,030 during that span. Most of that growth happened before 1999, when income peaked at $54,932 in 2011 dollars. It has fallen more or less steadily since then to today's level. Between 2000 and 2010 the number of families earning $50,000 to $150,000 (a rough approximation of the middle and upper middle class) declined by 2.6 million households, according to my analysis of census data.[5] During that time, average household income in constant dollars for all U.S. households fell about $2,500—a 4 percent drop. Added up, that's a $292 billion drop in total consumer income. The middle-class

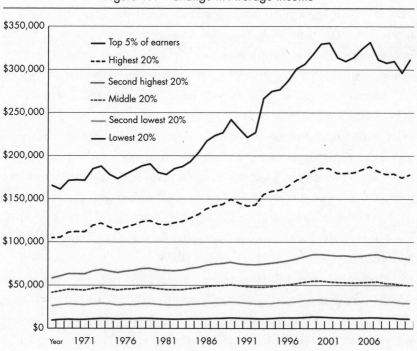

Figure 1.1   Change in Average Income

Source: U.S. Census Bureau, figures in 2011 dollars

loss was responsible for about half (53 percent) of that. The other 47 percent was lost almost entirely by households earning less than $25,000.

Middle-class incomes are even down slightly from 1988 in inflation-adjusted dollars. More importantly, the median household income in the U.S. has been fairly stagnant for the last half century.

That's pretty incredible when you consider that as recently as 1970, when there were more people in the middle class, those families were typically living on one paycheck.[6]

Women, and mothers especially, have finally been given the attention they deserve as important decision makers and spenders in the household, but it's their role as earners that is remaking the American middle class—or rather keeping the middle class alive. As more and more women have taken more and more lucrative jobs in the workplace and in traditionally male-dominated professions, those dual-earning households have kept the middle class afloat. Sort of. Adding a second paycheck has allowed the middle class to tread water, but not to make substantive gains. We will talk about this more in chapter four.

As I said, incomes have remained relatively flat for decades, when adjusted for inflation. The only growth has come by adding that second income. Since 1980, dual-earning families have seen their incomes rise more than $80,000 in 2011 dollars, which is nearly twice the growth seen by single-earning households and four times the growth within the no-earning households, according to my analysis of census data.[7]

Adding a second income can add additional costs, too. For instance, in households with children the gains of a second income are offset somewhat by the costs of caring for those kids. Often if both parents are working, they need another commuter car. With the costs of health care and other items (which we'll discuss more in chapter eight), that leaves less money to spend on discretionary goods and services like entertainment, education, personal care, clothing, and furniture. More than a third of households have less than $7,000 to spend on those non-essential goods each year. Just over half have less than $10,000.[8]

If we factor all of this in when comparing today's dual earners to yesterday's single-earning households, we find that today's middle class actually has *less* discretionary income to spend or save.[9] In fact, in the last ten years dual-income households have cut their average household expenditures more than 2 percent in 2011 dollars.

So these key consumers are earning less and spending less. That presents a challenge for brands. But it's not an insurmountable one.

All these changes have taken place so slowly that most Americans and, it seems, most brands haven't entirely noticed. The behavioral economist Dan Ariely coauthored an eye-opening study that asked Americans how they think wealth should be distributed across income brackets and how they think it actually is distributed.[10] The people interviewed thought that wealth should be somewhat evenly distributed with very few living in poverty and a smooth rise to those on the upper income levels who would understandably make more than everyone else. They thought that reality wasn't all that far off from their ideal. They were really, really wrong.

The top 1 percent of earners hold 40 percent of the nation's wealth. The bottom 80 percent only hold 7 percent.[11]

Many factors are at play here. You could look at student loan debt, the changing job market, the rut in which the Millennial generation finds itself, and how that differs from the other generations, and of course how the issues facing the entire rest of the planet impact the U.S. economic situation.

Let's look at two more pieces of the economic puzzle: consumer debt, which can fuel spending even when income is down, and net worth, which impacts access to credit.

Are consumers loading up on debt in order to afford a little more than they would otherwise?

As of this writing, it's difficult to find a trend in the most current data. Consumer debt fluctuates pretty widely from quarter to quarter these days. In geek parlance, we say that it's "noisy"—as in it's hard to find a signal with all the noise. According to the Federal Reserve, total revolving consumer credit has generally been trending downward since the start of the recession, meaning that people are paying down their credit card debt or are having a harder time accessing credit in the first place.[12] The Credit Card Act of 2009 changed a lot of the ways banks did their credit card lending.[13] Tougher regulation led to banks issuing less credit to certain riskier consumers. By 2012 that started to turn around, albeit unevenly.[14] Uncertainty due to the continued economic malaise, the debt ceiling crisis, and the impending elections meant that access to credit, especially by the middle class, was up some months and down others.[15]

In the longer term, anything other than a steady increase in consumer debt is a reversal of decades-long trends. In a panel discussion about the middle class hosted by the Brookings Institution, senior fellow and moderator E. J. Dionne Jr. introduced a panel on "The Endangered Middle Class" with the following observation:

From roughly 1950 through the early 1970s the American middle class increased its standard of living by increasing its income. As productivity went up, so did middle-class incomes. Since the late '70s, there has been a stagnation of middle-class incomes, and in order to keep up, people have had to resort to debt rather than increases in their wages. This has caused an enormous set of problems in our country, and while there is a tendency to talk about individual indebtedness entirely in moral terms as if there is something wrong with people trying to keep up their living standards, I think this underlying force, a stagnation of incomes, has forced people to do things that they would really rather not do. I can bet you that most people would rather increase their living standards by increasing their incomes, not their indebtedness.[16]

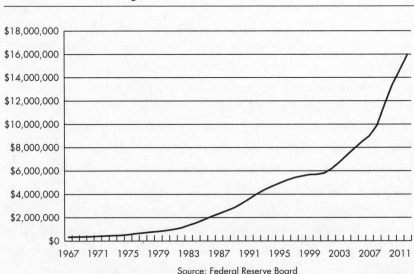

Figure 1.2 Total Consumer Debt

Source: Federal Reserve Board

Indeed, the Federal Reserve shows that in August 2012, revolving household debt (essentially representing credit cards and short-term loans) was $855 billion. Just thirty years earlier that figure was less than $65 billion. Non-revolving debt in that time went from $318 billion to $1.9 trillion.

Yet, as noted, since the recession we've seen Americans reducing the debt figures. Between paying down loans, having a harder time getting new loans, decreasing incomes, and gutted housing values, the new challenge for the U.S. economy is that, increasingly, the middle class can't access as much money.

The story on net worth is a little more clear cut. The bursting of the housing bubble wiped out at least a decade's worth of gains overall and more than that for many consumers. As the Federal Reserve notes, "The decline in median net worth was especially large for families in groups where housing was a larger share of assets, such as families headed by someone 35 to 44 years old (median net worth fell 54.4 percent) and families in the West region (median net worth fell 55.3 percent)."[17]

The Census Bureau reports that median net worth dropped 35 percent between 2005 and 2010.[18] Most of that decrease was related to housing equity and stock performance. If you exclude home equity, median net worth actually increased 8 percent. Therefore, the Gen-Xers were the most crushed during this period. As the age cohort most likely to have invested a large portion of their money to buy a house, they lost nearly 60 percent of their net worth. Older generations, whose houses are more likely to be paid off, lost less, as did those under thirty-five, who are less likely to own property. As with the other trends, it's clear that the higher one's level of education, the more insulated one is likely to be. On its blog, the Census states, "In 2000, those with a bachelor's degree had a median net worth value almost twice as large as those with a high-school diploma; by 2010, this number had risen to almost three and half times as large. The same pattern can be seen when examining the graduate or professional degree to high school diploma ratio; this ratio has increased from 3.5 to 5.8 over the period of 2000–2010."[19]

So where is the middle class going? D'Vera Cohn, a senior writer at the Pew Research Center, and I discussed that after the release of Pew's report "The Lost Decade of the Middle Class." The report states that, demographically speaking, there were definite winners and losers. "Over the

Figure 1.3   Family Net Worth by Percentile of Income

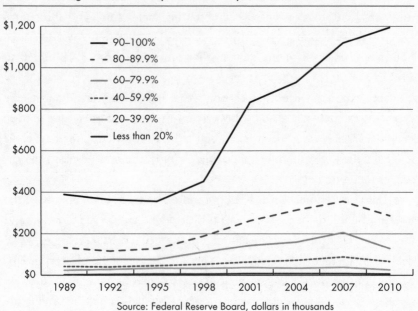

Source: Federal Reserve Board, dollars in thousands

longer term—1971 to 2011—older adults fared better than younger ones, married adults fared better than the unmarried, and college-educated adults fared better than those with less education." Not everyone was a success story. In the last decade, all non-white racial and ethnic groups showed economic declines, according to Pew.[20] "When there are people moving from the middle class to a lower class, that is a concern," said Ms. Cohn.[21] "Polarization gives us less in common as a people."

You can read that last sentence as "It's harder to create a mass-market message."

Who's Winning?

If the middle class is struggling, who is succeeding? The next chapter will focus on what's happening to the upper class, but for now what you need to fully understand is that those in the top tier are doing better at a much faster rate than those in the lower tiers. To put some numbers behind that, the Congressional Budget Office prepared a comprehensive look at income trends and found that "between 1979 and 2007, for the 1 percent of the population with the highest income, average real after-tax household income grew by 275 percent. For others in the 20 percent of the population with the highest income, average real after-tax household income grew by 65 percent. For the 60 percent of the population in the middle of the income scale, the growth in average real after-tax household income was just under 40 percent. For the 20 percent of the population with the lowest income, the growth in average real after-tax household income was about 18 percent."[22]

The Census shows that the top quintile saw its share of aggregate income rise from 43.3 percent in 1970 to more than 50 percent in 2009.[23] The top 5 percent of earners saw their share grow from 16.6 percent to 21.7 percent over that time. All the other quintiles saw their shares decline over that period. The recession took a little wind out of the sails, but now the bifurcation is growing again. During the period between 2009 and 2011, as the recovery was getting underway, only the highest tier fully recovered. The 8 million households with the highest net worths (more than $836,000) gained $5.6 trillion in wealth. The rest of America—more than 111 million households—saw their collective net worth decline more than $600 billion.[24]

These trends aren't new, but they're getting worse. How this happened isn't so much the story for us here, although one could certainly look at the tax code. In a *New York Times* op-ed article, Wall Street executive and Obama's car czar Steven Rattner examines changes since the Bush-era tax cuts were put into place.[25] The result, he writes, "is that the top 1 percent has done progressively better in each economic recovery of the past two decades. In the Clinton era expansion, 45 percent of the total income gains went to the top 1 percent; in the Bush recovery, the figure was 65 percent."[26] They did even better during this recession. According to economist Emmanuel Saez, "the top 1% captured 93% of the income gains in the first year of recovery."[27]

How Are Marketers Reacting?

When marketers talk about the middle class, the conversation tends to go in one of three directions.

First, there is certainly a school of marketers who aren't paying much attention to this at all. Consumers are still buying their products, so perhaps it's not as important that they're buying slightly fewer of them, or buying them with slightly less frequency. It's certainly not important that consumers have stopped buying someone else's product in order to afford theirs. If you're on the winning side of the trade-offs that consumers are making, you might not notice the change as quickly.

Even with the passing of Steve Jobs, Apple continues to gain market share without really altering its price point or its marketing message.

If you think about it, though, the nation now adds more than 2 million people a year—that's 2 million potential new customers. If your target audience isn't growing that rapidly, it could signal problems down the road. Some segments grow faster than others. If your target segment grows more quickly than that, so should your share. If your target is everyone, you should have a representative breakdown. For instance, if 16 percent of your customers aren't Hispanic, then you're looking at potential to grow in that marketplace.

A second school of marketers quickly turns to discussion of the major post-recession buzzword. The most influential trend is "value." I've had conversations about the topic and its changing definitions with marketers from Kia to Lexus and in between.

The most obvious manifestations of this are in the meteoric rise in the immediate post-recession times of the daily deal space led by Groupon and LivingSocial. Companies in this space created a multibillion-dollar industry out of nowhere by using smarter technology to link value-seeking customers with merchants looking to develop or regain lost scale.

Some leading marketers like Procter & Gamble, Target Corporation, and PepsiCo's Frito-Lay are evolving strategies that address the shrinking middle class. Despite Tide's dominance in the liquid laundry detergent world, P&G introduced a less expensive line of products geared toward a lower-income and more diverse audience. Gain liquid detergent has performed well but still drastically undersells its higher-priced cousin.[28]

Other brand extensions have been mixed according to IRI. Unit sales of Gain powdered laundry detergent were down far more than the category as a whole, but the fabric softener sheets outperformed the category considerably.[29] The acknowledgment that the middle class, which has been P&G's bread and butter for its 175-year history, is changing is significant. If there's a marketer who will figure out how to deal with economic bifurcation, it's Procter & Gamble. But it's a tricky adjustment to make. Even P&G isn't immune to the new economic realities—the company laid off 10 percent of its workforce in 2012.[30]

Likewise, Frito-Lay in a 2012 earnings call made a point to call out its performance in both the "value" segment and the "premium" segment while maintaining its dominance in the "mainstream" or middle-class market. It's not an easy task because marketers don't want to undercut their own products by creating lower-tier brands.[31] As Indra Nooyi, PepsiCo's chairman and CEO, stated, "We were looking for the right model to compete against the value segment of the business and the premium segment. We wanted to make sure we did it the right way and not take down the pricing level of the middle."[32]

Finally, and somewhat disturbingly, there are marketers who are taking a more global perspective. Given the iconic stature of the middle class in the fabric of the American quilt, it's hard to imagine a future in which the nation is divided even more into haves and have-nots. *The Atlantic's* Don Peck raised an interesting point in his book *Pinched: How the Great Recession Has Narrowed Our Futures and What We Can Do about It*. While attending the Aspen Institute's gathering of big thinkers, he noticed that many of the leaders were looking at the market in so completely global a manner that the plight of the American middle class didn't seem all that important. As one market fades, another rises up to take its place. Whether that's in India or Indiana doesn't matter to the almighty bottom dollar or the shareholder.

On the surface there are some issues with this thinking, but the idea merits discussion here. First, the American middle class still spends a ton of money. Looking at those who rank in the third and fourth quintiles of income (i.e., the fortieth to the eightieth percentile), you'll find a group who spent $2.45 trillion in 2011, according to the Bureau of Labor Statistics.[33] That amounts to 40 percent of all spending on food, 43 percent of transportation spending, 44 percent of health-care spending, and so forth. The entire spending output of the so-called emerging BRIC (Brazil, Russia, India, and China) markets with a combined population roughly sixteen times that of the American middle class was estimated by a 2010 McKinsey report at just $6.9 trillion in 2010. McKinsey projects that number will grow to $20 billion in the next decade.[34] Others aren't quite so sure if the BRICs are the world's future spending leaders; they point to their recently slowing growth and contrast it with rising growth in a number of other countries like South Korea.[35] Regardless of the rates of growth, these markets will grow in importance and purchasing power.

If the wealth is increasingly concentrated on the high end, the spending is more democratic. Some marketers can make up for lost volume with higher-priced items, but that doesn't work for everyone. A higher-priced, higher-margin car can make up for fewer sales of cheaper cars. But an affluent household making three or four times the median household income doesn't suddenly need three or four times the amount of toilet paper or soap or ground chuck. There are also all kinds of products and brands they might not buy at all and for which lower-income households make up the main market.

Chrystia Freeland, the global editor at large for Reuters, attended the same Aspen talks as Don Peck. In a piece she wrote for *The Atlantic* headlined "The Rise of the New Global Elite," she quoted Allstate CEO Thomas Wilson as saying, "I can get [workers] anywhere in the world. It is a problem for America, but it is not necessarily a problem for American business . . . American businesses will adapt."[36]

She also quotes (anonymously) the CEO of one of the world's largest hedge funds, who told her that a colleague of his felt that the hollowing-out of the American middle class didn't really matter. "His point was that if the transformation of the world economy lifts four people in China and India out of poverty and into the middle class, and meanwhile means one American drops out of the middle class, that's not such a bad trade."

Rom Hendler, chief marketing officer of the Las Vegas Sands Corporation, also believes the global market will compensate for the changing demographics here in the U.S. When I asked him about the declining middle class in the U.S., his quick response was to spin the metaphorical globe. "Most of our profitability is coming from Asia and what you describe is the opposite in Asia where the middle class and upper class are growing rapidly. [The decline] is nonexistent in that market. The profits coming from those segments are increasing and grabbing a bigger and bigger share."[37]

He goes on to talk about what he sees happening domestically, as well. "As far as the U.S. is concerned, the properties in Las Vegas did feel the overall decline. In the past you would say the gaming industry is considered recession proof." He cites an example of a typical consumer trade-off. A trip to Hawaii likely costs more than a trip to Las Vegas and the vacationers would just burn their money. In the recession Las Vegas is seen as a cheaper alternative with an added benefit that other destinations typically lack: the chance to win enough to cover your costs.

Even before 2000, Las Vegas was to some extent making a play for the value-conscious consumer. The reputation of cheap flights, cheap rooms, and all-you-can-eat buffets, any of which might be comped if you spent enough gaming, lured the vast middle class. As the business model of Las Vegas changed, said Mr. Hendler, "Recession proof stopped being real."

Without saying the word "bifurcation," Mr. Hendler acknowledges it. Some casino properties gear their target market toward the lower end while his business is focusing on the high-roller market. "If you look at the industry's marketing since 2008 you will see a lot of value communication. Some of that is looking at the lowest price point. We're trying to stay away from that. Many of our peers and competitors are playing in that playground. In the U.S. we had to adjust and are still trying to position ourselves in the upper end of luxury. We had to be conscious of value. Even people who weren't hurt, even people who were doing just fine, they were looking for value."

There's that word: "value."

Some argue that Target's earnings have been hit by its focus on the middle class as shops like Neiman Marcus at the higher end and Dollar Store–types at the lower end of the spectrum have flourished. Gregg W. Steinhafel, Target's president and CEO, tried to paint some of that in a more positive light in a 2012 earnings call. He thinks that in times of economic uncertainty, even middle-market Target is a value trade-off for many shoppers. "Against these [economic] pressures, we believe that our value proposition and shopping experience will deliver continued market share gains. We believe our guests will continue to be both cautious and resilient, shopping and spending at Target in disciplined ways."[38]

How do you knock a consumer off the "disciplined" platform and get them to be a little more free spending? To see the answer, Mr. Hendler needs only to step outside and look past the Grand Canal of his Venetian property at the throngs of people returning to Las Vegas.

What Happens with Vegas Happens Everywhere

The city of Las Vegas can be seen as a microcosm for reaction to the changes in the U.S. economy as a whole. As the middle class has changed, relying on its members to let their precious few discretionary dollars ride on red, or pump their pennies into a slot machine became, well, a riskier gamble. At the same time, the proliferation of high-end entertainment and dining options in urban areas was a trend Vegas not only couldn't ignore but needed to capitalize on. Looking beyond the gaming high rollers, Las Vegas needed to bring in the dining and shopping high rollers. Interestingly, those aren't the same people. Mr. Hendler says there's nothing in demographic or behavioral data that correlates well with gambling behavior—except previous gambling behavior. "You can't just look at big data and find high rollers. Just because you're shopping at Louis Vuitton and flying a private jet doesn't make you a high roller. If you look at the *Forbes* 500 richest people, there will be just a handful of things that you can really pinpoint as saying there is in common to these people. If there is, it's stuff that you can't really find in big data."

Las Vegas would like those who do fly private jets to land them at the Henderson Executive Airport next to the strip. Even if the passengers never spend a dollar playing craps, they're going to spend some money in town. Mr. Hendler would like to make sure it gets spent at one of his properties. Las Vegas just wants them to come.

And so we have begun to see greater emphasis placed on the overall experience of Las Vegas, not just on the exciting luck-of-the-draw thrills of gambling itself. Gaming revenue as a share of overall revenue has declined, but dining and entertainment have more than made up for it. The new diversified revenue model lures just about everyone who is looking for a good time—regardless of demographics.

Las Vegas is more than just a city; it's a brand and a very tightly managed one at that. It's a brand that traditionally has been heavily reliant on the middle class. It takes a lot of bodies to fill all those hotel rooms. It's also a brand that's heavily reliant on having a *healthy* middle class. When everything about your product screams "discretionary spending," you have to constantly remind consumers just how much they *want* it. Except for conventions, few people really *need* to go to Las Vegas.

And yet, Vegas didn't just fold up and go away when the bottom fell out of the economy. Why not?

From a product standpoint, as Mr. Hendler pointed out, the Las Vegas economy has been remaking itself into a more modern set of offerings, partially as a reaction to the shrinking of the middle class. Non-gaming revenue was growing and gambling itself had reached an all-time high of nearly $10.9 billion in 2007.[39] Developers responded to the growth. By mid-2008 more than 17,000 hotel rooms were under construction. Cranes were everywhere, giving the city a glittering new make-over with new hotel/casino/resort complexes all over the strip. It was boom time.

The marketing of Las-Vegas-the-brand is handled by the Las Vegas Convention and Visitors Authority. Its $127 million marketing budget means it has a sizable pool of money to spend by tourism standards.

That money was pumped into an incredibly popular campaign that resonated across demographics. The "What happens here stays here" tagline was so successful that it just integrated itself into popular culture.

But in late 2008 the warning bells started to ring. Fuel prices were surging, driving up costs for road trippers and air travelers alike. The hotels noticed a decrease in reservation call volume—a clear leading indicator that something was wrong. They called the Las Vegas Convention and Visitors Authority. Kevin Bagger is the Authority's senior director of marketing.

Mr. Bagger sits in a window office deep in the heart of the absurdly large Las Vegas Convention Center. To get there, look for a set of nondescript glass doors not too far from one of the main convention spaces on the second floor. When I arrived, what was easily one of the world's largest dump trucks was being assembled outside the center. It had been shipped piecemeal and was being reconstituted in the parking lot in preparation for a mining convention. Mr. Bagger said it's the trade show with the longest set-up time because the equipment is so large and elaborate.[40] As the monorail ran back and forth to the strip, he walked me through what the recession did to Sin City and how the Authority went agile in response.

The moves his department made helped bring Las Vegas back from the brink quickly, and the strategy could be seen as a model for reaching the middle class these days. He turned the focus from uninhibited fun bordering on (and maybe even crossing the border of) overindulgent partying into a focus on value, permission, and attainable entertainment. Even beyond that messaging hurdle, he had another obstacle to overcome. The Authority's marketing is funded by hotel taxes. So as demand for rooms decreases and prices are cut, as happened during the recession, so too are the dollars that fuel the marketing of the product. There's essentially no mechanism to double down on marketing in a recession—even if the Authority wanted to.

One of the first things the Authority did as the recession began to take hold was suspend its go-to tagline for what would turn into an eighteen-month stretch. It was time for secrets to be shouted. For the next few months, anything that happened in Vegas would be trumpeted throughout the land to anyone who would still listen.

The Authority and its agency spend a lot of time and money on research, which immediately picked up on the fact that long-term vacation planning had fallen apart, but short-term planning had become a little more prevalent. In the short term a near real-time "Vegas Right Now" campaign was developed that looked at what was happening in town in the next couple of weeks.

The bigger problem was twofold. One, a decent chunk of the population had lost a lot of money in a very public way. And two, those who weren't hurting as badly didn't want to rub it in. "People didn't want to be seen as having fun while their neighbors suffered," said Mr. Bagger. On the casino-property level, shifting focus to the higher-end luxury market is one way to deal with bifurcation. But if your job is to fill a city overflowing with hotel rooms, you need the middle class to visit and spend.

The Authority pivoted to a permission-giving campaign: "Crazy times call for crazy fun." The idea, of course, was to convince people that in turbulent times a little escape wasn't a luxury, it was a necessity.

Finally, they produced what is considered a low-budget campaign for this brand—they flew nearly the entire population of the small town of Cranfills Gap, Texas, to Las Vegas and filmed what amounted to a reality show about the experience. Many of the residents hadn't had a vacation in years, in some cases ever, and many had never left their county. Their reactions to being set loose on the strip ranged from excited to very, very excited.

The earned media from that campaign helped the Authority stretch its budget.

All of these efforts were created quickly and with a laser focus on the present to help Las Vegas weather the storm. Then the Authority sat down with its longtime agency, R&R Partners, to look forward. The billion-dollar question on the table was "Where does Las Vegas fit into a post-recession reality?"

Despite the enormousness of the convention center and the 19,000 business meetings hosted in town each year, convention goers made up slightly less than 5 million of the 39 million visitors to the city in 2011. While the convention business has typically provided some stability to the city's economy, it's been the leisure travel that has rebounded more quickly, according to the Authority's data. That is partially owing to the efforts of the Authority and the insights that came out of that session.

Much of the rebound—visitors have been returning steadily for the past few years now—is the result of smart advertising. Some of it is due to other efforts by the Authority, including working to bring in more inter-national guests. Globalization of the consumer base is happening here for sure. During the recession, airlines cut back on routes, which hurts when nearly half of the visitors arrive by plane. The Authority has been working hand-in-hand with the airlines to get old routes restored and new routes added, including nonstops from emerging markets like South America and Asia.

Some of the rebound is also coming as a result of the long-term re-making of Las Vegas as an entertainment center, not just a gambling desti-nation. It's harder to get the stretched American middle class to part with its money on the casino floor. Having high-end restaurants and big-ticket shows like Cirque du Soleil offers options for consumers across the eco-nomic spectrum.

Vegas has also remade itself as a family-friendly destination, through no fault of its own. Granted, a few of the hotel properties started to add some attractions that might appeal to adults traveling with children rather than just to adults behaving like children. But Mr. Bagger says that the success of the "family-friendly" meme was entirely out of his hands. "It's the most successful PR campaign we never launched. We can accommo-date families, but we don't target them. Adult freedom is the essence of what we're selling for Las Vegas."

Big Data, Small Stories

At the city level, Las Vegas has found a solid mix of marketing tactics to draw in more visitors. It uses demographic data to craft messages that will resonate with the changing middle class and is able to quick test different messages and rapidly assess the effectiveness of campaigns. If more bodies arrive and book hotels, the Authority is doing something right. Creating advertising that stresses "value" and gives permission for consumers to find some affordable entertainment and blow off some pent-up steam seems to be working as visitor volume continues to rise. The Authority also understands the value and limitations of various online and digital platforms such as mobile.

At the property level, Mr. Hendler is taking advantage of one of the key developments in marketing, one I'll talk about a lot in this book. He uses big data to maximize profits from the individual. Insights are driven largely by tracking customers through the property with a loyalty card that can be scanned and used to charge purchases back to the room at the casino, restaurants, spas, and shops.

That meant tearing down a lot of walls between departments so that a central team can see data from all of the different profit centers. With the potential to be profitable in a number of different places outside the casino floor, making sure the customer is incentivized in the right places at the right times became key.

"In the past we would just look at the gaming and everything else was secondary. Sometimes you would end up cannibalizing your own business. You'd see that someone was gambling a little bit and you'd give them a discount room or a comped room, and really they are not a good player; they're just OK but they spend more money in another area [of the property] and were much more profitable from another side. So it's been challenging because [each department] would say 'this is my data.' It's nobody's data. It's the company's data and it's going to be centralized."

If the internal issue with big data is sharing it between departments, the external issue with big data is privacy. Both the collection and use of big data set off alarm bells for consumers and regulators alike. One point you'll hear again and again in this book is how big data is providing both opportunities for marketers and all-important value for consumers. Perhaps no one knows that better than Scott Howe, CEO of Acxiom Corporation, one of the largest storehouses of consumer data. The problem, he says, is that marketers have done a poor job selling the benefits to consumers.[41]

Vegas's Mr. Hendler puts his big data to use making sure the right customer gets the right deal. For his purposes, he rightly puts that in terms of maximizing the *revenue from* an individual customer, but it could easily be put in the context of maximizing the *value for* that customer, too. If you're a foodie, getting the good deal at the profitable restaurant might be a much more alluring offer than having your drinks comped while you play blackjack. Just like the odds on the floor, you think you've won but, in reality, the house always wins.

Mr. Howe believes that the marketing world is moving toward a more consumer-driven focus and that big data has a big role to play in that process. With more than $1 billion in revenue in an industry that is increasingly under the spotlight, he has a lot at stake in getting consumers comfortable with how his customers use his product.[42] "Big data isn't big tobacco," he told me as we chatted after his talk at a conference put on by blog network Federated Media. The consumer, he says, needs to understand what they're getting in exchange for marketers like Mr. Hendler using data collected from loyalty reward cards, or companies like Acxiom using data it collects from a wide variety of online and offline sources. "They get the Super Bowl for free every year," he points out—and Facebook, too.

While he gets worked up about the topic, he has a very valid point. Consumers have a lot to gain by getting more and more relevant deals either pushed to them or made increasingly available for them to proactively seek out. What could be a better value than having all of the various messages one is exposed to in every conceivable medium be personally relevant?

"I turn cartwheels every time I go to my mailbox and get the $500 Valpak," says Mr. Howe. "Inevitably I use one of them. But I feel so empowered. Imagine if every coupon there were relevant to me. A consumer could control their world in such a way that they have their own personal Groupons, their own personal loyalty program, their own personal advertising agency. I don't think we're going to get to that extreme but the industry will make strides toward that."

The trends with the middle class aren't going away, so expect to hear more about these themes. Big data will help marketers get more agile, and marketers will learn to do a better job of communicating the payoff for consumers. The combination of big data and demographic data will help marketers craft messages and offers that are more tailored and more likely to get consumers to act in ways that they might have aspired to already. Throughout the book we'll also talk about the informed consumer. Big data cuts both ways, and more and more consumers are shopping armed with a cell phone offering access to all the knowledge of the Internet and real-time recommendations from their social networks. When dollars get stretched, spending them wisely takes on an extra level of importance.

Certainly expect to hear more about value from both likely and unlikely channels and parts of the price spectrum.

Because it's not just the middle class. These ideas trickle up. The affluent suffered as well during the recession—just in different ways and not for as long.

Earlier in the chapter we met Rosemary. Her story might sound like a middle-class dream—she's even the first generation of her family born in the U.S.—but really it's one of affluence in America. Her story is one of increasing success, of moving up the economic ladder, and of becoming what marketers like Rom Hendler and others are targeting: the emerging affluent market. We can't talk about what is happening to the middle class without spending a little time focusing on how that all-important top quintile lives. So for that, we'll leave Las Vegas and head to Maryland.

TWO

How the Other 18 Percent Live

Post-recession Realities for the Affluent and Luxury Marketers

LOGIC WOULD DICTATE THAT IF YOU HAVE A PRODUCT TO SELL, PITCHING IT to people who can afford it would be a good place to start. Thus the concept of "mass affluence" has become appealing to marketers in recent years. Simply put, in the growth period leading up to the recession, a growing upper middle class seemed to be forming with people both aspiring to luxury living and actually achieving it. Marketers and researchers dubbed them the "mass affluent." It was an easy concept to believe in because who wouldn't want to think that more and more people were prospering (or wanted to appear as though they were) and would then spend more and more on nicer and nicer things?

Then in 2007 the bottom fell out of the economy. A lot of people who were working toward moving up the economic ladder were suddenly faced with a new reality of an upside-down mortgage, a lost or decreased income, and other financial hardships. During the recession it appeared that the "mass" was gone and all that was left was the truly "affluent" sitting atop the farthest rungs.

The recession's impact was felt by everyone to some degree, but it certainly hit some groups harder than others. We talked in chapter one about the impacts on the middle class.

Many who were hoping to push up out of the middle class, or who had actually done so, found themselves squarely returned to that bracket. In other words, today's middle class contains a lot of yesterday's "mass affluents."

That's not to say that they've totally stopped buying.

Gen-Xers, now in their late thirties to mid-forties, who were in the "mass affluent" group prior to 2007 were among those hardest hit by the housing crunch. They had just reached their first-home-buying peak as they moved through their thirties, meaning that many bought in at the top of the market and saw whatever equity they had invested evaporate almost overnight. That financial ground will be tough for this group to make up. They're faced with a future that is much more middle class than they'd dreamed of.

Millennials who were on the economic rise owing to their early career success are quite possibly going to continue to rise as long as they hold onto their jobs. The aspirational among them are well poised for growth. Unlike the generation above them, they will begin settling their nests and buying homes in a housing market that is down considerably from peak years, which could set them up nicely for future growth. Will they be more cautious than previous generations and not view their house as a guaranteed investment? How will that caution shape their consumer behavior moving forward? These will be the trends experts focus on in the coming years.

As for the already affluent (i.e., those who weren't aspiring, but had already achieved) of all generations, they felt the recession much less than other groups. They (and their portfolios) also bounced back much more quickly than those in lower income tiers.

In this chapter we'll understand more about Rosemary and her family, whom we met in the first chapter. She lives in Howard County, Maryland, midway between Washington, D.C., and Baltimore. This geographic area ranks among the top five most affluent counties in the U.S.[1] It's in a pocket of some of the most concentrated wealth on the East Coast. Of the top ten counties ranked by highest median household income in 2011, seven were in the Washington, D.C., area, in either Maryland or northern Virginia.

Defining the "affluent" can be done in myriad ways; later on we will use some interesting statistics to understand who is in this group. According to the Mendelsohn Affluent Survey, whose data we'll discuss later

in the chapter, a good benchmark of who is affluent are households that
take in at least $100,000 per year.[2] In this chapter I plan to focus more
on the upper middle class than on the 1 percent of the truly wealthy with
private jets and households staffs. That makes Howard County, with its
high-but-not-too-high incomes, a great place to explore if you're looking
to understand what's going on with households who live comfortably. Of
course, we'll also layer in the leading research on the affluent consumer. By
the time we leave Maryland, you will be able to:

- Distinguish who the affluent are and are not;
- See how the affluent behave differently from other consumer
  groups;
- Understand how the recession impacted definitions of luxury and
  the profile of the buyers of those goods and services.

I met Rosemary when I was in Washington, D.C., speaking at the annual meeting of the Association of Public Data Users. I also had meetings
at Pew Research, the Brookings Institution, and the U.S. Census Bureau.
I thought squeezing in dinner with some of the people I would be getting
to know over the next few months would help remind me of the stories
behind the numbers I was speaking about.

I was surprised how rural much of Howard County felt as I drove
around exploring before my visit.

Ellicott City, the county seat, is a quaint town of a classic New England type with churches high on the hill and a winding little stretch of
shops that were likely thriving 150 years ago. The downtown runs along
a small creek and now has an odd mix of high-end boutiques and local
pet-care shops sandwiched between hippie crystal shops and palm-reading
storefronts. The city is home to the B&O (Baltimore & Ohio) Museum at
the nation's oldest surviving railroad station, and trains regularly pass over
the main street.[3] Rosemary and her husband, John, go there from time to
time to a favorite restaurant and for local shopping.

To get to their house, you pass a lot of trees and open countryside and
some fairly typical suburban malls, set well back from the road.

Their house sits on a short street that branches off one of the main
thoroughfares through the area. The street ends in a small cul-de-sac and
is lined by about a half dozen homes. This particular development was

built in the last decade, and the houses have a newer feel with clear attention to detail inside and out. A simple front door instead of a multistory
entrance feature greets you.

My plan was to get a tour of their home, take some pictures, and
maybe poke around in their cupboards to see what sort of brands lined
their pantries and their fridge. As it turned out, I still needed to sell them,
especially John, on participating in the project at all. They were understandably a little skeptical of the kinds of questions I would ask and the
information I would share, but over dinner we got to know each other
better, and they agreed to participate.

We talked about kids (their daughter is about the same age as my
twins) and dogs and the economy of the area. They're not overly concerned with their financial situation and are confident about their future.
Their house is fully furnished, they have two nice cars in the garage, they
dress well, and they have the latest gadgets such as iPads—items that
would be a stretch for many families. Larger expenditures, like a recent
basement remodel, get thought out and budgeted for, but rarely get turned
down because of cost.

How the Affluent Spend

That the recession didn't change the spending habits of Rosemary and
others in her bracket too much is important. People in their income range
are huge spenders. In the 2011 Consumer Expenditure Survey, the Bureau
of Labor Statistics found that the bottom two-thirds of households (those
earning less than $70,000 a year) accounted for less than half of all spend-
ing in the U.S.—some $2.85 trillion in aggregate.[4]

Meanwhile, the top 7 percent, earning $150,000 per year or more, ac-
counted for an oversized 17 percent of total spending. Comparing those
figures to the pre-recession year of 2006, we see that the share in that
$150,000+ range has increased slightly, as has its share of spending. Here
you start to see some significant differences as the upper incomes dominate spending in certain categories. For instance, the top 7 percent of consumers accounted for almost a third of spending in audio/video electronic
goods and nearly half of spending in the floor-covering market. More
generally, they accounted for an oversized share of aggregate spending in
nearly all of the 100+ categories tracked by the Consumer Expenditure

Figure 2.1   The Out-sized Spending of the Affluent

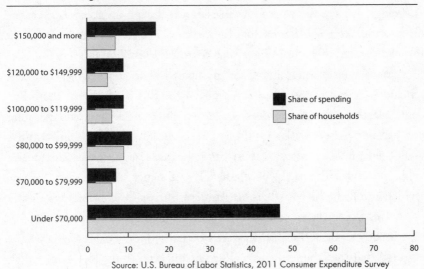

Source: U.S. Bureau of Labor Statistics, 2011 Consumer Expenditure Survey

Survey. Exceptions include tobacco and expenses like rent that don't really relate to the homeowner-heavy affluent lifestyle.

For our purposes, let's broaden our definition of "affluent." Roughly 18 percent of households earn more than $100,000 a year. Looking at this top earning group gives us a good chunk of "upper-middle-class" types as well as varying degrees of true affluence.

It's worth noting the cost-of-living problem that we run into any time we try to divide the national audience by income. Someone making $100,000 in the city of Champaign, Illinois (cost of living index 96), could appear much more affluent than someone earning the same salary in New York City (cost of living index 169). Housing in New York, according to Sperling's BestPlaces, is two and a half times as expensive as it is in Champaign, and overall the city is 75 percent more expensive.[5] A family of four in Manhattan can have an income almost $20,000 above the national median and still qualify for public housing assistance.[6]

Net worth is also a good measure of wealth. As I mentioned in chapter one, families that seem to be high income might not have much discretionary income to spend on luxury goods if they live in an expensive area, have high child-care costs, or have increasingly large student debt loads.

Unlike most income brackets, families in the top 10 percent of earners actually saw their net worth increase slightly during the recession according to the Federal Reserve Board's Survey of Consumer Finances, rising from a median of $1.17 million in 2007 to $1.19 million in 2010.[7]

Yet, the recession found a way to impact just about all of us personally, including most of the families I tracked for this book. With the affluent, questions about the recession garner different responses depending on exactly what you ask. "Optimism about themselves and their families has been pretty consistent," said Steve Kraus, senior vice president and chief insights officer of Ipsos MediaCT's Audience Measurement Group, which conducts the Mendelsohn Affluent Survey. "If you ask about optimism regarding the economy, that's been bouncing up and down a lot."

In other words, the affluent were worried about the country as a whole, but felt that they themselves would come out okay in the long run. So far, they've been dead-on with that assumption.

Shades of Affluence

The ad agency Digitas, which counts affluent-focused brands like American Express among its clients, partnered with *Ad Age* to produce a trend report about the affluent market in 2011 and did a follow-up in 2012. Digitas's research drew heavily on insights derived from the annual Mendelsohn Affluent Study.[8] Digitas broke the affluent market into five tiers:[9]

Aspirational affluents: Due to their age (35+) and career choices, they are
  unlikely to ever make it to true affluence.
Emerging affluents: Because they broke the $100,000 household income
  threshold before age 35 and chose careers in high-potential
  fields, they are well on their way to affluence.
Affluents: Those in "creative class careers" who have household incomes
  of $200,000 to $499,000 are described as "optimistic, stylish,
  financially savvy, and travel lovers."
The wealthy: With household incomes up to $1 million, these senior
  executives and CEOs still earn much of their affluence from
  a—granted large—paycheck. They "make time for luxury" and
  "prefer service and international destinations" when they travel.

The rich: These people are at the top of the income pyramid. They
    are "opinion leaders, trend followers, risk takers, and experience
    seekers."

If you look at the Mendelsohn data, Rosemary looks a lot like the
"affluent."

What separates her from true middle class is on some levels a
matter of degree. The daily-deal site for Rosemary is often Zulily, not
Groupon. For everyday shopping, she is more likely to be found at Target
than Walmart. Instead of Toyotas or Hondas, there are two Acuras parked
in Rosemary's garage. Rosemary's daughter tends to dress in trendy outfits from high-end children's clothiers or handmade from sites like Etsy
.com. What you see, therefore, isn't the ultra affluence of the truly rich.
They don't have a collection of cars in a five-car garage. The cars they own
are both needed and driven daily. The cars they do have, however, could
both be considered a luxury brand. Rosemary's husband had to trade in his
sporty BMW for something more car-seat friendly when their daughter
was born, but again, it's not on the same scale as driving a Ferrari. Nor-
dstrom is one of the most popular retailers and despite its premium con-
notation in many markets, she refers to it as "mainstream" and says that for
the most part Howard County lacks true luxury retail brands. Before their
daughter was born, they took annual vacations to global destinations such
as Greece and Korea. Like a majority in this group, she describes their
lifestyle as "upper middle class."

Rosemary uses popular culture cues to describe her situation, starting
with the 1980s blue-collar sitcom *Roseanne*.

"I think of *Roseanne* as middle class," she says. "But then I think of
Modern Family. I think of them as upper middle class. I think we live more
like *Modern Family* than *Roseanne*." She sees similarities between her family and the fictional ones on Modern Family—the houses they live in, the
cars they drive, and even the living situation of one of the couples, who has
a lawyer in the family, like her husband, and a young adopted daughter.

"We watch a lot of TV." She laughs. She's also not shy to admit that
she doesn't necessarily follow the slightly higher-brow trends of her demographic, which watches more of the Tennis Channel and the Science
Channel than average.[10] She watches a fair amount of reality TV and
her husband plays video games. Like many in their bracket, they watch

TV with iPads on their laps and iPhones on the table beside them. Their daughter had a very limited TV diet before age two but seemed to like having the *Today Show* on while her mom got ready for work.

The addition of their daughter to the family was a story you hear more and more. Women of all socioeconomic demographics are having children later and later in life. For many, that makes conceiving more difficult. But again, one of the big advantages the affluent have is the money to make choices. After five very expensive and failed IVF treatments, Rosemary and John had changed course and were in the final stages of adopting. That wasn't an inexpensive process. They had the nursery decorated and had been matched with a baby in Korea (where both their families are from and where John was born) when they found out Rosemary was pregnant. The agency canceled the adoption even though Rosemary and John wanted to go through with it.

As a couple now in their forties with plenty of income and savings and a young child, they are in the sweet spot for Jim Bacharach, vice president of advertising for John Hancock. Mr. Bacharach describes his market as the mass affluent, those having household incomes over $100,000.[11]

Those living in counties like Howard are far more likely to be investors than those living in other areas of the nation. Here's what I mean by that. The families you're meeting in this book live in counties that are representative of different segments of the U.S. population. I arrived at that by using two county-level segmentation tools, Patchwork Nation and Esri's Tapestry Segmentation. This is detailed in Appendix I. Each county represents one of the segments in each of those systems. In both segmentation systems, Howard County is in the top economic tier. For the Patchwork Nation, that means it's a "Monied 'Burb." Esri's Tapestry classifies it as a "High Society" county. In general, people who live in these areas tend to be at the top of the economic pyramid.

Consumer research firm Experian Marketing Services performed custom analysis of their data for me as I was working on the American Consumer Project stories for *Ad Age*. Taking data from its annual survey, it ran it through the Patchwork Nation and Esri's Tapestry Segmentation systems.[12] Areas like Howard County are more likely to have money in each major investment class, from stocks to bonds to mutual funds to Treasury bills.[13]

They're more likely to use a credit card but also more likely to pay off that card in full each month, and they generally have much more favorable attitudes about the economy.

Mendelsohn performed a similar Patchwork/Tapestry analysis for me as I was researching this book.[14] One piece of data that stuck out is that those in the affluent segment were 25 percent more likely than average Americans to believe they'd go back to work after retirement. That could take the form of continuing their previous careers or changing into new ones. That seems more like a lifestyle decision than one born of economic necessity. It's also a lot easier to return to a white-collar job in your sixties and beyond—think shifting into consulting or teaching—than to a manufacturing job.

As I mentioned earlier, the notion of "mass affluence" took a beating during the recession. In *Ad Age*'s 2012 white paper, Digitas all but declared the concept dead. As we've moved past the recession, the upper tiers have been quicker to recover and more confident of their own status.

That helps Mr. Bacharach take a longer view.

"You have to start with the fact that for the last thirty years and certainly for the last fifteen to twenty our primary demographic has been comprised of Baby Boomers. With that come the attitudinal qualities that define that generation in terms of high expectations for themselves and what they consider to be success. As those expectations have been reinforced in good economies and as they've been battered in difficult ones, that has had a significant impact on how we approach our target demographic in tone and the messages themselves. What has been consistent is being real and being human about it. But what constitutes reality at a given time over thirty years has ebbed and flowed."

During those last thirty years, John Hancock and its agency Hill Holliday have made commercials that make striking use of demographic and trend data, tailoring campaigns to the changing attitudes of its customers.

In watching the spots over the years, I was struck by the contrast of the pre-recession and post-recession spots.

"Pre-2008, our 'Cursor' campaign was focused on building the necessary sort of assets . . . and how to translate those assets into an income that will last up to thirty years. There was much more cause for optimism and people were concerned about retirement income," said Mr. Bacharach.

The spots show Boomers having these conversations play out via text messages and online chats, which was very calculated, based on John Hancock's research. "Decisions aren't necessarily made in that medium, but the ongoing conversations are taking place in electronic media. It gave us the opportunity from a creative standpoint to do something different. An added benefit is that it translated into campaigns that were quiet. [Our] target demo is doing something alongside watching TV half the time. The quiet gave them a reason to pick their heads up from the paper or their iPad."

Many Boomers (and, frankly, many Americans of all ages) have done a poor job of saving for retirement.[15] Losing a lot of money in the stock market and the housing crisis just as they were on the verge of retirement brought an extreme dose of reality to a generation whose generally free-spending and debt-driving ways had fueled the economy for decades. The focus became less on how to retire and more on whether retirement was a possibility.

John Hancock's post-recession "You are not alone" spots show husbands quoting TV talk shows advising that pulling money out of the market and socking it under the mattress might be the best financial course. Their wives reassure them that "the sky is not falling," and they all drift off to a comfortable sleep.

Part of the reason John Hancock's advertising has taken such obvious advantage of demographic trend data in crafting its creative is that it doesn't have a lot of other data available to it. Even as "big data" opportunities have emerged, that data is owned by the retail channel and its distribution partners. Having the data isn't good enough. The humans involved have to work together, too. Internal disputes about what departments "own" the data can keep it from being shared and utilized to its fullest advantage.

As we discussed in chapter one, Mr. Hendler at the Las Vegas Sands has been able to break down channel walls internally to facilitate the sharing and aggregating of data. But in businesses with outside partners, like John Hancock's, those boundaries are still firmly in place.

"We are far more dependent on the primary research we conduct than we are on mining data we have," Mr. Bacharach said.

One could argue that this would be a serious disadvantage as the Millennials move into more insurance-buying life stages and start to replace the aging Boomers as customers. Many Millennials have had an especially tough time during the recession. It's hit all demographics—even the increasing number of the highly educated among them who should be the most likely future affluents for John Hancock to target. As every retirement calculator tells us, the more money you save early, the better off you will be when it comes to retirement age. That's a problem when you have $150,000 in student loans and a job that requires you to wear aprons or fold sweaters.

Mr. Bacharach says that is a huge concern. I asked him if it's even possible to target Millennials at this point. "It's possible. It's certainly not the most efficient or profitable. It [purchase intent] tends to follow life stages or the arrival of a child. That's the point at which someone tends to think [about our products]."

Product development draws on many of the same demographic and behavioral trends that marketing does.

"At this stage in the game it's identifying where [Millennials] are in terms of expectations and then building products that can address them. In other words, would we expect that the products that their parents are investing in are going to be the same for the children? No, probably not. That's just the reality of the differences in the generations in both the difference in their financial situation and their attitudes. The same can be said for the generation that preceded the Boomers. Products evolved and that thing called 'pensions' went away. That then required the development of the products we know and have come to expect for Boomers."

That said, there is reason to be optimistic about the affluent Millennials. Experian Simmons's data showed that residents of counties like Howard are more likely than average to be planning major life events like engagements, weddings, and having children in the near term.

IT'S IMPORTANT TO NOTE THAT SOME OF THE ASPIRING AFFLUENTS WILL never get there. That was true when Digitas/*Ad Age* wrote the initial trend report in 2011 that showed that depending on career choice and other factors, some who get *pretty close* to affluence never get beyond that hope. That's more true now. The main difference is really the housing market. During the years leading up to the bursting of the bubble, the path to prosperity traveled through the home—buy one and sell it a few years later for a hefty profit and then buy an even bigger one. Or take out home equity loans, which were marketed as ways to upgrade kitchens with shiny new appliances or to pay for extravagances like boats and pricey vacations.

With the collapse of the housing market, that's no longer viable for most consumers, and no new path out of the middle class has magically appeared to take its place.

As I mentioned earlier, the Gen-Xers in their thirties and forties who fall into this "mass affluent" category haven't bounced back as quickly as the truly affluent. That leaves those previously aspirational affluents in the $100,000 to $199,000 range a lot more likely to look like middle-class consumers than luxury buyers.

Mendelsohn pegs this income range overall as about 70 percent of affluents.

On the other hand, the roughly 13.2 million Millennials in the $100,000 to $199,000 range are still aspiring to climb all the way to the upper tiers of affluence.

It's an interesting fact for luxury brands. Many of their customers aren't affluent. We tend to assume that people behave rationally. That's simply not true at all, and one could argue that it's especially not true when it comes to money. You need look no further than the fact that individual investors have underperformed in every major investment class in the last twenty years, according to the investment giant BlackRock. They have even underperformed inflation. The reason BlackRock cites? Emotion.[16] We're fueled by it and it leads us to make irrational purchasing decisions.

Behavioral economists would point out that we behave irrationally in predictable ways. While marketers often forget that people are irrational— or at least rarely put it in those terms—it's the very premise that makes advertising work. If we behaved rationally, all advertisers would have to do is convince us that their product is better than the other guy's. But it doesn't work that way. They still have to sell us on the product, on our emotional connection to the brand, and on our fundamental desire to own it in the first place.

As Rose Cameron, head of Global Brand Strategy at Hornall Anderson Design Works, put it when I interviewed her for this book, "Household income has little or nothing to do with regard to buying luxury products."[17] For those who are on the verge of affluence, and even many of those who don't even dream of it, being able to project a look of affluence leads them to buy at least some products that should realistically be out of their reach. "People who don't have a lot of money want to connote their affluence," she said. "People who do [have a lot of money] want to connote their influence. The smaller the bank account, the larger the bling."

She points to invitation-only marketplaces like Gilt.com, but the fictional jeans brand Gabriel Hounds in William Gibson's novel *Zero History* would work, too. The brand is so exclusive no one even knows who makes it.

Bob Shullman, who heads the Shullman Research Center, surveys affluent and non-affluent consumers to tease out the differences in their attitudes. He advises his luxury clients not to ignore the huge base of customers who aren't typically the target of "luxury" marketers. For example, he says, a champagne marketer might sell half its bottles to a select group of its best and most frequent customers but also sell half its products to customers who only buy one bottle a year—and consider that purchase a splurge.[18]

Shullman's research shows that at the high-income levels of $250,000 and above, 40 percent have purchased luxury goods in the past year. It's not too surprising to find the rich buying luxury goods. However, 18 percent of all households and 25 percent of households making between $75,000 and $250,000 are also purchasing luxury goods. Taken together, these consumers can make up a noticeable share of the luxury market.[19]

They exhibit different buying patterns, too. They typically purchase luxury items less frequently and are typically buying the item for themselves. They're much less likely to pay cash, opting for credit and often saving up for the splurge.

All of this indicates that there's still some aspirational behavior left in the non-affluent. It's just getting stretched thinner and has become a more challenging behavior to target.

MENDELSOHN'S SENIOR VICE PRESIDENT AND CHIEF INSIGHTS OFFICER, Steve Kraus, says that luxury brands have had to refocus on the truly affluent. The 2012 Digitas/*Ad Age* trend report found that "luxury" itself had shifted from a concept shared among the affluent to one that was "in the eye of the beholder." In other words, there wasn't a single definition of exactly what a luxury item or service is. Almost all agreed that small indulgences were meaningful. Increasingly a new concept had filtered up to the affluent market: price comparison. Almost nine in every ten respondents in the Mendelsohn Affluent Survey said that they "go out of their way" to find the best price on high-end items.

That doesn't mean luxury marketers should take the obvious approach and start touting their prices. It still takes a soft touch to market to high-end consumers.

Mark Miller is the chief strategy officer at Team One Advertising in Los Angeles, the agency of record for luxury brands including Lexus and the Ritz-Carlton. When he talks about "value" in the premium and luxury brand space, he's not talking about price at all. "We started talking about the term 'meaningful value.' What are the things that we could offer people that have emotional resonance for them and that are worth paying a premium for? Having a story you can share forever has a different kind of value," he told me.[20] For the Ritz-Carlton that meant accepting an important change in their consumers' behavior in and around the recession: they were traveling with less frequency. The pitch then centered around the idea that if you're going to travel less, it's even more critical that the trip be memorable. He felt that pitching value as "how many nights can I get for how few dollars" wouldn't work in the long term because as the recovery started up, it would be hard to get away from that idea.

"How do you justify going back to your customers and charging high premiums when you just slashed and burned prices in the short term? If you used to charge $500 a night and then you charged $250 a night, why would I go back to paying $500?" Mr. Miller said.

Lexus is another brand, like John Hancock, that has really grown up with the Boomers and the aspirational affluents. It also more or less invented one of the quintessential "special" moments in luxury marketing: the gifted car with the big red bow. In the beginning of the "December to Remember" campaign, it was primarily a marketing construct invented by Team One creatives working with the Lexus Dealers Association and Lexus clients. Now, the brand actually ships thousands of big red bows to its dealerships because the customers started demanding them. When the recession hit, Lexus tried to be considerate of the economic climate. Lexus and Team One ran a number of focus groups and conducted a lot of research trying to understand how best to be sensitive. Once it was revealed that the brand behind the research was Lexus, the consumer reaction surprised everyone involved. Instead of being outraged by luxury advertising in tough times, the consumers felt that the Lexus commercials were so ingrained in the popular culture that it almost wouldn't seem like Christmas without them.

Lexus continues to sell a lot of cars in December.

Mr. Miller represents brands that tried to maintain and justify their premium status during the recession. Many brands—especially those slightly less premium brands—did cut prices. Conventional wisdom had always stated that the value of the item would seem diminished in the eyes of affluents if it took part in anything as gauche as a sale. Mr. Kraus says that current research refutes that. "Only one in five [affluents] question the quality of a luxury item if it goes on sale." Like that of Mr. Miller, his research has led him to the conclusion that value means more than that. While the recession has trained consumers to expect to get a better deal on luxury, expectations on quality haven't changed. The affluent haven't given up on quality, but might have scaled back on quantity. The Ritz-Carlton embraced reduced frequency among travelers during the recession. Travel is now increasing again, but the brand remains focused on treating its guests as if they might come only once a year. Even handbag makers might see their customers buying two designer bags a year instead of four. Customers haven't given up on luxury categories, says Mr. Kraus, but they have changed the way they shop for them.

"We did reel back on the summer vacation," Rosemary told me. "Going to the house in [North Carolina's] Outer Banks was much cheaper than other options that we were considering such as an all-inclusive resort in the Caribbean or a cruise."

Sites that have benefited the middle class have also benefited the affluent. The daily-deal sites are stocked full of "luxury" goods and services—fine dining, spa treatments, massages, and golf outings. For the aspirational affluent, it's allowed careful consumers to achieve many of the trappings of affluent life at up to 60 percent off. The affluent have taken notice, too. One in five households in the Mendelsohn study used a daily-deal site in some way in 2012, reflecting a significant uptick from 2011.

The flip side is true, too. Traditionally middle-class categories are trying to move into the luxury space. Cinépolis Luxury Cinemas has expanded into the U.S. market to provide luxury moviegoing experiences for those who find paying twice as much for a movie to be totally fine if they get a fully reclining leather seat and sushi menu out of it.[21] Its site describes the theaters as "a revolutionary concept that has forever changed the movie-going experience. [Its goal] is to pamper guests in an intimate and comfortable environment."

Choices, Choices

In chapter one, we talked about the importance of dual incomes in raising families into and sometimes up out of the middle class. We also talked about the ability to make choices. For Rosemary the decision to become a stay-at-home mom and forgo her income came almost as a whim. She saw a Facebook posting from a stay-at-home-mom friend who was taking her young daughter to ballet class. She realized she was missing out on those moments and had her resignation letter written almost immediately. She and her husband had discussed the issue, certainly. Months earlier she'd mentioned the talks to me. "I knew that if I stayed home we would have to change our lifestyle. I would be okay with that. I was worried John would be unhappy with a lifestyle change. And my husband is such a saver. He likes to have a nice nest egg cushion so I thought if I stopped working, we wouldn't be able to save as much and that would probably cause a lot of anxiety."

They'd even come up with a makeshift budget limit for Rosemary to practice staying under. But in the end, she made the choice, and they are content to save less for now. When she was working, they were mostly saving her paycheck, which meant they were saving more than a typical U.S. household earns in a year. But in the end, their day-to-day lifestyle hasn't altered much.

"I think I stuck to [that budget] one month over the course of three or four months. I do sort of have this budget. It's not a concrete number . . . I figure now that I'm not working I don't need to buy the work clothes; I'm not using as much gas, not eating out for lunch as much. But I was only going in two days a week. We'll see how that goes. It hasn't stopped me from buying clothes for [my daughter]. I still buy clothes for her."

She's trying not to over-program her toddler, but she did enroll in a gymnastics class she got a good price on through a daily-deal site.

Previously they were able to pay extra into their mortgage each month to bring down the principal owed on the loan. Now they're not saving as much but are still over-paying their housing bill. "I suppose if we really had to buckle down, we could," she said.

That's the key. In the recession, the middle class was forced to buckle down by an actual decrease in income and financial well-being. The affluent buckled down out of a perception of economic unease and concern about the appearance of looking as if they weren't suffering when others were. Again, it comes down to choices. Rosemary and other top earners had them.

In Clark County, Nevada, Chris doesn't have the same choices. He, like many middle-class homeowners, is just plain stuck. As a divorced dad in North Las Vegas he's developed a likely unhealthy fascination with the home valuation site Zillow.com. It rarely brings him good news.

Living alone (except for the days when he has custody of his daughter), he is living on a single income. He works in the hospitality industry, and his pay and bonuses are partially performance based. When the economy takes a hit, so does he.

Median household income in the U.S. is roughly $50,000. For a family household it's $62,000—double that of a non-family household.[22] You can see how that would impact choices for a growing segment of households. How much is that segment growing? That's the subject of the next two chapters, which will force you to rethink the term "typical American household."

THREE
Home Economics

How Changes in Homes and Who Lives in Them Impact How We Spend

CHRIS IS A DIVORCED FATHER WITH CUSTODY OF HIS TEENAGE DAUGHTER on weekends. Sandra is a single mom with two daughters—one in college and one in kindergarten. Liz is a single woman who plans to move in with her boyfriend when their respective leases run out. Andrew lived with his girlfriend before proposing. Michael lives with his boyfriend and a roommate. Basha and her husband are empty nesters. Jay lives with a roommate who is a friend from high school. These people range in age from their early twenties to their seventies. Each of them could be considered a "typical" American household these days. Yet you'd be surprised at how many people—marketers included—still think that married couples with kids are the norm.

As of 2010, simply put, they're wrong.

Demographically, the U.S. hit a number of milestones in the past several years. Married couples with children now make up fewer than one in five households. Married couples as a whole make up just 48 percent of households.[1] That means that most U.S. households do not include a married couple. This tipped only recently, marking the first time in recorded (and likely unrecorded) history that we can say that. Both of these figures are so important and yet are understood by so few.

By the end of this chapter, you'll be one of the folks who get it. You'll know all about:

- The changing makeup of the household structure;
- The rise of the single-person household and the different age groups it represents;
- Why multigenerational households are and are not important to consider.

The bottom line is that there is no "typical" any longer. Changes in the family structure are wide-reaching—so much so that I'll touch on them here in the broader discussion of households and then devote the next chapter entirely to them. Also remarkable are the changes to the "non-family" households. The incredible explosion of people living alone, coupled with the urban and driving-related trends I'll talk about in later chapters, are remaking the landscape for big box stores, grocers, automotive marketers, and other big spending categories. But not all marketers are responding in smart ways.

Because so many of these changes have taken place during the lifetime of the average *Fortune* 500 CEO, it is more difficult to see shifts, and the data is so overwhelming that it is hard to digest and react to.[2] The bottom line is that the world that these men (and they're still roughly 95 percent men) grew up in doesn't exist anymore.[3]

In 1950, more than three-quarters of households looked more or less alike—they were married-couple families. That share has dropped an astonishing 30 percentage points in just sixty years. Since 1950, the U.S. has added more than 77 million households. But in that time, married couples have only increased by 25 million.[4]

Now, 13 percent of households are led by single mothers and another 5 percent by single dads.[5] One in three households is a "non-family" household.

What's going on? One thing to look at is the rate at which people formed their own households. It's a basic building block of society and the economy. The rate at which households formed dropped to an anemic

Figure 3.1   Share of Selected Household Types

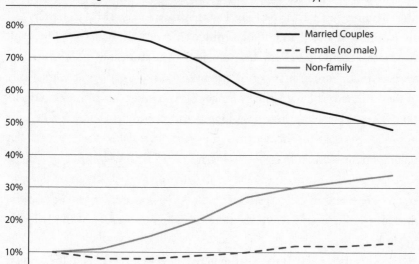

Source: U.S. Census Bureau

level of just 357,000 new households formed in 2010.[6] That helped push the average age of a householder up over fifty for the first time in history.

Thankfully for the economy, growth has since rebounded somewhat, and the U.S. added more than a million households each year in 2011 and 2012.[7]

Demographics might solve many of the problems for business in coming years. The Millennials aren't getting any younger. Now reaching their thirties, they will be increasingly looking at moving into the next life stages. Whether they'll do so in traditional ways (get married, buy a house, have kids) or not is certainly open to debate. As the largest generation in history, if even a reasonable percentage of them follow that pattern, it will lead to a big uptick in demand for housing and all the new spending that goes with having kids. That's good news for home goods, baby goods, packaged goods, car makers, and more. Trends regarding households are complicated. They're driven by marriage rates, education rates, and economic and social factors.

The majority of women over age fifteen in this country are unmarried. One in three has never married. For their male counterparts, barely half are currently married and 36 percent have never tied the knot.[8] The marriage rate, according to Pew Research, is at an all-time low, and the median age at which women first get married (26.5) is at an all-time high.[9] Part of that is due to the increasing number of women getting a higher education. They are staying in school longer and putting off marriage at least until they graduate or further, until they have established their careers. I'm talking about women here because there are now three women in college for every two men. If marriage is a partnership, it's typically never been an equal one. Economically, the scales are tipping toward the females for the first time in history. It's hard to understate the importance of this increasing imbalance.

This isn't to say that these women will never marry. In fact, for women with higher levels of education, the marriage rate is *rising*, not falling.[10] You'll notice a recurring theme in this book about bifurcation. There are two important splits in marriage rates along the lines of education and income and race. The rate is declining much more for poorer, less-educated women and for blacks.

Part of the equation is the student loan debt that graduates carry. It's much harder to start a household for today's graduates who are saddled with $27,000 (average) in debt. Ten percent of borrowers owe at least twice the average. All told, there is nearly $1 trillion in outstanding student debt in the U.S. That's a lot of money not being spent on household goods.[11]

College is certainly one factor in marriage rates, but it's not the only one. A majority of women (and men) never get a college education at all. In fact, only 28.5 percent of Americans have a bachelor's degree or higher.[12] So gaining the benefits of a college education (read: vastly improved earning potential) doesn't explain the story entirely.

Liz, a Millennial in her late twenties who lives in Champaign County, Illinois, is unmarried and lives alone at the moment, although she plans to move in with her boyfriend when their leases run out. She isn't necessarily delaying marriage while she sorts out her career and makes plans for graduate school, but she's not in a hurry either. This despite the onslaught of weddings she has to attend herself as a bridesmaid or a guest. At one point she was forced to put off plans to get a new computer for herself because she was spending so much money on other people's weddings. When budgets are tight—Liz had a 5 percent pay cut during the recession that led her to pick up a second job—it can often be the unexpected changes in day-to-day spending that push people to the limits of their budgets. For some, that's medical costs. For others, it's having too many eligible friends.

In Hampden County, Massachusetts, Andrew's girlfriend moved in with him last year, partially to save on expenses while she was out of work and attending graduate school. She's a little older than he is—nearing thirty while Andrew is in his mid-twenties. When she graduated in the spring, she got a new job and they found themselves on surer economic footing. Now they're ready to "formally" start their lives together. Since I began reporting for this book, they have gotten engaged and by the time it's published they should be married with their first child. That process has brought about more changes. Andrew's parents own a three-flat apartment building and live in one of the apartments. Andrew and his now-fiancée have moved into a flat on another floor and are living rent-free while they save toward buying their family's first home. She has stopped working to become a full-time mother.

Sandra in East Baton Rouge Parish, Louisiana, is a lower-income college graduate who might never marry. Her job and her role as a single mother don't leave her a lot of time to focus on herself. That was a realization she kept coming back to in our discussions. She has spent very little time or money on herself, channeling it all into her daughters. She is African American, and the marriage rate for her race is barely 30 percent.

In Los Angeles County, Alfredo went to a technical school instead of college. He works for a trucking company and, with business down since the recession, he lives a life with few splurges. He and his family have a lot of challenges financially, but he has high hopes for his daughter. She was able to tour Ivy League colleges as part of a program funded by her high school for selected high-achieving students. She started at Smith in fall 2013.

The size and makeup of a household impact everything as far as income and spending are concerned. For instance, the average household spends about $50,000 a year, according to the Bureau of Labor Statistics. A household with a married couple and no kids typically spends about $58,000 a year. Married couples with children tend to be the highest-earning household type, but their spending also increases by more than $10,000 over that of a married couple with no kids. Dropping down to a single-person household cuts spending down to $31,000.

It's always good to be asking yourself what the drivers of trends are, especially in tumultuous times like those we saw leading up to, during, and following the recession. We're already starting to see some of the big "trends" of recent years reversing themselves. One area of growth between 2008 and 2010 was the number of households that had an "additional adult" living in them. That included a significant number of parents with adult non-student children living with them. Various factors were judged to be part of that growth, most notably the economy but also the strong relationship between many "helicopter-parent" Boomers and their Millennial progeny and the increasing footprint of the American house itself. It's only in recent decades that children started having their own bedrooms in houses.[13] Larger houses have made it possible to accommodate an extra adult while still providing "space" for everyone.

In 2011 roughly one in five households had an "extra" adult. All told, that adds up to more than 41 million "extra" adults. That's a really big number. About half are children of the householder, one in ten are parents of the householder, and about one in five are non-related roommates. Nearly two in three of the "extra" adults are under the age of thirty-five. However, as soon as the economy started to improve, the number of "shared" households in the U.S. started dropping—from an increase of 1.2 million in 2010 to a decrease of 200,000 in 2011.[14]

The economy is certainly one factor driving the rise in multigenerational households, too. Between 1990 and 2010, the number of households with at least three generations living together rose dramatically on a percentage basis, increasing 67 percent.[15] My hunch is that we'll continue to see a rise in those figures. We'll see fewer of the adult children living at home as the economy improves and they can get jobs and start their own households. We will instead see the rise in the multigenerational households fueled by an aging population that eventually, but not immediately, will need more care. Specifically, we'll see more of these households in cases where one spouse has passed away and the widow/widower isn't able to live alone. Culturally, we also see this as a more common trend among the two racial/ethnic groups that are fast growing in the U.S., Hispanics and Asians.

The reason it's not a big deal for marketers is that we're still talking about a very small proportion of all households. Even with the steep rise, only 4 percent of households are multigenerational.[16]

In talking with marketers, it's also hard to come up with a message to reach this umbrella of households and it's unclear how they shop differently from one- or two-generation households. Some brands like Comcast have at least been focusing more on showing this type of household in their advertising—especially when targeting the Hispanic market.[17]

The much more important trend for media and brands is not the small number of people now living in larger households. It's the enormous number of people now living in very, very small households.

A whopping 28 percent of Americans now live alone.[18] To give you a sense of scale, that's a figure roughly equal to the number living in empty-nester households. That figure has more than doubled since 1960.[19] This is a global trend—the U.S. actually lags behind many European countries in the numbers. Here, a little over 40 percent of those living alone are under the age of thirty-four, which you would probably expect. But a greater and more overlooked proportion are over the age of sixty-five. One good thing about the rise of single-person households is that they're a group who are actually spending more than they used to. In the last ten years dual-income households have cut their average household expenditures more than 2 percent in 2011 dollars.[20] Single-earning single households (in other words, someone with an income living alone) raised their spending a little over 1 percent.

Sociologically, this is all very fascinating. People are living alone on the younger end because they can. It takes money to live alone and enjoy the kind of independence that comes with city living, which is where most of these households can be found. They can have networks of coworkers and friends and plenty of dining and entertainment options without having to actually live with any of these people. On the older end, many women are outliving their spouses. Since older Americans are generally living longer, healthier, more active lives, they can survive without assistance much later into life.

For brands, these situations provide all kinds of opportunities for new products and markets. It's just a matter of reaching them.

Between 2003 and 2012, the amount of time Americans reported spending on shopping activities dropped nearly 33 hours annually to 263 hours.[21] Women saw their share drop faster than men did.

People living alone have to balance work, social life, and household upkeep without anyone to split the chores and errands. For Liz, this leads to more online shopping. Chris sometimes stops at the market (Vaughn's) or Walmart on the way home from work. That limits his choices in that he doesn't want to lengthen his commute by more than a couple of minutes in any direction.

Chris is representative of another kind of single-person household on the rise, especially for Baby Boomers—divorced people.[22] Since he has custody of his daughter only on weekends, the census would count him as single. But that weekend custody is the kind of twist you don't find in the data. You find it by visiting Las Vegas.

Chris lives in Clark County, Nevada. In the Patchwork Nation archetypes, that's considered a "Boom Town." Boom towns were some of the fastest growing in the run-up to the recession. Then they were among the hardest hit. Chris lives in what seems sort of like a bachelor pad. In the sparsely furnished living room, a large comfy couch looks out over a flat panel TV and gaming center. Were it not for the bedroom decorated for a pre-teen girl, you'd think he was just another single man.

But while she's there—and even to a large extent when she's not—his daughter has a huge impact on his life and his buying habits. A single guy who lives alone, Chris often talks about "we."

He shops primarily on Saturdays, with his daughter. "I always ask her opinion on everything," Chris said. "She's getting to that age where she needs her own things, so I'm always making sure we get her stuff, whether it's shampoo or clothes." She also drives his adventurousness in food buying.

"We like trying something new for dinner, but there are some things that remain consistent from week to week. When it's time to buy cereal, she always picks something different. I pretty much pick the same thing."

Therefore, his kitchen is stocked with a lot of items he normally wouldn't buy on his own. His daughter has two bedrooms, one at his house and one at her mom's house across town. Each is more or less fully stocked. She has clothes, furniture, toiletries, and all the usual kinds of things that you would find in the room of a teenage girl. That means that if you can sell her on a product or brand, she's liable to buy *two* of them.

In talking to the ten families I tracked during the research for this book, it was interesting to hear them talk about the opinions they solicit about purchasing decisions, major and minor. It seemed important for the single adults especially to get advice and ideas from someone of the opposite gender. Even as household structure changes, our need for relationships is still critical. Increasingly, it's these indirect relationships that are important for marketers. In other words, the challenge now often isn't in reaching the person who will actually use the product but rather the person who will buy it for them or recommend it to them. But since "mom" or "Mrs." isn't doing all the shopping anymore, that's a big change. I'll talk about the technology side of this phenomenon more in chapter nine when I discuss the connected consumer and the rise of social media. For now, let's look at the direct relationships impacting shopping.

For Chris, the woman in his life is his daughter. For Sandra in Baton Rouge, Louisiana, the key man in her life is her dad. She works full-time and cares for her two daughters, who, despite being fourteen years apart in age, both have the same father. He's a trucker and lives in town, passing through their lives on an infrequent and irregular basis.

Sandra's dad, however, is a rock in her life. He spent twenty-five years in the army, moving his family from Germany (where Sandra was born) to Kentucky, Ohio, Louisiana, Massachusetts, and back to Baton Rouge. He retired from that career when she and her sister were in high school. "[He was a] very strict father, with very strict rules and expectations and high standards for us. We didn't appreciate it at the time, but we appreciate it now. All of his kids graduated high school and all went to college."

Even from across town, he still exerts a lot of influence in her household, including major purchases like the 2006 Impala she drives today.

"This is the first car that I've actually bought. My dad's bought cars for [my sister and me] in the past. But he had to be a major part in this purchase, because he actually gave me a lot of money to help get it.

"He actually did a lot of research on the Impala. He took me to Mississippi to get this car, because he wanted me to have a certain car with a certain interior, with the kids. He didn't want it to be a light color. He wanted it to be a darker color for stain purposes. I really liked the Impala, and I just really didn't think I could afford it. He gave me money for a nice down payment on it, which gave me an affordable note."

Missing Signs in the Housing Market

There's not much point in having a discussion of households without having a discussion of housing as well. Who lives in your household has a pretty big impact on the kind of housing you need. Singles need less space and want more access to friends and places to be social. Families need more room and more rooms. Seniors can live in huge communities of like-aged folks to get both the activities and the support they need. All of these decisions impact spending patterns.

Housing is the single biggest expenditure most Americans make both in a lifetime (assuming they purchase a home at some point) and as a monthly mortgage or rental expense. The housing market went berserk in the 2000s as the bubble inflated and popped in rather spectacular fashion. As we discussed in the first chapter, this hit middle-class homeowners especially hard by sucking a lot of their net worth away.

The market is still trying to find some equilibrium.

While I was visiting Chris in North Las Vegas, I expected to see For Sale signs everywhere. But I didn't. Chris told me about a foreclosure near him, but there were still no signs. Since real estate is such an issue today, especially in areas like this, I stopped by the real estate office of Jamie Cox. He and his partner, Josephine Picerno, gave me a crash course in the area market. Legislative changes in 2012 dried up the foreclosure market, resulting in a rush on properties by investors. They would swoop in within hours of a home going on the market with full-price, all-cash offers.

"Families that want to buy a house don't have a shot if they're trying to finance it," Mr. Cox told me.

The market was so out of hand in the fall of 2012 that buyers were offering side deals to homeowners. Generally, owners doing a short sale—selling below the amount owed on a mortgage and forcing the bank to eat some or all of the difference—won't see a dollar from the transaction and are often out whatever money they had put into the house. If one buyer offers them thousands of dollars in cash for their dishwasher—which they get to pocket legally themselves—it's not hard to see which offer they'll take.

All of this craziness is why I didn't see any For Sale signs. Ms. Picerno said, "Signs are just a big joke to us. It's passive marketing. Most of the time those properties are already gone a long time ago. Realtors put them up just so people will call them about the property and they can try to get another client." She said that they now sell the properties faster than the day or two it can take to get the sign ordered and installed, so they just don't bother.

Most markets aren't quite that out of whack, but all except the wealthiest are still in recovery mode. In most of America, it's merely harder to get a loan in the post-crash era. That means that fewer people own homes, and many who used to own are now forced to rent. Homeownership rates have fallen somewhat consistently since the bubble-era peak of 69 percent in the third quarter of 2006 down to 65.5 percent of all households at the end of 2012.[23]

How Does This Matter for Marketers?

It probably won't surprise you to learn that owners and renters spend in very different ways. In the last twenty-five years or so, homeowners and renters haven't really changed their average expenditures, which makes a lot of sense in that, as we noted in chapter one, incomes haven't been increasing for most Americans. The average homeowner spends roughly $56,000 a year and the average renter spends about $33,500, according to the Bureau of Labor Statistics. Housing remains the biggest expenditure for both groups. The percent of expenditure on housing has increased faster for renters, now making up nearly 40 percent of all money spent.

It's also no secret that health-care costs have risen. The only way most families have been able to make that work is by buying fewer or cheaper staples such as food and clothing. Thankfully, costs for those two budget items have been decreasing. Here's where the surprising data comes in.

Health-care costs have risen *more than 2.6 times as fast* for owners than they have for renters—up 42 percent in the last quarter century. These rising expenses have been offset somewhat by long-term downward trends in the cost of food and apparel. The costs of growing and transporting food, changes in our wardrobes, and the decreasing cost of manufacturing clothing have led to decreased spending on apparel (41 percent) and food (14 percent). Of course, there's been some belt-tightening as well. We're also holding on to our cars longer, leading to decreased spending on transportation.

Renters cut back on those expenses as well, but not as severely. Interestingly, renters have cut back on entertainment while owners have increased those expenditures by 11 percent.

I know what you're thinking. "Insurance costs are rising for owners because they are more likely to be families and insuring spouses and kids is costly." Here again, the data tells a somewhat counterintuitive story. The gap between owners and renters in terms of the number of children living with them fell consistently and has actually tipped in recent years. Renters now have more children living with them than owners do. That's largely the result of the increasing number of home-owning empty nesters as the Boomers age and their kids move out. On the Boomer front, it's worth noting that among households headed by someone over the age of sixty-five, more than one in five are renters. About 13.5 percent of all renters are in that age range. Neither of those stats have changed much in the last decade.[24]

A Marketer Throws an Allen Wrench into the Equation

IKEA spends a lot of time thinking about trends like these. Each year, as part of its planning process, the marketers do a deep dive into the data. It's a process called "STEEPR" because it looks for changes that are social, technological, environmental, economic, and political as well as changes to retail. Demographic shifts have impacted the very spaces we live in. I'll talk more about the house itself in chapter six but here are some key takeaways for now:

- The number of people living in each house has decreased.
- Houses have gotten bigger.
- The layout of the home has changed.
- Housing is eating up more of our income.

In the last century the average number of people living in an American home has dropped 40 percent to just 2.7 people (only 2.5 in rented units). That might not be too surprising. Even households on TV have gotten smaller. Gone is *Eight Is Enough* and in are the smaller households in *Modern Family*. Meanwhile, houses themselves have gotten larger. All we see on housing shows that populate networks like TLC and HGTV are sprawling McMansions and the gluttonous houses Americans are supposed to live in with all their granite countertops and stainless steel appliances. Indeed, the average square footage of a new-construction home increased from 1,740 square feet in 1980 to 2,392 square feet in 2010 and was near 2,500 square feet in 2011.[25] There have been dips in the growth from time to time, including the recent recession. Those dips can cause breathless headlines to declare that the age of the McMansion is finally over. But as soon as the economy picks up again, so does the size of American homes.

I've seen some but not a lot of research on the topic, but I suspect that the growth in home size has helped make it easier for multigenerational households to exist. Having mom or dad move in or letting your kids keep living at home as they're supposedly entering adulthood is less strenuous when you have enough rooms for everyone to have their alone space.

Within the overarching growth trend are some surprising sub-trends. Houses within metro areas (which include the suburbs but also all the properties in the city center) are larger than their more rural counterparts. Also, houses in the more established, tighter-packed Northeast region are the largest by as much as 200 to 300 square feet when compared to other regions in the U.S.

And those McMansions? Well, that trend is a little misleading and here's another form of bifurcation. Houses on the whole have gotten larger. As of 2011, one in five new homes built had at least a three-car garage. The majority of homes had a fireplace, two stories, and air conditioning. Nearly half had three bedrooms, and four in ten had at least four bedrooms.[26] But a majority of Americans are still living in homes with five or fewer rooms. A majority are also living in homes built before 1980.[27] Fewer and fewer new homes have formal dining rooms, but kids now have their own bedrooms.[28]

At the same time, more and more people are living alone and dealing with adverse economic conditions. Story after story in the press talk about how people are living in smaller spaces as part of a revival of downtown and urban living. The recession has also forced people to economize. Housing is the largest living expense, so it's an area where downsizing even a little can lead to big savings during tough times.

In 2012, IKEA's theme for its annual catalog was focused on small spaces. It seemed like fortuitous timing. I spoke with Mary Lunghi, strategic insights manager at IKEA. She says that "small spaces" is a core theme at IKEA and rotates through every few years. "No matter how much or how little space people have, they tend to fill it with stuff.

"We've done some research here in the U.S. where we've talked to people in various size homes and no matter how large your home (even over 3,000 square feet), they will say they still don't have enough space in their home. No matter the size of your home, you are constantly filling it with stuff so there is always a need for smart and clever solutions that will help you organize and make the most use of your space."[29]

That said, IKEA still tries to be cognizant that more than a quarter of potential customers near its U.S. stores live in spaces that are smaller than 1,000 square feet. That's a challenge for product designers as well as for marketers.

IKEA also recognizes that the busy consumer, as well as the consumer who's driving less and living in more urban spaces (which we'll talk about more later), doesn't necessarily have the same luxury of trading their time for price. While initially the you-build-it/you-save-money proposition of IKEA was a huge draw in the U.S. market, people are increasingly also driving up sales at the retail end because they like the design and simplicity. IKEA has increased its marketing push behind its services. Customers can choose to pay a bit more and have IKEA staff pick the items out of the warehouse-like ground floor, load them in/on your car or rented truck, or even deliver them. Most of these services have been around for years, but with an increased marketing push, deliveries shot up 40 percent in 2011. IKEA has even targeted owners and renters with different campaigns. Owners, for instance, are more likely to get the mailers for kitchen counters and cabinets than are renters, who are not typically in the remodeling market.

The Swedish furniture maker has had to make many changes to its strategies based on the altered shape of homes and those who live in them. For instance, an ad for a table tested well with Hispanics when it was used as a dining table with a family gathered around it, enjoying a meal together. Showing the table for other uses didn't work as well for Hispanics. The key takeaway is that there isn't one solution for each demographic. IKEA couldn't simply assume that a dining table made sense to every type of household because many just don't have dining rooms anymore. Instead, it had to develop, test, and measure different approaches to reach an increasingly fragmented consumer base.

One critical part of the family that has changed radically over the past decade and beyond is the father. Once again, there's bifurcation to discuss. Father figures just aren't what they used to be.

But let's start by talking to the most traditional-sounding father figure possible, a family farmer. I had to search long and hard to find him. Way up in Montana—Teton County, to be exact—I met up with Dale, his wife,

Frankie, and one of their three daughters (the third was away at college in nearby Helena). Dale is the third generation of his family on the farm. His daughters, who all drive combines in the summer, are generation four. It's a tightly knit family, and Dale and Frankie work hard to provide for their daughters despite the long odds facing family farmers in today's economy. I can honestly say I haven't met too many dads like him in today's world. Even his role has changed.

In the next chapter we'll home in on the all-important consumer group that is parents. Even more specifically, I'm going to write about a group of underappreciated consumers that for me hits close to, um, home: dads. So let's head for Montana.

FOUR

The Buyographics of Family

Can Advertising Catch
Up to Changing Gender
Roles in the Home?

THE TRADITIONAL ROLE OF "DAD" IS THAT OF THE PROVIDER. HE'S THE GUY who makes sure the money is earned, the bills are paid, and the family's future is secure. Dale fits that model pretty well—what could be more representative of traditional American dads than a third-going-on-fourth-generation family farmer?

Dale is typical of an America that used to exist but doesn't so much anymore. Now, fewer than one in five households look like Dale's, a married couple with kids. In order to find Dale, I headed all the way out to Teton County, Montana, population 6,073.[1] Even here the roles of dads and moms are shifting.

Dale is a hardworking family man who makes time for his community when he can.

So why are so many marketers, TV shows, and agencies spending so much time and money mocking him and his fellow fathers? Big brands like Huggies, Hyundai, and others have aired ads showing dads in such a poor light that they have raised the ire of dads and daddy bloggers. In the latter camp is 8BitDad, which even tracks this genre under the heading "Bad Dadvertising."[2]

As the makeup of the American household changes shape, so do the jobs that dads and moms do within those households.

In this chapter we'll focus on parents. Married-couple households with children spent more than $2 trillion in 2011—more than any other type in aggregate.[3] On average these (often dual-income) households spend $70,000 a year—$20,000 more than the overall median U.S. income, which of course includes lower-earning and lower-spending household types. So while they're declining in numbers, married couples with kids are still very important to brands.

This chapter will help you understand:

- The changing roles of moms and dads;
- The ways in which marketers are adjusting to the changing roles of parents—some doing so successfully and some not so much;
- The bifurcation of dads.

Dale is on the young end of the Baby Boom. He lives with his wife and one of his three Millennial daughters. Another daughter recently graduated college and lives and works nearby; the third is attending college elsewhere in Montana. To get to Dale's farm, you'll need to fly into Great Falls International Airport. You'll land at one of six gates—three of which often aren't even in use. The restaurant (singular) is called "Restaurant." Head down the escalator, pick up your rental car right outside the door, and drive an hour or two farther north and farther west. Just hope that the roads aren't too icy.

This part of Montana runs along the foothills of the Rockies near Glacier National Park. The grandeur of the sprawling landscape with the distant mountains is hard to capture on film. On the way to Dale's farm you'll pass through the county seat of Choteau, home to one in three of Teton County's 6,000 residents. Stop in at the county building, where David Letterman got married—he owns a ranch here—or shop along Main Street at the Trading Post. Grab a bite at John Henry's or the Elk Country Grill. Fuel yourself and your car because there's basically nothing but land between here and Dale's farm.

I visited in September. It was 22 degrees. Granted, it was unusually cold for that time of year, but still. Twenty-two degrees. And snowing. Nothing but clouds in the big sky.

Admittedly, Dale's situation isn't particularly common these days. When all three daughters were living at home, they raised the population density of the county due to the size of their homestead. In the Patchwork Nation framework, Dale lives in what is called "Tractor Country," a sparsely populated, mostly rural part of America. In Esri's Tapestry Segmentation system, Teton County is dominated by the "Factories and Farms" LifeMode group. The population looks a lot like the America of the 1950s: mostly white married two-parent families with children. This is not an area with much diversity. Incomes in areas like this are often low due to the heavy concentration of jobs in agriculture and manufacturing as well as an older than average population.

Dale is far enough off the grid that he doesn't even get mail service every day, although AT&T has a surprisingly strong signal and you can find Dale on Facebook most days.

You'd think this area would be Walmart country but only to some extent. The nearest Walmart is back in Great Falls. Therefore, the day-to-day shopping is often done in town at the local grocery store, Rex's. Area residents stock up on supplies during day-long shopping trips to the big city.

I dropped in at Rex's to pick up a bottle of wine to take out to Dale's. I was not alone. "It's amazing how much wine we sell in a week," Dan Nyberg, the store's manager, told me. The store has spent quite a lot of time honing its beer and wine selections and displays. He was proud of the store's ability to adapt and change, which has helped it to be the last standing independent grocer in the town.

A Farmer and a Father

Dale is a pretty traditional guy. He still helps his daughters (each of whom checks in nightly on the phone) with financial decisions. As long as they're in school, he manages to pay off their expenses as best he can so that they can concentrate on their grades and not have to get an outside job. He's still very much the provider—now also for his mother, who is technically a dependent. But there's a lot of new-look dad in Dale, too. He's very family-centric, preferring to spend time at home rather than going hunting with the other area dads. He says he likes to invest in his family because it's a stock that pays dividends forever.

His wife is pretty traditional, too, but with all the modern twists. Like many of today's moms, she works. She has a part-time job as a dental hygienist. She does the shopping (because she's in town several days a week, whereas Dale might not leave the farm for weeks during harvest season), and she did the bulk of the child care when the girls were younger.

But certainly not all of it.

Dale never missed a birthday treat at school or a parent meeting. Since he is self-employed, it was often easier for him to "slip out" to pick a kid up at school and take her to the doctor than it was for his wife. Typically, he says, whoever got home first at night would get dinner going, although Dale concedes he's not the best cook. He'd often even have the wine ready when she got home. "I'd have to mellow her out because it's probably going to be a [bad] dinner I made. A couple glasses of wine and everything tastes better."

And despite sticking to jeans and plaid himself, he was perfectly capable of getting his daughters out of the house with their hair brushed and wearing outfits that matched. French braids were beyond his skill set, he admits, but clearly he takes pride in being a fully competent part of the parenting team.

Fatherhood is changing. It's becoming much more of a partnership. Roughly one in five dads with kids under five identifies himself as the primary caretaker of his kids. Among fathers with a wife who works, a third took care of their kids at least one day a week in 2010, according to the U.S. Census Bureau. That's up from 26 percent in 2002.[4]

Since 1965, dads have tripled the amount of time they spend with their children each week and more than doubled the housekeeping they do. Even so, fathers are two times more likely than mothers to say they don't spend enough time with their children.[5]

Moms, meanwhile, have cut their housekeeping hours by 44 percent, increased their parenting time by roughly the same amount, and nearly tripled the time spent doing paid work. In dual-income families the numbers converge even further for working moms and dads. Working moms still spend more time doing housework and child care than dads do but they spend fewer hours at the office. Overall, both parents spend nearly identical amounts of time each week on the combination of paid work, child care, and housework.

As we said in chapter one, having two incomes is more of a necessity than a luxury for most families. Nearly six in ten married couples with children have both parents in the labor force.[6] That's almost a twenty-percentage-point increase from 2000.[7] In 15 percent of those households, mom is the primary provider.[8] But having both parents working often comes with a price. Child-care costs eat up a lot of a family's budget. Families with a working mom and children under the age of fifteen paid an average of $138 per week for child care in 2010, up 70 percent from 1985, the first year that this data was collected.[9]

Clearly that leaves fewer stay-at-home parents. While *Time*,[10] the *New York Times*,[11] and others have produced trend pieces on stay-at-home dads, there are still fewer than 200,000 of them in the U.S.[12] That number has doubled in the last decade, but it's still a sliver of the population of dads. Stay-at-home moms aren't all that common either. There are only 5.1 million of them in the U.S.

Figure 4.1   Percent of Parents Who Stay at Home

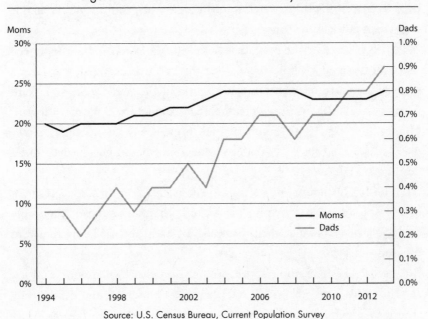

Source: U.S. Census Bureau, Current Population Survey

Working moms outnumber stay-at-home moms nearly three to one although stay-at-home moms have actually been a growing share, increasing from 20 percent in 1994 to 24 percent in 2012.

Not surprisingly, nearly a quarter of households with a stay-at-home mom are relying on the $100,000 or more in annual income brought in by dad. The ratio of high-income stay-at-home-dad households is only slightly lower. When mom is the sole provider, it's often because she's more than capable of providing well by herself.[13]

Gender Pitfalls

You might think that you would see the greater parity between moms and dads reflected in media and advertising. That's often not the case.

Finding examples is easier than it should be. For instance, Amazon created a service for caregivers, which is great and wonderful. But clearly "1-Click" ordering must be too big a hassle for fathers, because Amazon (a recent *Ad Age* marketer of the year, mind you) called its service Amazon *Mom*.

AT&T's spot showing the multitasking available for iPhones on its network chose to show a dad who seemed incapable of one of the basics of child care—changing a diaper. He got a scornful glare from mom as he tried to change his child, watch football highlights, and talk on the phone to a friend at the same time.

Dads used to be the patriarchs both in real life and in their representation in the media. Somewhere along the line that changed, and fathers stopped being strong, smart, capable figures like *Leave It to Beaver*'s Ward Cleaver or *The Cosby Show*'s Heathcliff Huxtable, trending more toward Homer Simpson.[14] The "bumbling dad" trope is now so ingrained in media that one site calls it an "undead horse," meaning it gets beaten "like a dead horse" but lives on.[15]

The big change we're starting to see is that consumers are pushing back. With the rise of parenting blogs (for both moms and dads), consumers have a place to voice their displeasure. Marketers are being forced to respond.

In the AT&T example above, or in a Clorox spot where Dad's efforts at helping his daughter with a science project go wrong and need a serious clean-up effort from Mom, the dad probably thought he was doing a good job of parenting by changing diapers or helping with homework. The moms in the commercials seemed to have a different read on the situations—one that involved eye-rolling.

It's an interesting tension—the way each gender thinks about its own role in the household. Here's another example: I'd seen some data from a Yahoo survey in which more than half of men identified themselves as the primary grocery shopper.[16] That got me curious. So in an *Ad Age/Ipsos Observer American Consumer Survey* I asked a similar question and broke out the data by gender. Our survey agreed: a majority of men said they were the primary grocery shoppers. But 85 percent of women surveyed said *they* were the primary grocery shoppers. When asked independently, each gender thought it was doing the majority of the work, which clearly isn't mathematically realistic.

My takeaway is that it's important to play not to the perceptions each gender has of the other, but to the perception each gender has of itself. Those two concepts are not the same.

Unilever's research showed that nearly three-quarters of men felt that they were poorly and unfairly represented in advertising. The packaged-goods giant launched a campaign in 2013 for its Dove Men+Care brand aiming to show men as they saw themselves—taking care of household duties, and being first and foremost a dad.[17]

Kimberly-Clark's own research shows that dads are involved in about 25 percent of diaper-buying decisions, yet it still managed to anger fathers to the breaking point with a series of "bumbling dad" spots for its Huggies brand diapers.[18] After blowback on social media, a petition on change.org, and some really bad press, Huggies pulled the offensive ads, promised to do better, and quickly rolled out new spots showing dads in a more positive, caring, and nurturing light.[19]

Amazingly, it's not just dads who are poorly represented in advertising.

Somewhere in the last decade or so, marketers ratcheted up their love for moms and caught on to just how much spending power this demographic controls. Babies cost a lot of money. A BabyCenter survey of 1,900 moms found that they typically spent up to $10,000 on baby products and services—in just the first year after a baby is born![20]

There are many ways to reach out to women and moms. They are increasingly balancing work and home-life demands. Demonstrating ways your brand can make their lives easier would seem to be a good strategy.

Jewel supermarkets chose the wrong way to go about it. In 2010 Jewel (then owned by Supervalu) developed an initiative—like many grocers— to streamline the number of products it sells. In general industry jargon this process was called "SKU Rationalization" and was seen as a logical refocusing on the products that were most purchased by consumers. Jewel, however, decided to dub their efforts "Project SHE." SHE was an acronym for "Simplify Her Experience."[21] The theory was that women were just overwhelmed by all the product choices and couldn't deal with the pressure of choosing among four different brands of chili. Not surprisingly, it led many shoppers to *complicate* their experiences because they had to shop at multiple stores in order to find all the brands they relied on. They took to the Internet to complain.[22] For one thing, it's possible that the underlying business strategy wasn't sound—Walmart, for example, when facing declining sales, started adding products back onto its shelves. Jewel started an about-face by 2011. But why risk alienating your consumers by demeaning them? It would be bad enough if Project SHE were some snarky internal code name that leaked out, but no, this was something executives at the time were willing to talk about on the record. Technology marketers are especially bad at speaking to women. Among the headlines from the 2013 Consumer Electronics Show was Michael Learmonth's in *Ad Age:* "CES's Biggest Miss: Marketing That Just Doesn't Get Women." Gadgets in advertising are often as hard for women to understand as babies are for men.[23]

Men in the Media

2011 was billed as the TV season of men as "TV Wimps." A CBS executive was quoted in the *Wall Street Journal* as saying that he'd seen twenty pitches that cited a well-shared article in *The Atlantic* titled "The End of Men" about the "mancession."[24] Some of these shows, like the Tim Allen vehicle *Last Man Standing,* even made it on air on the various networks.

The "mancession" is in some ways nothing new. Adjusting for inflation, men's wages peaked in 1973.[25] The recent recessionary acceleration of "mancession" didn't last. Men got the worst of the recession, true. They lost twice as many jobs as women did when industries like manufacturing and construction tanked. Once the recession started receding, they gained back the lion's share of the jobs that were being created.[26]

Yes, there are three women in college for every two guys, so in the long term women are going to be taking more and more of a leadership role in absolutely everything. If there's a statistic in this book that will impact everything everywhere moving forward, it's likely that one.

I like to think that things are turning around a little bit. As a dad and someone who studies this kind of stuff, I was heartened to see a show pop up on NBC's fall 2012 schedule called *Guys with Kids.* Even though it's a comedy, the humor doesn't come at the expense of the three dads at the center of the show.

I met with one of the creators of the series, writer and co-producer Charlie Grandy, on the lot at Universal Studios.

Seated outside, having coffee in an area populated by writers and producers, we talked about the changing role of dads in the media.

"I never wanted to make a statement," he said. "I think there have been hands-on dads forever. I think it's becoming more accepted. I never wanted to acknowledge that within the show. When you try to make it more than what it is—which is just a silly TV show—you get in big trouble because you're just inviting backlash."[27]

He has kept a bit of advice close to the heart for the show. His brother-in-law, who's also in the industry, told him, "You don't want to reinvent 100 percent. You want to shift 10 percent. You can't portray something too far off because it won't be credible."

But given that the show was canceled after its first season, maybe things aren't turning around that quickly after all.[28]

The changing role of parents is an issue for brands and society as a whole. It's interesting to talk to marketers about these issues in all their roles—as advertisers, as managers of their own staff resources, and as parents.

I sat down with Facebook's vice president of Global Marketing Solutions, Carolyn Everson.[29] We were mostly talking about mobile and social advertising, but I wanted to ask her about some comments she'd made about moms in the workplace. I pointed out that the workplace hasn't entirely caught up to involved dads. It somehow seems less acceptable to sacrifice work time for child-care time if you're a dad. To put some data behind that, the Families and Work Institute's National Study of the Changing Workforce found that fathers in dual-earner couples feel significantly greater work-life conflict than mothers do, and this level of conflict has risen steadily and relatively rapidly.[30] This is exacerbated by public and corporate policy in the U.S. Nearly 178 nations offer paid maternity leave, and more than 60 have paid paternity leave. In the U.S., parents have no such guarantees.

"I think nothing is going to change for women to be more comfortable until men are more comfortable," Ms. Everson said. "To me this is a topic that affects both genders. It's really more important that companies create an environment that men can feel comfortable leaving to coach a game, go to a doctor's appointment, or be at a school.

"So many marketers in the last decade caught on to what powerful decision makers moms are. If this goes the way I think it's going to go, with dads taking 50 percent of the work and really being very involved, then you could see a whole wave of new marketing where your diaper products and packaged goods become more targetable towards dads. It will be really interesting if we really get rid of the stereotypes of men and women in marketing. We've made progress on the female side."

One place that seems to understand the holistic nature of being a parent as a lifestyle as well as a targetable demographic is the blogosphere. So-called mommy blogs have proliferated and thrived, driving page-views and attendance at conferences where marketers shower the bloggers with Oscar-like gift suites in hopes of good buzz and positive product reviews. I spoke with Deanna Brown, then-CEO of Federated Media—a blog network that is host to one of the most popular mommy blogs, Dooce.com. She made an interesting point. Parenting blogs are rarely about parenting. They're about technology, employment issues, family, cars, shopping, religion, education, and yes, kids.

Some Dads Have Stepped Out, Not Up

Not all dads have become more involved like the dads we've been talking about until now. Some dads aren't present at all. Four in ten children are born to unmarried mothers. For mothers under thirty, it's more than half. That's right: the majority of children being born to younger moms are born to unwed mothers.[31]

Now, "unwed" doesn't necessarily mean "single." Here's an oft-overlooked stat: more than half of those kids born to unwed mothers are born into couples who are living together. That varies significantly by race/ethnicity. Black women were almost twice as likely as white or Hispanic women to be single mothers living alone.[32] Unfortunately, there is another often overlooked stat. The poverty rates for single mothers are disturbing. In a city like Chicago, for instance, nearly half of all unwed mothers with no father present are living below federal poverty standards—more than three times the rate for married couples with kids. In the U.S. as a whole, 41 percent of single moms are living in poverty: that's more than four and a half times the rate for married parents.[33]

You met Sandra from East Baton Rouge Parish, Louisiana, back in chapter three, where we discussed changing household structures. Lacking a second income, she's on the lower-end of middle class, a perch that she could get knocked off of with just a missed paycheck or two. She's a Gen-X mother to two daughters, one in college and one in kindergarten.

Both daughters have the same father, a trucker who passes through town infrequently. He's not completely out of the picture, but he certainly doesn't fit the Dale model of an engaged parent by any stretch.

So for Sandra we see a world without choices. She must work. She must have some flexibility in her work because there is almost no one else to pick up a sick kid or run someone to a ballet lesson. When she's running errands, her younger daughter is typically with her because there's no one to watch her back home. She is having an easier time now with her older daughter able to watch her younger one from time to time. The gaps are filled in not with her daughters' dad, but with her own. He lives nearby and lends a hand and a dollar when needed.

In the case of Sandra's dad, support is unpredictable, unstructured, and on his terms. When her oldest daughter started college, he called Sandra to his office and gave her a sizable check to help with a loan she had taken out to help with tuition. He said the money could also be used for books and school supplies. He handed her the money and told her to "issue it out accordingly."

"This is kind of how he operates . . . You don't know it's coming. He just calls and says, 'Okay, this is what I'm going to do,' and he does it."

Instead of choices, she has trade-offs. Does she try to save a little bit this month, or pay down some of her debt? Does she have time and energy to cook once she gets everyone home, or does it become a "breakfast for dinner" night with frozen waffles?

The scenario of the mom coming home to find Dad making a mess while he clumsily tries to take care of the kids is as foreign to her life as the competent dad is. Remember this important statistic: 40 percent of kids are born into families without a married father present. That's up from just 5 percent in 1960.[34] It's a societal problem that arguably needs some high-level attention. Recent studies show that the 24 million children living apart from their biological fathers are two to three times more likely to be poor, to abuse drugs and alcohol, to experience emotional, health, behavioral, and educational problems, and to engage in criminal activity, according to Fatherhood.gov, a government website set up to discuss these issues. For our purposes, it's also a creative problem. Under the theory that big data is a boon to targeting and demographics help inform good creative, you'd expect to see more marketers reaching out to the dichotomy set up by the bifurcation of dads: fathers becoming more involved because they're in dual-income households and have to help carry the load and mothers with no husbands trying to keep up on their own.

But you don't see marketers reaching out this way. John Hancock tried in 1997. It aired a spot only a few years after the sitcom *Murphy Brown* featured a plot line in which the title character becomes a single mother. The resulting brouhaha drew commentary from a wide range of Americans including then-vice president Dan Quayle, who derided the fictional character as "mocking the importance of fathers by bearing a child alone."[35]

The rise of single-parent households was well documented but not well reflected in popular culture. John Hancock's Jim Bacharach says the spot was "controversial both internally and externally." In addition to recognizing the social reality that mothers raise kids without a father present, it also made the leap to the practical reality. If there's no other adult in the household, Mom is making all the traditionally Dad-centric decisions. Therefore, the mother in the Hancock spot was shown as the sole decision maker regarding financial concerns like insurance. That reality existed then and is the norm now in all kinds of households.

Reaching across gender lines is something you are starting to see from brands. Sometimes it's in product development, like the 2012 launch of a Barbie construction set geared toward dads buying gifts for their daughters.[36] Mattel thought that men would feel more comfortable interacting with their daughters and playing with "girl" toys if they were at least put in "boy" contexts.

The NFL has put a lot of emphasis on helping football appeal to women, too. It's part of the reason you see the story lines of the drafts and the personalities of the players highlighted much more, according to CMO Mark Waller. This has been predictably good for business. "As we were able to add significant viewers to our female fan base over the last five years or so, we were able to bring in advertisers like P&G with brands like Tide."[37]

On the other side, IKEA played into the stereotype of man-as-bored-shopper but at least tried to have some fun with it and make it better for all the men who did fit the stereotype. It launched a man-cave section in some of its Australian stores. In true IKEA form, it was called Mänland.[38]

IKEA's Mary Lunghi said the brand has no plans to bring that particular store feature to the U.S. Women are still 70 percent of IKEA's customer base—that hasn't shifted. But the company recognizes the growing importance of men. "We want to treat men with respect," she told me. "We recognize his contribution and his role . . . We are in the process of executing against this. We don't want to make it seem like mom is always the hero."

Mom might not always be the hero, but by Charlie Grandy's 10 percent shift rule, we're a long way from Dad as the hero. Sure, every father has his limits—Dale's self-described "weak stomach" led him to avoid some of the messiest diaper changes—but hopefully we'll see more dads reaching the heretofore unachievable plateau of competence.

Teton County might be a great place to meet a great dad, but it's probably not the best place to talk about our next trend. Of the 6,000 residents, a total of two said they were black, according to the 2010 Census. Add in fewer than one hundred self-described Mexican-Americans and a handful of other racial/ethnic groups and the county is still nearly 100% white. Teton clearly lacks diversity.

So let's go meet Andrew in Hampden County, Massachusetts. If you're looking to encapsulate almost all of the diversification trends going on in the U.S. these days, you can basically start and stop at his house.

FIVE
The Majority Myth
How Multicultural Marketing Fares as the Nation Becomes Truly Diverse

IT'S NOT FAR-FETCHED TO IMAGINE ANDREW AS THE FIRST HISPANIC PRESI-dent. As a Millennial in his mid-twenties he has won elected office and is very involved in politics in Hampden County, Massachusetts.[1] He's already dreaming of the statehouse in Boston, a goal that a new fellowship at the Massachusetts Institute of Technology could help propel. "I love walking around the statehouse," he said. "I would like to lead large amounts of people. Maybe not 365 million, but start with 40,000 or 50,000 and go from there."

Western Massachusetts is a pretty depressed part of the country. Much of it is rural and scenic, stretching up north along the Berkshire Mountains toward Vermont and Upstate New York. Springfield, the county seat, saw its population peak some fifty years ago. The area has a lot going for it, including an increasingly upscale mall that draws business from nearby states like Connecticut, but it also has a lot of problems.

"The education system in this region is one of the worst in Massachu-setts," Andrew told me. "We're number one in a lot of negative things."

Hampden County is dominant in Esri's Tapestry "Traditional Liv-ing" LifeMode group, personifying the area's legacy dominated by a hard-working, somewhat industrial middle class. In the Patchwork Nation, it's a "Service Worker Center," which is consistent with the county's present—where service-sector jobs dominate. The hospital and electric plant are two of the largest employers, along with the mall.

Millennials like Andrew are often credited with being more civic minded than other generations, and Andrew is part of this movement. When he finds something amiss, he tries to fix it and doesn't let his age stand in his way. Now, as a literacy coordinator, he has been focusing on education.

Andrew's town has the largest percentage of Puerto Ricans of any city in the continental U.S. Although he's fully acculturated, he is proud of his ethnicity and the role he plays as a Hispanic leader. His current position has him working actively to encourage reading. "We have such a small community that I'm comfortable we can make dramatic change in a short period. I can be a role model. I can be the person who drives down the street, and people look twice if they see me. They see me in the schools, they see me in the newspaper, they see me on the news."

The city where he lives has no racial or ethnic majority. In this respect, Hampden County today looks a lot like what America will look like in coming decades. Many demographers believe that in 2010 we crossed the threshold from a white majority to a plurality in terms of the children being born in America. Put simply, for today's kids there is no majority. Sometime between 2040 and 2045 there will be no racial or ethnic majority in the U.S.[2]

By the time you read this, Andrew and his fiancée will have had their first child, who will add to this trend. His fiancée's heritage is a European mix, and she's Jewish. Even though demographics are changing, it doesn't mean that everyone's attitudes about race have changed. Among the older generations, Andrew encounters people who sometimes wonder why a Hispanic leader is engaged to someone from outside his community. Now that he's a prospective father, he does worry a little about what his daughter may face. "I think it will be easy for her to grow up in this liberal state, but it would hurt me to have her come home and have had someone call her 'Jewrican.' I'm not sure as a society that it's something we're ever going to get away from."

We're reaching a tipping point where diversity becomes less of a concept and construct and more of a firm reality. That means a major shift in how this country views itself and its community. From a marketing perspective, the question is what multicultural marketing even means in this landscape.

There are two ways to talk about diversity in marketing. One is to look at niches and decide how to segment groups out by traits that are perceived to be unique to their cultures. The other is by looking at the smaller and smaller set of places where we all still come together regardless of demographic. That universe has shrunk to the point where there are arguably only three places to reach everyone at once: so-called tent-pole events like awards shows, live sports—specifically NFL football—and Facebook.

Two groups are predominantly responsible for this demographic tilt: Hispanics and non-Hispanic whites. The Asian population factors into the shift to a lesser extent. It's the fastest-growing racial segment of the population by percentages (43 percent), but it still makes up an overall small portion (less than 5 percent) of the total U.S. population.[3] That share is projected to grow slowly to about 7.4 percent in 2045. The black population, on the other hand, has been pretty consistent as a share. After declining until about 1930,[4] it grew from about 10 percent of the population to 14 percent in 2010 and is projected to remain more or less flat until 2050.[5]

The bulk of the shift is the flatlining population of whites, which is projected to remain nearly constant while the overall population increases, and the rapidly growing population of Hispanics. Therefore, we're going to focus mostly on those segments for this chapter.

In this chapter you will:

- Get a better understanding of the composition of today's America, including which markets are growing and which aren't;
- Understand the geography of race/ethnicity;
- Uncover strategies for reaching certain groups and for reaching everyone.

Race and ethnicity are subjects demographers like to talk about. The 2010 census found that the Hispanic population in the U.S. had grown to more than 50 million, or just over 16 percent. But it's now growing more slowly than it was early in the 2000s. According to my analysis of U.S. census data, the annual growth rate for the Hispanic population actually declined steadily over the course of the 2000s, falling to 3.2 percent at the end of the first decade.[6] Fewer jobs and tougher immigration standards factored in. Much of the growth now is coming from births, not immigration. The growth trajectory is still impressive, although the Census Bureau revised its projections downward slightly based on the 2010 census.[7] Now, 28 percent of the population is projected to be Hispanic by 2050, down from 30 percent in earlier projections.

Big, round numbers like 50 million get people's attention. It's not as if this is a new phenomenon because you don't get to 50 million overnight, but milestones are important to our psyche as Americans and as marketers. The number is important because the population is large enough that we can really start to segment it in meaningful ways.

The easiest is geography.

As of 2010, nearly 20 percent of all Hispanics lived in the Los Angeles and New York metro areas, meaning that one in five of this group lived in just two places.[8] Nearly half lived in just ten places. At the state level, we can find nearly half of all Hispanics in California and Texas. To reach three-quarters we only have to add six more states: Florida, New York, Illinois, Arizona, New Jersey, and Colorado.

If the Hispanic population follows past immigration patterns, this will change as education and job opportunities move around the country. The majority of states now have at least a 5 percent Hispanic population and seventeen states have more than 10 percent—up seven states from 2000. In New Mexico, Hispanics are rapidly approaching the majority of the population. The last decade saw growth of the Hispanic population in almost every county and in all but one city (Arlington, Virginia).[9]

The Asian population is even more dense. One in three Asians lives in California. More than half of foreign-born Asians live in just four states: California, New York, Texas, and New Jersey.[10]

The black population is a little more evenly distributed with greater than 5 percent in thirty states and more than 10 percent in twenty-one states. Blacks account for 20 percent or more of the population in nine states.

One way to digest this is to view the *USA Today* Diversity Index. For decades, the newspaper has tracked the chances that two people living next to each other in a certain county are different racially or ethnically. Based on the 2010 census data, the national average was fifty-two, meaning that it's even odds that two people would be different. That's up from thirty-four in 1980, but a map of the index at the county level shows that the South and the West are markedly more diverse than the Midwest and the Northeast.[11]

You could start to segment by income. Racial and ethnic groups show very different income distributions. The Asian population is more affluent than other groups. One in three Asian households makes more than $100,000 a year, compared to just one in five for the U.S. as a whole. Blacks have a higher percentage of the population making under the median income of roughly $50,000. Nearly two-thirds of black households make less than this benchmark. Hispanics are doing slightly better, although their median income is $10,000 less than the national median.[12] Six in ten Hispanic households fall below the median, and 12 percent are making over $100,000, a couple of points more than the black population, but still less than the U.S. totals.[13]

Education is the key predictor of income. As educational level increases, so does income. Meanwhile, unemployment drops.[14] So while today we see an overall lower education level for Hispanics as a whole, the younger Hispanics, who are more likely to have been born here and more likely to speak English, are also more likely to be staying in school. High-school graduation rates are setting records (76 percent in 2011) and nearly half of those graduates are moving on to some sort of post-secondary education.[15]

Figure 5.1   Median Income by Select Race/Ethnicity

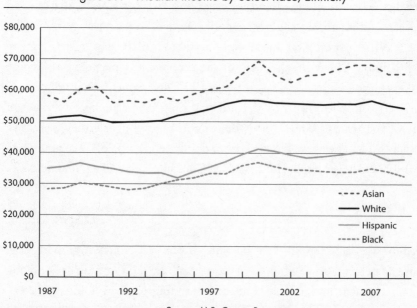

Source: U.S. Census Bureau

Finally, let's look at the bottom line: consumer spending. Naturally, this mirrors income to some degree. The highest-earning racial and ethnic groups are also the highest spending. A typical Asian-headed household in the U.S. spends just over $60,000 a year, compared to $37,000 for blacks, $42,000 for Hispanics, and $53,000 for whites.[16]

It is difficult to divorce a discussion of the Hispanic marketplace from a discussion of immigration and acculturation. These are polarizing issues in polarized times. It's also easy to get so caught up in the big data moment of measuring everything by real-time Twitter sentiment that we forget our history. We are, after all, a nation of immigrants.

I chatted with D'Vera Cohn, a senior writer at the Pew Research Center, about historical and current population trends and asked her, "Are things changing more rapidly than they have in the past?"

"Can I say it's more tumultuous than the early part of the twentieth century when the share of immigrants was even larger than it is now? No, but the variety of changes we're seeing both in the racial and ethnic makeup of society and in how life is lived at the individual level has been quite dramatic," she said.

Here are a couple of other stats from Pew to keep in mind. First, nearly two-thirds of all Hispanics in the U.S. are proficient in English. Bilingualism is common in second-generation Hispanics. As you move into the third generation, nearly three-quarters don't speak or read Spanish fluently.[17] This follows the trends of other immigrant groups (European and Asian), although to a slightly lesser degree than in the past.

While working on an *Ad Age* story about 2010 census data, I spoke with Barry Chiswick, chairman of the economics department at George Washington University and author of *The Economics of Immigration*.

"If you called me in 1890, you'd be saying, 'There are large increases of Jews, Italians and Greeks. They don't know much English, they don't have many skills. They have little chance of doing well,'" he said. "I see nothing in the data to suggest that [Hispanics] will become a permanent underclass."[18]

Andrew's Offspring

Andrew's daughter will be a member of one of the fastest-growing segments percentage-wise: those of more than one racial/ethnic background. This segment presents all kinds of interesting challenges for marketers.

The population reporting multiple races numbers 9 million and grew by 32 percent from 2000 to 2010, compared with those who reported a single race, which grew by 9.2 percent.[19] It's the fastest-growing group among children—rising almost 50 percent in the last decade to 4.2 million. Even more impressive, the subgroup who identified as both black and white exploded more than 134 percent to 1.8 million.[20]

If they identify more as one than the other, it's less of a big challenge—you simply target them as the dominant identifier. Take President Obama, for example. He technically misrepresented himself on his 2010 census form by checking "Black" instead of acknowledging his multiracial background.[21] This group will continue to grow, thanks to the Millennials. They are growing up as the most diverse generation and are considered more tolerant than previous generations.[22] It's therefore interesting to note that of the Millennials I've been tracking for this project, three out of four are in multiracial couples. Michael, who is black, lives in New York County (otherwise known as Manhattan) with his Hispanic partner. Liz, who is white and lives in Champaign County, Illinois, plans to move in with her black boyfriend when their apartment leases run out. Trends are just that, however. Trends. These couples represent a more tolerant Millennial generation. That's the trend. But that doesn't mean we're suddenly living in utopia or that it's easy for all of them. Liz learned the hard way that some of her friends aren't quite open to the new diversity of America. She says that her boyfriend has helped her to better understand the different experiences that people go through and the different backgrounds that people come from. She has reveled in that, but not everyone feels the same. "Friends that I had for a long time might have been a tad bit bigoted. That's been a hard pill to swallow because people don't tend to show those colors until they're confronted with it."

Demographic Bingo

Andrew, our budding politician in Hampden County, is a fully acculturated, English-speaking, American-born member of his family's third generation in Massachusetts. His family came from Puerto Rico in the 1940s. His grandmother and parents speak perfect Spanish. English is Andrew's first language, and he rates his Spanish as about 60 percent to 70 percent fluent, putting him a little ahead of the curve for third generation.

His grandmother gets her news from the Spanish-language network Tel-emundo. He gets most of his news online, surfing sites like MassLive on his phone and laptop—he doesn't like to pay for Web content. By necessity as well as interest, he also watches local TV news. He likes the NBC af-filiate because he feels it covers more positive stories about the Hispanic community than the local ABC and Fox affiliates.

All of this tracks with trends. But perhaps the most important trend to discuss in Andrew's household isn't about him at all. It's about his fi-ancée. She is slightly older (in her late twenties) and was living with him while she finished a graduate degree and looked for work. It was a help-ful budget-saver for both of them. So at the time I met them, they were an unmarried, biethnic, cohabiting Millennial couple in which she had a higher degree of educational attainment than he did. That's the demo-graphic equivalent of a full bingo card.

Now they're trend-buckers. She's no longer a girlfriend, she's his fi-ancée, and as of this writing, they have had their first baby. Purchase deci-sions in couples are a pretty standard example of cases in which one person is buying for the other and vice versa. It's a bit of a media conundrum to sell men's shampoo to women who shop for them or to market toys to the children who demand (loudly) to play with them but really market to the parent who has to actually pay for them. This idea of "selling through" one consumer to get to another has long been a challenge for marketers. Typi-cally, gender and generation have been the big obstacles here. Now we're adding race and ethnicity to the mix.

Coming from two different cultures, Andrew and his fiancée influence each other's shopping and lifestyle. Since she does most of the cooking, they often wind up with more Italian-influenced dishes than the Puerto Rican fare he grew up with and favors. On the other hand, she's now a big fan of Christmas, a holiday that Andrew describes as "American" and that she had to teach him isn't universally celebrated.

He sees their differences more in terms of their families. She grew up in rural Vermont, he in the city. Their families had different dynamics. "I don't think there's a right or wrong way," he says, but he leans toward her more soft-spoken way of dealing with conflict and decision making as op-posed to the more emotional setting he grew up in.

As a noted member of the Hispanic community where he lives, An-drew certainly pays attention to the product offerings and the media representation of his own culture. When he wants Hispanic-targeted products, he knows he has to go to the Save-A-Lot, where he also turns when he wants to cut a few dollars out of his overall grocery bill.

"I Don't See Race"

Satirist Stephen Colbert has a running joke on his *Colbert Report* about how he doesn't see people's race. He tells jokes like this: "People tell me I'm white, and I believe them, because I own a lot of Jimmy Buffett albums."[23]

I especially like this quote because it's taking a behavioral look at demographic targeting. As the historically important lines of race and ethnicity continue to blur, it's an increasingly impressive argument for the need for targeting by nondemographic means. Not surprisingly, I am of the opinion that demographics are as important as ever, too. As Pew's Ms. Cohn told me, "It's important to know that all thirty-five-year-olds are not alike and all Hispanics are not alike, but it's certainly important to know how the age structure and racial structure of a population is changing because that often speaks to the kinds of priorities and values that people will have. It's crucial

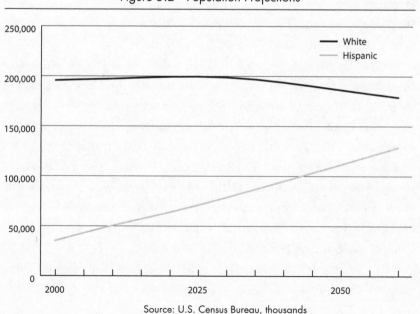

Figure 5.2   Population Projections

Source: U.S. Census Bureau, thousands

to keep an eye on the basic demographics of a society because that gives you important clues about how the population is changing."

Certainly one of the major themes of this book is that demographics drive consumer behavior, and that's as true today as ever. We just have better means, thanks to more data sources, of measuring those behavioral impacts and targeting around them. All data needs to be considered through a broader lens and put into context. You have to understand the context and the nuances around it. For instance, market research is impacted down to the very wording of survey questions to make sure that they are interpreted by all cultures in the same way.[24] But once you get the big picture, behavioral data can lead to much greater efficiencies than we've had before. If you want to reach soccer fans, Hispanics are a good broad target. But many Hispanics don't follow soccer, and many non-Hispanics do. Behavioral targeting can help you separate the good leads from the overly broad generalizations. So what are some strategies for reaching Hispanics and other racial and ethnic groups?

Cultural and language decisions are important. Simply running ads in Spanish will miss a growing number of the demographic, but so does running ads solely in English.

Target's CMO, Shawn Gensch, told *Ad Age* that in its Spanish-language spots, a family might be eating flan, but in English spots they'd be eating cake. The retailer is also trying to find the right product mix in Hispanic-heavy markets. "We're bringing in the right food or cleaning products that are relevant. Products like Goya or Fabuloso."[25]

Similarly, Mary Lunghi and I discussed some of IKEA's challenges in addressing Hispanic audiences. More and more, the furniture maker is targeting the bilingual audience. Among other things, the marketer tries to keep as many product names (which are made to *sound* Swedish) in its campaigns. "There are still nuances we have to pay attention to that don't translate well. Sometimes it's cultural cues."[26] We talked in the last chapter about an ad for an IKEA table. For Hispanic audiences, the table was shown in the context of a family dinner. For other audiences, who are less likely to gather for a nightly meal, it didn't click, so ads for other targets used the table in a different way.

Recent research has reached some surprising conclusions. First, groups want to feel included in a brand experience and message. It's more important than the cultural differences they bring when viewing an ad. Aronté Bennett, an assistant professor of marketing and business law at Villanova University, discussed a study she conducted in *Ad Age*: "We found uncanny similarities in minorities' responses to advertising; this, despite their deep-set cultural differences. Contrary to popular belief, it's not their racial or ethnic identity that determines minorities' response to a brand, but rather, how welcoming they feel the brand is toward them."[27] Often that can take the form of such simple steps as representing them in marketing messages. As we discussed in chapter four, it's helpful to do so in a meaningful way while avoiding talking down to groups or downright insulting them. A study in the *Journal of Advertising Research* says that one popular approach, reminiscent of the United Colors of Benetton campaigns, isn't the way to go about this.[28] If you look at early ads for the retailer—or, for that matter, at a lot of group photos in stock art collections—you'll see a demographically mixed group of black, white, Asian, and Hispanic men and women all together smiling and looking beautiful. The research argues that by including all these groups, none of them feel special in seeing the ad, which works against the goal of being inclusive in the first place. Therefore, targeting each group individually, in the appropriate context for that group, is ideal.

Laura Desmond, Global CEO of media-buying giant Starcom MediaVest Group, feels this is a real opportunity to develop good creative and content marketing. "[Groups] know they're unique and they want to be marketed to with relevance. This is where I think content can come into real play. With big data we're going to be able to aggregate to those groups much better than before. If you're doing your first job, which is reaching them, but you don't have relative content that is unique to them and that can follow them across screens, you'll blow it. I think that's the piece marketers miss."[29]

We're All Ready for Some Football

As the population is diversifying, the media landscape is as well. We'll talk about the proliferation of devices later on, but let's take a look at TV for a moment. The year 2013 saw a huge milestone as Univision pushed NBC to the fifth-rated network during February sweeps.[30]

NBC was reeling for a number of reasons, but perhaps the biggest was the missing driver of their ratings: the NFL. An *Ad Age* headline said it all: "NBC's 44% Plunge Reveals: Football Has Become TV's Addiction."[31]

It's certainly not news that the Super Bowl is the most watched show in any given year. The only small suspense year-in and year-out is whether the game is going to post record numbers or not. Less noticed is that the weekly telecasts are often the most watched shows of the week as well, throughout the season. It's not unusual for five or six of the top ten shows to be NFL-related.

What's remarkable is not just the NFL's ratings dominance, but its dominance among so many different demographics. Sure, it dominates with men, but it's drawing women in increasing numbers. Sunday night football ranks highly among women in the eighteen to forty-nine demographic.[32] As we mentioned in chapter four, the league is speaking to different groups in different ways. For women, this has involved generating narratives and developing the biographies of the players more—especially during the off-season draft and as the season kick-off nears. It's important to keep the audience engaged year-round.

Then there is the Hispanic audience. It's easy to think of soccer, or *futbol*, as the dominant sport for that culture. But nearly half of all U.S. Hispanics watch NFL football, according to the league's media kit. Further, citing Nielsen data, the league claims that the "NFL's 2011 season average Hispanic viewership is more than triple the combined average of NBA, MLB, NASCAR, MLS and NHL." And the league's reach is only growing.

I moderated an Advertising Week panel in New York about diversity marketing that included the chief marketing officer of the NFL, Mark Waller. As I was doing the research for this book, I knew he was someone I needed to talk to. We chatted via phone and talked about how the NFL appeals to everyone.

We started by discussing a line that's been attributed to him but that he admits came out of a big brainstorming session with the league's agency, Grey Advertising. It's the image of football as the last great American campfire.

"If you were to fly over the U.S., you'd see the glows from the stadia and the TVs in homes, and bars . . . people huddled around laptops and cell phones and all glued to our games. Football is that one thing that everybody gathers around and it brings weekly hope to people. It brings communities together almost like nothing else anymore, and nowadays even families. Our games have become one of the few times families actually get together and hang."[33]

That sounds like overreaching until you really consider it, and he cites some stats to back up the claims: more people watch football on any given Sunday than go to church or than voted in the last general elections.

"You think about your life. Your routine changes at the beginning of September when football starts. It's coincidental with the start of school and the end of the summer holidays and going back to work but football is a huge expression of that transition. High school on Friday, college on Saturday. NFL on Thursday, Sunday and Monday."

Staying ubiquitous as the population shifts in numbers and importance to advertisers presents opportunities. How does the NFL capitalize?

"It starts with protecting the essence of what brings in people in the first place," he said. "Keeping the integrity of the model is key because that's what's attracted the consumers in the first place and then working hard to adapt content to demographics that are emerging." By "model" he means things like the scarcity of the games so that each week counts for every team, and the promotion across all networks. Everyone who has a piece of the NFL sells not just their slice, but the entire pie.

"If you look at the Hispanic demographic almost by definition that means the youth demographic too. If you want to appeal to youth, you're going to have to appeal to Hispanics and vice versa. We're doing a lot of work with our teams about how do you bring young Hispanics into the game and teach them the fundamentals of the game and how it's played."

It's more than just marketing. It's community outreach. The NFL and even the players are in your community and in your schools interacting with kids through the "Play 60" program, which promotes sports, athleticism, and a healthier lifestyle for kids. The campaign encourages kids to be active for sixty minutes each day in order to reduce obesity.

Sponsors help the program and the program helps sponsors.

"You bring in a Quaker or a National Dairy Council. You bring in partners that are able to help you reach a youth demographic and give them a program like 'Play 60'—something that is a powerful, meaningful expression of football in their local communities. We help each other."

The NFL has ways to reach targeted groups; for instance, it has developed partnerships and custom programming on Spanish-language media.

It also has the biggest tent of all, with an audience bigger than anything on TV: the Super Bowl.

Marketers turn to the big game when they need to get a broad message out to just about everyone. I spoke to Michael Sprague, the executive vice president, Marketing and Communications, at Kia Motors America. He told me about launching the Sorento at the Super Bowl in 2009.

"We were virtually unknown here in the U.S. We saw an opportunity as others were pulling out of the Super Bowl [due to the economy] to jump in and launch a new product that was being built in the U.S. at a time when a lot of U.S. manufacturers were closing plants.

"Even if half the people weren't paying attention, there were still 50 million people whom I had an opportunity to speak to about my brand."[34]

One more thing about NFL football: Tickets in most markets are expensive and hard to come by. Not very many people get to experience it in person. "The percentage of people who have actually attended a game is actually pretty low," concedes Mr. Waller. "That goes to the beauty of the model we built decades ago—it's free for you on TV."

In many ways football is made for TV. With modern technology, you can get the cameras right down in the action—something that's impossible with a game like soccer, where the nature of the movement across a large field means that the cameras have to be pulled out most of the time.

Bridging the gap are high-school and college games, each of which get a dedicated night of the week.

When I was up in Teton County, Montana, visiting Dale, the passage from one community to another along desolate roads was marked by the triumphant painting of hay bales heralding the changing territory from one school district to another. One set proclaims that you're in Bulldog Country. Later down the road, "Win with Character." Dale actually met his wife at a college football game. He's a long way from a professional team of any sport, but he tells me that on Friday nights everyone in town is at the game. If it's an away game, the town is deserted as many of the games are hours away in a state with as little density and as much land as Montana.

IT'S HARD TO WRITE A BOOK ABOUT ADVERTISING AND NOT SPEND SOME time in the industry's mecca, otherwise known as the island of Manhattan. So let's head to New York County, and spend some time with Michael.

He's not too into football, but he grew up and went to college in Ohio, and he'll always be an Ohio State Buckeye fan. It's just another aspect of the power of sports in the fabric of our world: rivalries are strong, deeply ingrained, and not always rational. So let's go to New York, where we will focus the discussion on the increasing importance and complexity of cities.

SIX

The Buyographics of City Living

How Product Design, Messaging, and Shopping Itself Change as We Become Increasingly Urbanized

MICHAEL AND I ARE STANDING IN HIS SMALL MANHATTAN KITCHEN LOOKING through his window, which faces south over Central Park. Skyscrapers loom on the other side of the expansive green space. Michael is in his early thirties, right on the Gen-X/Millennial cusp. He lives in Harlem and exemplifies a number of trends in today's urban living. He is part of a growing black professional class. His income would make him affluent in most parts of the world, but not so much here. So he and his Hispanic partner also have a third roommate in their apartment. He keeps a lot of his expenses low and therefore has enough discretionary income for entertaining, dining out, and other social activities.

He talks about a few of his friends who have left the densely populated city and moved to the other side of the East River in search of more living space. These things are all relative in New York terms. He tells me that they love looking out over the Williamsburg or Queensboro Bridge and seeing the city spread across their new view.

"But I don't want to look at the view," he says. "I want to live in the view."

Michael is not alone.

The overarching trend is that people are moving to urban areas. There are different trends within that, and we need to look at each of them separately as well as understanding how they interplay. This brings us to two questions: Which trends will last? and How can marketers and cities learn from each other?

In this chapter we'll try to answer those questions. We'll talk about one big brand that took great advantage of urban dynamics with a perfect combination of big data and demographic savvy. By the time we move on, you will understand:

- Why the Millennials aren't changing everything (yet why they are);
- How big data can help brands escape geography (finally);
- Why politics and place matter, even to brands.

When we think of cities, we think of density, skyscrapers, hustle, bustle, and probably a fair amount of grit. In other words, when we think of cities, we think of their downtown cores. But that's just one part of the city. Let's start there and work outward.

The Census Bureau chooses City Hall as the geographic center of a city. From there, anything within a two-mile radius is considered the urban core. For most cities, it's as good a definition as any but clearly there are exceptions. Most any study of New York City, for example, is going to find that it differs from any other U.S. city in many key ways, this being one of them.

Throughout the U.S., the urban cores in nearly every major metro area grew in large percentages during the 2000s. These are dense areas (remember, it's only a two-mile radius). They are also areas that before 2000 weren't necessarily teeming with residential development. Chicago, for instance, saw a crane-dotted skyline for much of the decade as high-rise condo complexes rose throughout the urban core. That led to a 36.2 percent gain in population, but that gain equated to fewer than 50,000 people out of a metro area population of more than 9 million.[1] One critical thing to note is that the people moving into downtowns like that of Chicago were often affluent. The number of households with annual incomes of more than $200,000 grew throughout the region during that time, but much faster in the urban core.[2]

The two groups that are driving the trend toward urban living are Millennials and Boomers, but especially the Millennials.[3] They don't have cars. They live in small spaces. They traverse the Internet on small, mobile devices. They love their urban lifestyle.

As I was interviewing Jeff Speck, the author of *Walkable City: How Downtown Can Save America*, he pointed out something critical. An influx of even small raw numbers of people in a downtown can be disproportionately impactful.

"A boom that transforms a city center would probably be statistically insignificant compared to what's happening in the suburbs because there's so much more suburban land."[4]

Moving outward, there's a ring from two miles to five miles around the core of the city. These areas don't offer the density of the urban core that so many find appealing. Nor do they offer the amenities of the suburbs. So these caught-in-between areas tended to lose population in the early 2000s.

Then you hit the suburbs and the exurbs. They're huge and take up a lot of space. Elizabeth Plater-Zyberk, a scholar, author, and one of the founders of the New Urbanism movement, told me that "the extreme low density of the suburbs could be seen as an overreaction to the crowding of the city."[5]

It's easy to look at the suburban data and see big numbers. That's important if you're looking for a mass audience. Each one of those people has a wallet, after all. I interviewed Ed Glaeser, Harvard professor and author of *Triumph of the City: How Our Greatest Invention Makes Us Richer, Smarter, Greener, Healthier, and Happier*, for an *Ad Age* story, and he pointed out that in some parts of the country cities are growing because of the economic opportunity they offer new residents. These are not necessarily the older, more established dense areas like Chicago and New York, but rather sprawling metro areas like Houston. Urban theorists might not think areas like Houston's sprawl are ideal and sustainable, but suburbs are still popular and people choose to move to them and live there.

"When it comes down to considering a home and [shoppers] look at what it costs to get a home and a yard in the city versus the suburbs, people choose the suburbs," said Jed Kolko, chief economist for the real estate site Trulia.com.[6]

Less dense areas like Raleigh, Austin, Charlotte, Las Vegas, Jacksonville, and Orlando were some of the fastest growing in the 2000s.[7]

Cost of living is also a factor. As you look at the data, you see that the dollar goes further in some cities than in others. "You begin to understand why a million people moved to Houston. A family that starts off with 20 percent higher [than average] earnings in Houston [after taxes, housing costs, and adjustments for final prices] ends up being 50 percent richer in real terms even including transportation and cars. That's a huge difference and it's easy to see why Houston would appeal," said Mr. Glaeser.[8]

Not all of these growth areas are as cheap as Houston. Many suburbs, in fact, cost a lot more than the urban areas they surround when you factor in the high cost of transportation.[9]

These three geographies (urban core, surrounding city, and suburbs and exurbs) collectively constitute a metropolitan area.

In the 2000s, the national metropolitan areas picked up nearly all population growth. The overwhelming majority of Americans, 84 percent, chose to live either in or in the vicinity of a city of 50,000 people or more. Nearly one in three Americans lives in one of the fifteen largest metro areas, each of which has more than 4 million residents. The fifty largest metropolitan areas are home to 53 percent of the nation's residents.[10]

Let's not overlook the smaller cities. Nearly 30 percent of Americans live in towns with populations between 25,000 and 200,000. Many of these places are suburbs of larger cities. True, forty-five of the fifty largest metropolitan areas grew in the 2000s, but these smaller towns grew almost three times faster, according to my analysis of U.S. Census Bureau data. Totaled up, 90 percent of the growth in the nation's metropolitan areas took place in the nation's suburbs, *not* in its central cities.[11] Again, there's a lot more land for the growth to occur so that's not too surprising.

Like aging and diversification, suburban growth is a global trend. More than half of the earth's population now lives in cities. With the huge growth of urbanization in the population powerhouses of China and India, that number will only increase.[12]

Cities are paying attention to the data and remaking themselves to accommodate these two desirable groups—Boomers and Millenials. Urban pundits like Richard Florida point to the rise of a "creative class" of younger, more educated professionals who thrive in cities.[13] The thought of a downtown teeming with a tax base fueled by such a group is enough to get many mayors thinking like planners. Remember the growth of the affluent in Chicago. Mayors are taking notice and developing livability initiatives following in the same molds of walkable streets, better public transit, mixed-use downtowns, loft-like residential development, and more.

You see it in large cities like New York and Chicago, both of which started large-scale bike-sharing programs in 2013, all the way down through Oklahoma City, Grand Rapids, Michigan, and Bellevue, Washington. The largest "complete streets" remake in North America, which will incorporate transit, bike lanes, and pedestrian-friendly features, is being planned in Detroit ("Motown"), Michigan, of all places.

Livability

Why are both the Millennials and Boomers moving to downtown areas? Both groups want easy access to amenities. The Millennials have never been big on car ownership and driving, for reasons we'll detail in chapter ten.[14] Big cities tend to offer better public transportation. Cities big and small can be places to be mobile even if you stay on foot. Besides public transportation, walkability is also big with the retiring Boomers who foresee a future for themselves in which driving becomes more of a chore and the benefits of getting a little exercise and getting out on a quick grocery run are obvious.

We've previously talked about the rise of the single-person household, and you'll notice that the two groups driving that trend are also driving this one. That's not a coincidence at all. What could be more adaptable for singletons than an urban (or at least a walkable, mixed-use suburban) environment?

Target Corporation, for instance, has been keeping a close watch on the urban trends. In a video produced for the Census Bureau it noted that urban consumers are more likely to live alone and in smaller spaces and are more likely to be renters. Target is tailoring its mix accordingly. "We used the Census Bureau data to notice the trend in urbanization, especially among our younger consumers and younger guests," Kate Whittington, director of guest insights, said in the video. "We've carried the merchandise that we think is most appealing to that guest. So a little bit more apparel and younger fashions for example than some of the more classic styles that we might carry in our suburban stores."[15]

For the near term, expect the urban core growth to continue. Each day 10,000 Boomers turn sixty-five. That seems like a huge number until you consider that each day nearly 12,000 twenty-four-year-olds are turning twenty-five and further entering adulthood.

Cities advertising to tourists and convention goers is not new. We read a lot about Las Vegas's efforts in chapter one, for instance. But these are examples of cities remaking themselves physically and philosophically in response to market conditions. You'll find cities big and small concerned about how to make themselves more pedestrian-friendly for age groups who are decreasingly dependent on cars. Fighting crime and improving schools are also constant battles throughout the nation. Cities are using technology both to collect data about how services get used and to communicate results to constituents. Sustainability, in forms such as urban agriculture, is a movement gaining momentum, especially with organic-enthused Millennials. Incubating technology start-ups is now the purview of mayors as well as venture capitalists. In other words, cities are engaging in smart product development to attract a greater base of a desirable and growing consumer segment. In Tampa Bay, researchers are using Foursquare check-in data to inform urban planning decisions. Cities are starting to think like marketers. How can marketers learn from cities and how can brands adapt to the changes in the urban and suburban environments?

Understanding the Geography of Targeting

Segregating markets into broad geographical demographics can be misleading, yet that's how marketers are trained to think about the divisions of our national geography. Buying TV or radio air time or even newspaper ads have confined traditional advertising to these broad geographies. Metro areas, or designated marketing areas (DMAs) in Nielsen parlance, encompass all the geographies we've been discussing. So marketers have historically been stuck with some really bad and archaic geographic frameworks for looking at the world.

Because the suburbs, the city, and the urban core are very, very different places—especially when you're talking about the most densely populated areas—lumping them all together can be counterproductive or at the very least inefficient. Unless your target is literally everyone, you're buying a lot of audience that you don't need.

Suburbs themselves can take a variety of different shapes. Some were previously outlying cities with their own distinct downtown shopping districts and personality that eventually got subsumed by the expansion of the central city. Some are more modern cookie-cutter cul-de-sac planned communities. Each lends itself to a certain kind of lifestyle and each is following a different set of trends. All of these impact the shopping environment and the fundamental ways in which urban core consumers like Michael in New York or suburban shoppers like Chris in North Las Vegas spend their time and their money.

Suburbs are also notably not the economic bargain many expect. In some areas people are now spending more of their incomes on transportation than on housing.[16] Combining both of those costs can really strain a budget as gas prices increase. Lower-income families are especially at risk. The non-profit Center for Neighborhood Technologies brought this dilemma to light when it began publishing its Housing and Transportation Affordability Index a few years ago. The revised 2012 report notes: "For households earning 50 to 100 percent of the median income of their metropolitan area, nearly three-fifths (59 percent) of income goes to housing and transportation costs. For these households, the growing 'costs of place' are particularly burdensome, leaving relatively little left over for expenses such as food, education, and health care."[17]

It doesn't leave much left over for savings either.

Looking Forward: Will the Millennials Change Everything?

I think it's safe to say that, given all we know about Millennials today, it is likely that they will continue to thrive in dense urban areas—especially while they remain unattached and without children. There are so many of them coming of age for the next decade or so that it's important not to ignore that.

But don't assume that this cohort of people is suddenly going to upend either the entire narrative of the U.S. since 1950 or the biological imperatives of eons of evolution. In other words, many if not most will eventually have kids and will probably move to the suburbs for all the same reasons that previous generations have. The huge question is to what extent.

The Millennials' tendency to remain unmarried and childless, and often to put off living on their own, has been referred to as "delayed life stages."[18] The word that often gets overlooked is "delayed." In some ways, the Boomers putting off retirement is kind of like what the Millennials are going through now. It's a delayed life stage brought about partially by cultural differences from previous generations, but also by the timing of the recession. However, just as most Boomers will eventually retire, most of these Millennials will eventually get married, buy a house, and have kids.

Jay, who lives in Leavenworth, Kansas, is on the older end of the Millennials, having now entered his thirties. Not long after turning thirty, he became engaged. He and his fiancée, who is a few years younger than he is, are both public school teachers. They're changing many life stages at once by shopping for a house and thinking about having kids. As Jay's stage changes, so do his priorities. "You start to observe a lot of things that you don't normally look at. I could care less about street lights but my future wife lives on a street with no street lights and she's scared half to death. I want her to feel safe if I'm not there."

Even as the Millennials age and potentially start to look more like older generations in terms of their housing choices, I believe that people in their twenties will continue to be drawn to urban cores and, like the Millennials before them, will stick around as long as they can.

The School Issue

Since the Millennials are proving to be the most well-educated generation in history, it's hard to imagine them settling for anything less than a great education for their little ones. No generation has ever wanted to provide *less* opportunity for its children.

Will Chicago, New York, and Los Angeles solve their school problems before today's twenty-five-year-olds turn thirty and start having kids? Let's bet no.

As you've noticed, kids are expensive, and they and all their "stuff" take up an outsized amount of space for such small people. For all but the most wealthy or most adventurous, that spells one thing that is confirmed by the data: once individuals begin families, they also begin packing up for the suburbs or even moving to less costly cities.

The impact of the Boomers moving downtown could help or hinder the desire of Millennials to stick around. On one hand, the Boomers have very close relationships to their Millennial kids. Having Grandma and Grandpa around (maybe even within walking distance) when the little ones are born is a huge boon and can make urban childrearing a little bit better.

On the other hand, one can certainly argue that the Boomer generation hasn't shown itself to be particularly altruistic.

Peter Francese, the founder of *American Demographics,* has studied the Boomers extensively. He says, "I suspect that the dominant thinking among Boomers has shifted from any concern about the needs of someone else's children (or their own) to heavy worry about themselves having enough assets to retire."

Therefore, the thought of them voting to raise their taxes to fund better schools for their grandkids seems unlikely.

As for the Boomers themselves, they might well be enjoying urban living in their sixties, but as they start turning seventy and eighty, will that continue? I asked Joel Kotkin, noted urban scholar, author, and executive editor of NewGeography.com. He's skeptical of the entire urban trend.

"We looked at people aged forty-five to fifty-four in 2000 and saw where they were ten years later. They were leaving the core cities by a huge amount. They were also leaving the suburbs by a small amount and moving to small towns.

"Why would an older person who has lived in the suburbs all their life, with their friends in the suburbs, why would they want to sell their home and put their equity into a very expensive downtown condo to live away from their friends and live a lifestyle that they're probably not used to? It would seem to make much more sense to sell their home and go someplace that's much cheaper and keep the equity if you're going to move."[19]

I bring Kotkin's perspective in for two reasons. One, to show that what we're talking about here are *trends,* which are hard to predict. Experts, often looking at the same data, sometimes disagree. But I also want to get back to my earlier comments that small changes can still be transformative. Cities are making efforts to court these urban Boomers and Millennials because they're desirable residents. Marketers can take a lesson from this.

Just looking at housing costs, the suburbs are generally cheaper than housing in the city. You can get a lot more space for your money. Moving to the suburbs that have the best schools, however, still costs money. A Brookings Institution report quantified that.[20] Families can expect to pay a premium of more than $200,000 to live near the best school—assuming they can afford that.

There is research showing that we're growing more and more clustered economically, especially in fast-growing markets in the South and West. According to Pew Research, income is replacing race as the leading type of segregation.[21] High-income households are clustering in "affluent" neighborhoods (up 18 percent between 1980 and 2010) and low-income households are clustering in "poor" neighborhoods with the share rising 5 percent.

Since we know from previous chapters that most people can't afford to pay a premium like that for good public education, and since education is strongly correlated to income, it's likely that income bifurcation will only get more pronounced.[22] It's also safe to say that you are probably living in a world where you're more and more surrounded by people like yourself. I'd argue that it's much more difficult than it used to be for you to imagine what people who are not like you are thinking/feeling/reacting to/dealing with. Your customers are in a similar situation. They look more like their neighbors than they ever have before.[23] Being able to reach across media and down into finer geographies to find the clusters you're targeting is going to be hugely important.

Twenty-Somethings Will Be Twenty-Somethings

Even if today's Millennials eventually move out of the city, other people will move in. In looking at these urban trends, it might be a good idea to stop thinking so rigidly about the generations and start shifting to more of a life-stage view. Data suggests that the Millennials will not live in the cities forever. However, it's entirely likely that people in their twenties will continue to delay getting married, having kids, and buying homes. There are a lot of iGens (the name I've given to the post-Millennial generation, now in their teens and younger) on the verge of heading off to college and making their way in the world.[24] I think they'll behave much like Millennials did in their twenties, if not more so. You're seeing a shift in the meaning of "being in your twenties" (especially among the more educated) from the years people get married and settle down to the years people live in a city on their own or with roommates, learn more about themselves, maybe get a master's degree, and then move on to their thirties, which is when they get married and have kids.

Likewise, the Boomers in their sixties might very well enjoy moving into downtown and reducing the size of their empty nests. We'll talk more in chapter seven about the different retirement options for the aging Boomers, but while some are moving into downtowns, many others are going to follow more traditional routes of moving to the Sun Belt or "retiring in place" and staying in their current homes longer. That's partially the result of desire and partially the result of the housing crisis, which has left them with homes worth less than they'd anticipated.[25]

Will the Gen-Xers want to move into downtown communities when they hit their sixties? That seems perfectly plausible, especially as cities work to make themselves more livable for a population advancing in age.

These urban and suburban trends, therefore, will continue in their importance for marketers for the foreseeable future. As you can imagine, consumer attitudes differ in these two geographies about such major components of the budget as transportation, housing, food, and education. Let's head back to New York for a moment and think about the life Michael leads.

Michael doesn't own a car. That's understandable in a city like New York. Parking can be absurdly expensive and public transportation is easily accessible. He rents a car from time to time when he needs one, or he gets friends to drive him places when he needs to purchase something big. He divides his friends (and really the city as a whole) between areas he can easily access along certain subway lines and those he can't. As a renter, he doesn't have a lot of room for storage either. Costco doesn't have a lot to offer someone like Michael. Buying thirty rolls of toilet paper at a time might be economical, but not when you're renting the six square feet it takes to store the package at Manhattan prices. To say that has an impact on how he shops is an understatement. Chris in North Las Vegas might drive a couple of miles out of his way to stop at the market on the way home and grab something for dinner. Michael has nearly infinite choices right on his commute. One of his favorites is to stop in at the market in Grand Central Terminal while he switches trains. With just a quick indoor detour he can pick up some sushi or something fresh to make for dinner as soon as he gets off the train on the other end. No parking spot or shopping cart needed.

I stopped in at Pescatore Seafood Company to talk to Jerry, Grand Central's resident fishmonger. He knows his transient customers very well, including their media habits and their buying habits. He doesn't need any big data, he just talks to his customers. For instance, his Wednesday routine is to grab the dining section of the *New York Times* and see what the recipes are. If any of the dishes have fish as an ingredient, he knows to stock up before the weekend.

He also knows that he gets his customers going and coming. Even if they're not buying any product in the morning, they're browsing as they go by on their way to work, planning what they'll pick up that night. Maybe they'll Google some recipes in the meantime for whatever is on sale that day.

For the most part, he thinks New Yorkers are unique because his customers are very educated about his product. "You might get clams for half price in Chinatown, but they're 'wet' and injected with filler to appear larger and weigh more," he tells me, pausing to flick a leaning price sign back in place with his pen as we talk.

For the most part, however, they want the best and they know the best. He'll sell them the same fish they'd get at the Four Seasons—because it's the same customer.

Jerry even has a customer loyalty program even though he has only the one retail outlet. Returning customers get a punch card—get ten punches and get a free pound of anything you like.

"When I hear 'I'll take a pound of Chilean sea bass,' I know they've got their card punched because that's my most expensive fish."

And he smiles because then he knows the card is working.

Data and Democracy

Once we have moved past all the physical aspects of urban and suburban life, let's look at how these consumers actually *behave* differently.

In 2012, a heavily divided electorate voted to put President Obama back in office. During the race the candidates and their surrogates spent billions on advertising trying to sway the swing voters. The final margin: 5

million votes, or roughly 4 percent of all votes cast.[26] In today's polarized climate, that almost qualifies as a landslide. But in terms of actual numbers, that's really a pretty slim difference. The red/blue maps show stark divisions at the state level, yet the margin of victory is nearly identical in the swing states and the non-swing states. So where is there a difference in voting patterns? It's in the breakdown where there is no split at all: the city level. President Obama won *all but two* major U.S. cities: Jacksonville, Florida, and Salt Lake City.[27] That includes cities in Texas. And Ohio. And Florida. And Louisiana.

If the urban/suburban/exurban divide can be seen as a political one, what else can we look at through that lens?

First, we can look at brand affinity. YouGov, a global market research company, measures brands favored by Democrats and Republicans as part of its BrandIndex analysis. There's not a lot of crossover between so-called red and blue brands. Out of the top ten, only Cheerios, Clorox, and Craftsman make both lists.[28]

I asked Experian Marketing Services, a global provider of consumer insights, to run its TV preference data through the Patchwork Nation framework.[29] Essentially, it coded each response based on the county, and each county based on its dominant Patchwork Nation segment. Since Patchwork Nation types are based on geography, demographics, and voting patterns, they give us a pretty good way of discerning viewing habits based on urban/suburban breakdowns and also based on politics. Some areas like "Industrialized Metro" are more Democratic and urban, whereas "Military Bastions" are more suburban/rural and Republican. Looking at data for more than 500 shows, we can see that the "Industrialized Metro" segment is way more likely than average to watch *Tyler Perry's House of Payne* and shows on PBS and BET—owing to the diversity in these large counties. What's especially helpful about layering this data through the Patchwork segments is that you can contrast the "Industrialized Metro" counties with their neighboring counterparts, the "Monied 'Burbs" county types. The "Monied 'Burbs," which would often be included in the same designated marketing area or DMA as their urban neighbors, are much more likely than average to watch *Modern Family, The Office, Saturday Night Live,* and a host of other network shows. Four of the top five shows for the "Military Bastions" are courtroom reality shows like *Judge Joe Brown, Judge Mathis,* and *Divorce Court.* "Service Work Centers" like

Hampden County, Massachusetts, which are mostly small to mid-sized areas with economies fueled by hotels, stores, hospitals, and restaurants, are more likely to watch top-rated CBS shows like *Mike & Molly* and *NCIS*, but also *Antiques Roadshow* on PBS.

A survey—even a survey this large—isn't quite what we consider "big data," but it's certainly big enough to draw some broad conclusions. As we just demonstrated, using a segmentation tool like the Patchwork Nation, Esri's Tapestry, or Experian's own Mosaic, you can find a show that will do an optimal job of targeting the specific demographic you want. But there's another way if you have the data.

Winning with Demographics

So how did President Obama win the election with demographics? Think of him as a CEO, the head of product development. The product here is public policy. He's kind of like a Richard Branson or a Steve Jobs in that it's hard to separate his personal brand from the company he heads. In this scenario the campaign staff is the marketing department. (Granted, I'm oversimplifying a bit.)

In this case, you never know when the CEO is going to come out and make a new product announcement such as supporting gay marriage. Some of the campaign's senior staff learned about the president's statement from lower-level staff who were reading reports on the Internet. A quick meeting was called and then everyone had to hit the ground running.

"It seemed like we were on a caboose and the president was driving the train. We didn't know when we were whipping around the corner what was going to be up that hill," Harper Reed, the chief technology officer (CTO) of Obama for America (OFA), told me.[30]

As pundits and politicians on both sides of the aisle have pointed out in post-election hindsight, Obama and the Democratic Party policies better reflect the realities of today's demographics. Shortly after the election, Mitt Romney said that he lost because President Obama had given too many "gifts" to special interest groups.[31] That's a pretty blunt way of putting it. Another way to say it would be to say that the president had spent his time in office engaging in smart, data-driven product development. He courted the segments of the population that are growing in numbers and in influence. It's simple math.

Obama won 70.6 percent of Hispanic voters. He also won 73.2 percent of Asians and virtually all black voters. He won the single-women vote by almost 40 percent.

He stayed competitive with the sixty-five and older demographic and won 60 percent of voters under thirty—by far his best age group.[32]

All of this bodes well for the Democrats in the future. I talked with Nate Silver, the stats guru who correctly predicted the results of all fifty states for his FiveThirtyEight blog.

"A lot of the swing states are pretty diverse so the fact that they [the Republicans] lost all the swing states except for North Carolina would be a little frightening to me if I were the GOP. In the long run the parties are supposed to adapt to the changing circumstances. If you have more Hispanics or Asian Americans, if you have Americans changing their views on gay rights, then the parties are supposed to adapt to that. If the Republican Party decided to remain the same party they were for the last four or eight years or become even more conservative, then you might see some sort of inefficiency where the Democrats would be able to win a series of elections."[33]

Running for president is clearly more than just a marketing exercise and appealing to target niches. It's about as mass-market play as you can get. As with any brand, the bottom line still matters. In this case, any number of consumer actions is helpful (like sharing content, donating, volunteering time or services) but all that counts in the end is that they make good on their intent and purchase the product, in this case by voting.

For this, the Obama campaign made a concerted and ambitious effort to make decisions based on the best available data. More importantly, they realized that they needed to be able to tie the available data together from a number of sources in order for that data to be most impactful. The campaign took a risk and decided to build out its team in-house rather than relying on a bevy of consultants as every other campaign in recent history had.

The use of data and technology was central to the campaign from day one and it built a dream team of coders, analytic wonks, and user-experience gurus and put these experts right in the physical heart of the campaign's central offices.

So you can look at the 2012 election cycle as the combination of using big data to market a product built in response to demographic trends on one side and a failure to acknowledge the demographic realities of 2012 America on the other.

For a guy who describes himself on his website as "pretty awesome" and "probably one of the coolest guys ever," Harper Reed is rather humble about what he and the campaign accomplished.

He says that taking the voter rolls (neither a particularly clean nor small data set) and matching them to things like Facebook, cable subscribers, and other public and private databases was no big deal.

"We stood on the shoulders of a lot of companies that have been doing this for years." To an extent, he's right that marketers have been dealing with these challenges for a long time. To an extent, he's just being modest.

"A lot of what the campaign did was take ad tech and make it physical," Reed told me. Before he ran the tech team for Obama for America, he was, among other things, the former CTO of a Chicago-based hipster T-shirt maker, skinnyCorp's Threadless. One could argue that his challenge there was exactly the opposite—taking something physical like T-shirts, and making it social and user-driven. The company's shirts are designed and voted on by customers.

For the re-election, Facebook was key to the work his team did. As we will discuss in chapter nine, it's a good place to achieve scale. Facebook knows a lot about its users and can make that data available, in accordance with its privacy policies, to third parties via apps and other share mechanisms.

"We spent a lot of resources getting our people matching set. We were able to really dig into Facebook," Reed said.

Once OFA had connected with people on Facebook, it could then look into who their friends are. Reed was conscious of but not overly concerned about the privacy implications. "It's hard for it to be Orwellian. A lot of this data is self-reported and a lot of it is public [like the voter records]."

Getting smart about those connections was one of the strengths of the operation. The share button became an important tool. OFA would filter whom it asked people to share content with. If a person was in a non-battleground like Chicago, it might only pull up that person's friends in Ohio and Wisconsin. It could then track how well he or she worked as an influencer.

In the real world, a campaign worker might say, "Hey, tell your friends," and have no way to track that. In the digital world, OFA was able to replicate that experience on Facebook and put analytics behind it. A campaign worker might also ask if someone would go and knock on some doors. OFA developed a score for each voter that gauged the strength of support for the candidate. It would use that and its people matcher to utilize its campaign assets as efficiently as possible. If the campaign felt it would be a waste of time to knock on three doors out of a block because there was no hope (Romney supporter) or no need (strong Obama supporter), then it would instruct the volunteer to skip those doors.

That's something that wasn't as possible in previous elections. Transferring calls to action back and forth between the digital and physical worlds—in an automated and scalable way—was something the campaign excelled at. It's a model that we'll see more of in campaigns for brands.

The Obama campaign was able to leverage this to solve some of the geographic riddles marketers encounter every day. Buying ads for a DMA means you're reaching a lot of people who are out of target. With a modern campaign that can be even more true. There was essentially no chance that Romney would win California, nor that Obama would win Texas. Why spend precious TV dollars advertising in markets you're going to lose?

Part of the answer is the city/non-city divide. OFA had a lot of supporters in blue cities within red states. Technology like this allowed them not just to reach out to those important customers but to engage them and put them to work. Think of it as turning your loyal customers into brand ambassadors.

A frequent-voter loyalty card isn't the right thing (well, maybe in "vote-early, vote-often" Chicago). OFA thought like a modern city. Like adding bike lanes to attract creative class Millennials, it made tools that helped enable people to work in modern ways. The tools were mobile, sleek, and easy to use and understand. The campaign drew in young, enthusiastic workers and gave them simple tasks that could easily be accomplished by people with time constraints.

The tools themselves are critical. "The interface is really important," said Reed. "It's a tool of big data that I don't think people realize. People underestimate the power of the user experience."

E-mails from Julianna Smoot (one of the campaign's public faces) would conclude by asking people directly to "make three phone calls today" or "donate $3." But not everyone would get the same e-mail. Some would open an e-mail from the campaign and be asked to give $8. One of the subject lines that tested best wasn't a call to action, or an alarmist headline (although those did well, too). It was a simple greeting from the president: "Hey."[34]

Tests were run at breakneck speed and at incredible scale to determine which worked better and for what groups the larger request led to increased donations.

In other cases, an e-mail might offer a prize like dinner at Sarah Jessica Parker's home. Why? Because the Obama campaign ferreted around in its big data to find that SJP would play as well with educated, liberal-leaning East Coast women as George Clooney did on the West Coast.[35]

Other parts of OFA were working on using technologies like these to solve offline inefficiencies.

Using people matching, they were able to attach the voter files to data from cable companies and understand what people watched on TV.[36] Armed with this information, the campaign then eschewed traditional ad-buying techniques and found the exact shows in the exact markets that the "leaning Obama" crowd were watching. This led to some ad buys that made little sense to the outside world and to the opposition. For instance, the Obama campaign purchased 1,710 spots on the relatively cheap TV Land network (at the national cable level). The Romney campaign bought none.[37]

It all hinged on the data, which led to Reed's biggest fear. It was very possible that the data they were mining could lead them to the wrong decisions, from spending precious ad dollars in the wrong markets to deploying last-minute get-out-the-vote volunteers in the wrong precincts. This fear wasn't helped by the fact that the competition was looking at much of the same data and publicly drawing the conclusion that their guy was going to win.

"They had drastically different answers," he said.

Think about it: With all the polling. With all the market research. With all the consultants. With all the pundits. With all the Nate Silvers of the world keeping a watchful eye on the numbers, the outcome of this election should have surprised no one.

The stakes for the data couldn't have been higher. Reed's team did extensive testing. The culture of testing rigor and methodology is one of his proudest accomplishments. "We had to be right. We knew we couldn't [mess] it up. So we were just careful."

Getting it wrong wouldn't mean losing a point of market share or having the *USA Today* Ad Meter say your Super Bowl spot wasn't funny.

Getting it wrong would mean your candidate's speech airs first. He'll thank his supporters and hop back into his own car instead of one driven by earpiece-wearing guys in suits.

Retirement

I didn't ask Michael whom he voted for, but I can make a pretty educated guess. He's a city dweller who is black, young, educated, and gay. His partner, whom he lives with, is also urban, young, educated, and gay. Except he's Hispanic. Their household income would make them affluent in many markets, but this is New York—a city where luxury trade-offs can mean not having room for a bathroom in your $800-a-month 78-square-foot apartment.[38]

New York City is clearly a great place to be young. It also has pockets that are great places to be old. Areas like the Upper East Side are densely packed with (mostly affluent) older Americans content to retire in the city. It's a phenomenon whose numbers are increasing, but it's not what most people think of when they imagine "retirement."

Retirement is on a lot of people's minds these days. Ten thousand people a day are reaching age sixty-five. To talk about trends in aging, I headed to the epicenter of senior living, central Florida. Lake County is home to the largest senior living center in the U.S., The Villages. The census counts it as its own city. So let's go meet Basha and see how retirement is changing.

SEVEN

The Buyographics of Aging

How Boomers' Transition to
Seniors Will Define the Economy

BASHA AND HER HUSBAND ARE GETTING OLDER. YOU MIGHT NOT GUESS that by listening to their daily activity log. They still work—she at a department store and he at a major sports complex—they are active in their community, and he teaches his neighbors how to play tennis.

Nearly every single one of their neighbors is at least fifty-five years old. Most are much older. I met several of them when I visited Basha in Clermont, a town in Lake County, Florida. I took a tour (by golf cart, of course) of their retirement complex with the community manager, Kim Myers. She explained that many of the complex's roughly 4,000 seniors moved there when the community opened fifteen years ago. Then they all got older. That's pushed the median age of the community into the seventies.

Lake County is an interesting microcosm of two trends. During the 2000s, its population both aged and grew more diverse. Each of those trends is impacting different communities differently. In chapter five, we spoke of the uneven geography of diversity. The aging population also shows a spectrum. Some areas are getting older. Some are getting younger. I visited today's seniors in order to get some perspective of what America (and the rest of the developed world) will look more and more like for the next few decades as the nation grays. In this chapter we'll look at:

- How the recession knocked the soon-to-retire off their plan;
- The uneven aging of America;
- How marketers are responding to the challenges of a non-heterogeneous aging consumer population.

The Baby Boomers have long been the darlings of marketers and have quite literally driven the economy for decades. Every day for the next two decades, 10,000 people from this generation will celebrate their sixty-fifth birthday. They will move from an age bracket that spends an average of $54,000 per household to one that spends just $45,000.[1] They will be put out to pasture—entering the marketing wasteland of "seniors." If they don't already, many of them will wind up living in places like this, not far from Orlando, but largely forgotten by Madison Avenue.

But they're getting harder to ignore. While the coveted demographic of TV advertising is the eighteen to forty-nine cohort, 2010 found a new record in the census data. It's an often overlooked statistic, but the median age of an American head of household is now over fifty.[2] That's right, more than half of households in the U.S. are outside of the marketer's favorite age range.

Today's seniors display a lot of differences from previous generations: they're living longer, they're more active, and they're working later in life. They're the best model we have of what this enormous Boomer cohort (roughly age forty-five to age sixty-five) will look and behave like in coming years and decades. There are differences. The Boomers are often considered more free spending than the frugal generation before them, which was more likely to have seen the impacts of the Great Depression firsthand. Perhaps just as importantly, today's retirees (from the generation ahead of the Boomers, often called the silent generation or the Pre-Boomers) generally made it out of the workforce before companies switched from defined pension plans to more volatile 401(k)s and before employers stopped offering or cut back matching contributions to those plans.[3] The timing of the recession coupled with often poor financial planning means that the Boomers themselves will have a tougher time of it than their parents did—especially in the short term.

When today's seniors looked into retirement a decade ago (then between ages fifty-five and sixty-four), nearly two-thirds had savings, according to the Federal Reserve Board. Comparing that to the older end of Boomers who are now in that age range, we see that just over half have saved. That's not even retirement savings; that's any savings at all.

The median net worth of retiring seniors a decade ago was $227,000. Now it's just $180,000. Today current retirees have a higher net worth than those about to retire. Ten years ago, the opposite was true.[4] The recession played a big part in this scenario. Income, in constant 2010 dollars, has remained flat for the fifty-five- to sixty-four-year-olds, but in 2007, the median net worth of that group was $85,000 more than it is today. They were the hardest hit of any age cohort between 2007 and 2010.

No wonder they're working longer. They have to. We talked about the Millennials and their "delayed life stages" in previous chapters. What's happening to the Boomers is somewhat analogous. They're not retiring in the same way, nor at the same time as their parents did. They're continuing to be active parents (i.e., supporting and sheltering their kids) longer and longer. This makes for an interesting marketplace on both ends of the age spectrum.

If you look at the labor participation rate of seniors (the percentage of that age range in the workforce) in 2007, it was 16 percent. That was much higher than the 10.8 percent in 1985. Let's go back further, all the way to 1948, which is when the Bureau of Labor Statistics started tracking this.[5] At that point, a whopping 27 percent of seniors were in the workplace and nearly *half* of senior men. So while the trend of working seniors is currently growing, it's a somewhat long-standing reversal of a long-standing decline. The more recent trend of note is that as recently as 2001, the majority were working part-time. Now more than 56 percent are working full-time.

Spending vs. Passing Down

Historically, the transfer of wealth from one generation to the next has been a safety net. Inheritance has provided a strong financial cushion for younger generations. Today, however, it's a much harder trend to understand. On the one hand, today's seniors have a greater net worth than seniors did in the past, and that wealth is more concentrated than ever. The other reality is that people are living longer, and seniors need their money to stretch over more years and provide for health-care costs that are rising exponentially each year. One study found that one in three adults in the U.S. is pretty sure they'll outlive their savings. More troubling is that this number is below the global average.[6] Another survey by health insurance giant WellPoint found that nearly three-fourths (73 percent) of consumers aged fifty to sixty-two who are still working said that obtaining health benefits was "the single biggest concern" or "one of the biggest concerns" they will face in retirement.

If you look at spending patterns, you'll find that age really does impact spending patterns. Seniors typically spend less on just about every product category than the nation does as a whole. The big exception is health care, where for younger seniors (aged sixty-five to seventy-four) their expenses are more than 80 percent higher than those of the typical U.S. household. Older seniors spend slightly less than younger seniors, probably because they are more likely to be in single-person households than the younger seniors are. Overall, seniors spend nearly as much on health care as they do on food. For comparison, households headed by someone aged thirty-five to forty-four spend nearly three times as much on food as on health care.[7]

"People are finding themselves not retiring when they thought they would," said Margaret Mueller, president of CarbonSix, a Chicago-based market research firm focused on health care. "A lot of people who want to stop are continuing to work purely for the health insurance. They're even taking lower-level jobs just to get the insurance."

The Gravity of Retirement

Typically, empty nesters move south. Better weather, year-round golf, and a climate where no one needs to shovel are all draws.

Basha and her husband left Miami to come to the then sparsely populated Clermont and the then-new 55+ community she and her husband both still call home. At the time, the area was largely orange groves. The malls, Olive Gardens, and other vestiges of sprawl would come later. They had to start their own temple because there wasn't one nearby. The lure was the community, and a chance to be closer to their kids.

More and more, seniors look like Basha: active, social, working, and independent. As the Boomers move into seniorhood with her, they're unlikely to take the inattention from marketers sitting down.

"We [Boomers] always changed the market to accommodate us, and we will continue to do so," says Patricia Lippe Davis, vice president marketing for AARP's media sales.[8]

Since many seniors are retired, their income is only 60 percent of the median household income for the U.S. It's easy to look at that data point and try to dismiss older folks as a low marketing priority, but wealth is the key factor here: despite the downturn, households headed by seniors have more than twenty times the net worth of households headed by those thirty-five or younger. That disparity has grown significantly since 1984, when the ratio was more like 10 to 1, according to Pew Research Center. Because of mandated cost-of-living increases in many pension and retirement plans, seniors are the only age group whose real income has grown since the recession that began in 2007.

The Geography of Aging

Today there are more than 40 million seniors in the U.S. Another 38 million will turn sixty-five in the next decade.[9] The senior population grew faster between 2000 and 2010 than did the population as a whole—15 percent versus 10 percent.

The growth is very uneven geographically. If you look at a county-level map, you'll see a lot of decline in the 65+ population running a

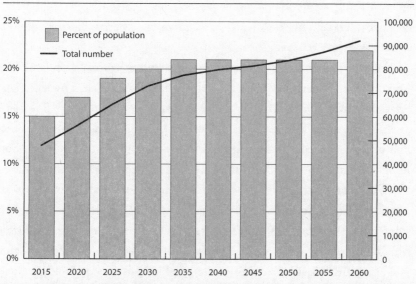

Figure 7.1   The Growing Senior Population

Source: U.S. Census Bureau, 2012 National Population Projections, thousands

line down the middle of the country from North Dakota into Texas. Partially this was due to below-average population expansion in those areas.[10] Partially it's due, frankly, to older generations dying and not being replaced.

The growth took place in expected places, such as parts of Florida, Arizona, and other Sun Belt counties, but also in the Pacific Northwest, northern Michigan, Virginia, and the Carolinas. Like the decline, this is partially migration and partially areas where the population is simply aging.

If you compare them to a demographic that gets a lot of marketer attention, that puts seniors as a whole (i.e., all 65+ consumers) just 10 million behind the fast-growing Hispanic population in terms of sheer numbers. Seniors spend about $39,000 a year per household, or roughly $3,000 less than the typical Hispanic household, according to the Bureau of Labor Statistics. And because their households tend to be much smaller empty nests, there are actually many more senior households than there are Hispanic households. Therefore, seniors spend nearly 60 percent more, in aggregate, than Hispanics do, accounting for more than a trillion dollars in annual outlay.

Marketers and merchants are taking notice. Quietly.

Paco Underhill, the retail guru who authored the seminal *Why We Buy: The Science of Shopping*, wrote an article for *American Demographics* in 1996 that outlined many techniques for making stores more senior friendly. We chatted about trends in targeting seniors, and the fundamentals haven't changed: bigger fonts on displays and price tags, better lighting, slower escalators, etc.

While visiting Lake County, I toured a Publix grocery store and saw some of Mr. Underhill's proposals being put into practice. The store sits adjacent to Kings Ridge, one of the several large communities of 55+ residents in the area. The residents can drive their golf carts right up to the Publix via a special entrance and park in designated parking spots. For some residents, the golf cart is the only mode of transportation they have.

This particular Publix has twice as many powered shopping carts as a typical branch. Several were in use as I toured. Responding to customer comments, the store has increased its selection of gluten-free products, which are popular with seniors. Those all have large green labels on the shelf, and the manager keeps printouts of gluten-free recipes and product information in a kiosk at the entrance. The store aisles are wide (to accommodate those carts) and well lit.

But a little seating area with free coffee is a big draw. The male seniors gather there in the late morning, socializing and playing scratch-off lottery tickets while their wives shop. The store manager likes to sit and visit with them as he's making his rounds. It's all meant to create a more inviting environment for the store's core demographic.

Publix creates an annual Thanksgiving-themed TV spot. The 2010 version featured a grandmother cooking for her family. It was a grocery store commercial set in a home. The in-store environment didn't receive a mention, although the spot focused on values that are key to the senior demographic.

"One of the problems that scare marketers is, if you actively market to seniors, is that a turnoff to everybody else?" says Mr. Underhill. "Do you want to go to the supermarket that caters to geriatrics? I don't know if that's a legitimate concern or not, but it is something that goes through the minds of both merchants and marketers."

For instance, Toyota created the Venza for the younger end of the Boomer cohort who are in their late forties through their fifties. The car is easy to get in and out of and has rear seats that fold with little effort, and its high ride offers open sight lines. This isn't about marketing; it's about product research.

"For us it starts with the fact that it was designed with active Boomers in mind. A lot of research was done by our engineering side to make a car that fits that lifestyle and that generation of buyer," says Russ Koble, Toyota advertising and planning manager. He noted that the model also does well with seniors—and Millennials. "We know that people are living longer and are staying much more active. The activities may change, but they still have active pursuits."

But you don't see seniors in the Saatchi & Saatchi, Los Angeles–created spots, which have been running since late 2010. They feature Boomers and their Millennial kids. (Though the sentiment, aimed at people in their fifties, should also resonate with seniors. In the spots, a Millennial frets over her parents having no online "friends" while in actuality her parents are out biking and exploring with real-life buddies.)

Southwest Airlines has many programs that are targeted toward seniors, including reduced fares, the bags-fly-free program, and "Honor

Flights" that bring World War II vets to Washington to visit the memorial there. However, a spokesperson from Southwest says that the airline "doesn't specifically target seniors with paid media."

Geriatric Supermarket

One morning during my visit to Lake County, I stopped in at a big senior hotspot, McDonald's. A group of older men sat together, socializing over coffee and other McTreats. They didn't come in together and they didn't show much sign of leaving any time soon. It's a scene reminiscent of the McDonald's "Joe and Frank" ad that won a Bronze Lion at the Cannes Lions International Festival of Creativity for DDB, Chicago, in 2010. In the spot, two senior men compete for the attention of a woman at a nearby table. The commercial wasn't created because of a specific senior-targeted brief from the client, but rather grew out of a conversation between DDB and the marketing team. The group was discussing how, in markets throughout the world, you'll find seniors gathering as they do here in Clermont. It wasn't even created for the purposes of airing. It was developed for the franchisee convention, but the response was so positive that the client approved putting it into rotation.

Bill Cimino, executive creative director at DDB, Chicago, touched on a point raised by many marketers and agency execs about the key to targeting seniors. "The way this spot treated the guys, it did so with dignity."

AARP's magazine actually mandates that advertisers in its pages avoid the "I've fallen and I can't get up" stereotype of the helpless senior. Dignity and respect are concepts that come up often in conversation. So does segmenting creative. By advertising in senior-heavy publications like *AARP: The Magazine* or by using online-targeting tools, brands can generate creative for seniors that other demographics will be unlikely to see. *AARP: The Magazine* even segments the audience further with three discrete editions for subscribers in their fifties, sixties, and beyond. That can help alleviate the "geriatric supermarket" issue Mr. Underhill alluded to.

Where's the Zumba Class?

Back in Lake County, my golf-cart tour began at the community center. We were shooed out of a very serious pool tournament against a rival 55+

community, but later welcomed back for a photo shoot once the competition had ended. In the lobby, Elvis's music played quietly until the King was drowned out by the blaring soundtrack from one of the fitness classes. This was the exchange I overheard:

"Do you know where the Zumba class is?"

"All the girls over there are waiting for it."

"Oh, I thought that was line dancing."

This community and others like it are self-selecting groups of aging adventurers. Basha's husband's tennis lessons are just one attraction. Like the pool tournament, they're taken very seriously. I'm told you wouldn't want your grandkids hearing some of the language used on the courts. Because they still work, Basha and her husband are out and about more than many residents whose activities are often managed through the complex, including weekly excursions to shopping and entertainment destinations. For the seniors who leave their communities, everything is close. Retailers are building, trying to keep up with demand caused during the boom times.

Clermont has a "historic" downtown, just a couple of blocks long. Most of the commercial action is along the two main stretches of highway. Much of this has been developed in the past fifteen years. As we dined at the Olive Garden near her complex, Basha told me more about how the area had changed since they moved here. "We only had one restaurant. And it was terrible," she says.

Ray San Fratello, president of the South Lake Chamber of Commerce, says the area hadn't had a movie theater for the past fifty years. Now there's a multiscreen movieplex and the standard slate of chains like Red Lobster and Outback Steakhouse. Along the highway sprawl you'll find a Walmart, strip malls, more senior housing and condo complexes, and a handful of golf courses.

Back home, Basha and her husband usher me into a living room with super cushy black leather furniture surrounding a TV blasting ESPN. They are sports nuts—her husband is a retired college athletic director and still works at a massive sports complex in Orlando.

They have all the premium sports packages and use their DVR to skip commercials. That makes Basha doubly hard to reach with TV ads. First, she often doesn't watch them, and second, she's often watching shows, like ESPN news programming, that aren't targeted to her.

Their house contains a museum-quality collection of memorabilia, including a coffee table with a glass top covering a sculpture of a life-size baseball player sliding into an imaginary base. Basha also has a good-size collection of Disney plush toys and figurines. They like to vacation, and they drive sporty cars. They also have family to buy presents for. In short, their spending profile looks a lot like that of a couple much younger.

So, to an extent, does their online profile. Basha claimed she wasn't very computer literate—and her @aol.com e-mail address lent some credence to that—but she pays her bills online and Skypes with her family.

"I pick up e-mails and play some games," she says. "I'm periodically on Facebook. But I do have some apps . . . not 'apps' but icons that I use." Basha doesn't like the Facebook messaging function, nor does she really understand the difference between wall posts and direct messages. She's taking part in many of the same online activities as other generations, just not on quite the same scale.

For marketers, this makes her a difficult nut to crack—if they even care to. But as this age group continues to grow and spend while taking on a profile more like that of younger generations, it's increasingly a group we should start to see in creative, not just in product-engineering, meetings.

Recessionary Impacts

Basha's life looks pretty good: Florida, friends, fitness, freedom, and family. She was lucky, to some extent. She'd retired from her career when the recession hit, and she and her husband still have incomes from their "retirement jobs" beyond their retirement savings and social security.

Others weren't so lucky.

Some $2.8 trillion in retirement investments was lost during the recession.[11] That includes both 401(k) retirement accounts and defined pension plans. Some, but not all of it came back. That doesn't include investments tied up in real estate—including the very homes the retirees lived in.

The real estate crisis hit areas like this hard. Down Highway 50 toward neighboring Mascotte sits the development of Knight's Lake Estates. Paved roads stretch beneath streetlights, but there are no driveways. Or houses.

Worse, head a little bit North and visit Bella Collina. The Tuscan-style development features a lush spa, a Nick Faldo golf course, and an opulent clubhouse. Lots originally sold for around $200,000, according to Diane Travis of Travis Realty Group, who gave me an insider's tour of Lake County real estate. As the economy boomed, the lots got flipped and re-flipped, trading at a peak of nearly $1 million. The success drove up prices in nearby developments as well. Then they all crashed.

Now, she says, you can buy a lot here for less than $10,000. But even at that price, they're not selling, because you would still need to build a home up to the standards of the community and pay the membership and other homeowner fees.

Things are improving slowly, but Basha sees the impact in the present, too.

"All our homes here where we live, it's like, 'Wow, what happened to our investments?'" She's made cuts in her budget and uses online coupon sites such as Coupon Mom. While she likes the idea of Groupon, she hasn't seen many deals that appeal to her age group, which to me spells an opportunity for the right brands.

Aging in Place

One aspect of retiring in the South that is often overlooked is that it's not necessarily a permanent change. According to Ms. Travis, the real estate market keeps afloat partially because seniors who retire to areas like this often end up missing their families and returning. So there is some churn: just as quickly as some flee back north, others come south seeking the warmth of central Florida.

Jeff Speck, author of *Walkable City: How Downtown Can Save America* and coauthor with Andres Duany and Elizabeth Plater-Zyberk of *Suburban Nation: The Rise of Sprawl and the Decline of the American Dream*, would say there's more to it than that. Many who move to retirement-heavy areas but not right into retirement communities find themselves cut off from the rest of the world if they reach a point when they can no longer drive. There is no plausible means for them to walk to any place that could support their daily needs. So they're forced to move again to some place that can better support them, or to some place where they can better support themselves. He says today's Boomers have watched this happen to their parents and are hoping to avoid what he calls "re-retirement."

"There's this myth that you can retire to a golf-course community. But if you retire to a sprawling community and the automobile is a key instrument of your daily life, then when you have to give up the car, you are no longer a viable member of society and re-retire somewhere else like a nursing home where, if you're lucky, a bus takes you to the mall on Wednesday."[12]

As we noted in chapter six, many Boomers are moving to cities and towns and out of the suburbs, looking for amenities like good restaurants and walkable locations that help them stay fit and stay mobile—with or without a car. You see this in neighborhoods like the Upper East Side of Manhattan or in smaller towns like Lexington, Massachusetts, where Mr. Speck's parents moved. Urban planners call areas where this is taking place NORCs, short for naturally occurring retirement communities.

As a result of the real estate crisis, many simply can't afford to move to a more suitable place than the large suburban homes where they raised their families. Either their mortgages are underwater or their home is worth so much less than they'd anticipated that it's not enough to buy into a new community. Many will "age in place," or continue to live in their own home for the next decade. It could be a feasible option for most sixty-somethings, but less than half of seniors in their seventies said they could live independently.[13]

On the other end, some Boomers are doing just fine financially and will take on a second home if they haven't already. According to noted demographer Peter Francese, the rate of second home ownership increased at a pace roughly double the rate of primary home ownership over the last decade. "Whether that will continue is a real question," he said.[14]

The Boomer population is so large that combinations of "retiring in place," buying second homes, and moving to other communities will happen. One thing to keep in mind is that the vast majority of Americans don't move, regardless of age. Over the five-year stretch from 2005 to 2010 more than 65 percent of the population stayed in place. Of those who moved, 80 percent stayed in the same state, and 61 percent stayed in the same county. Roughly eight in ten of the older Boomers stayed in their homes as they neared retirement.[15] In 2011 less than 3 percent of all seniors over age sixty-five moved.[16]

Global Graying

In the U.S., seniors make up about 15 percent of the population. By 2030 that will rise to 20 percent, and it will climb to 22 percent in 2060, according to Census Bureau predictions. At that point, there will be, for the first time, a higher percentage of seniors than of kids under eighteen. For a quick view at what that will look like, peek west to Japan and China. Japan is already the oldest nation on earth with more than 23 percent of its population over age sixty-five.[17] China is facing an interesting crisis, partially as a side effect of its so-called one-child policy. As its population has aged, it has a greatly diminished ratio of kids to take care of those adults both financially and physically. In China it's more common for parents to move back in with their kids as they get older and need more care. But now a married couple might not have any brothers and sisters to share that burden, meaning they could have four parents to care for.[18]

Caring for the elderly is an increasing concern for Boomers, and it is further impacting what their retirement will look like. Health care is in a very real sense becoming an issue not just for the aging but for everyone.

Every trend we've talked about up until now plays into health-care trends, and every family we've met has something to say about it. It's such a pervasive concern that even the Millennials are thinking about how they pay for it, and how they'll take care of their parents.

I'm going to start by introducing you to Alfredo in Los Angeles County. His story is becoming increasingly familiar and as the Boomers age, that will only become more prevalent. Alfredo essentially lives with his mom, who has Alzheimer's disease. It impacts just about everything in terms of how he spends his money and his time. So let's head to L.A. and learn more about how health care's increasing slice of the pie is affecting the rest of the household budget.

EIGHT

The Buyographics of Health Care

How We Re-prioritize as This Sector Takes Up More of Our Time and Money

ALFREDO LIVES WITH HIS WIFE AND TWO CHILDREN IN AN APARTMENT COMplex in Los Angeles County. His household isn't, strictly speaking, multigenerational, but his mother lives in the next unit over. She has health conditions that require around-the-clock care. Alfredo's wife is paid by the state to care for her part-time, and they have a nurse who also stays with her. Alfredo, who works in logistics, chips in what he can for her care, and his sister winds up paying for most of it. His sister also splits time on weekends staying with her.

His mother is lucky. She has health insurance for life as a retirement benefit from the factory where she worked making picture frames. Unfortunately, the assisted living homes where Alfredo has tried to place her either don't have rooms or aren't in the network of her particular insurance plan.

So caring for her not only is a full-time job spread among several members of the family but also has financial implications since insurance doesn't cover everything necessary for her care. It impacts where they live, the kind of jobs they can take, and, of course, the bottom line for all involved.

To say it's tough going is an understatement. To say it's an increasing phenomenon in America is, too.

Families in Alfredo's situation are commonly referred to as the "sandwich generation"—essentially middle-aged families taking care of their children and also their parents. In some cases that's direct care within households in which three generations are under one roof. We've said the numbers of multi-generational households are rising, but they are still less than 5 percent of the overall number of households in the U.S.

Technically, Alfredo wouldn't count in this statistic since his mother lives in the next unit, but he is an example of this demographic. It's a household structure we should expect to see more of in the coming years. Even for families who aren't actually living together, more and more Baby Boomers are finding themselves involved in financing the care of their parents or helping them make decisions in the marketplace.

The simple reason is that we're living longer. In the last fifty years the average life expectancy has increased almost a decade from just under seventy years in 1960 to over seventy-eight years in 2010. For women, it's over eighty-one years.[1] Couple that with a tremendous rise in health-care costs, and it foreshadows some pretty serious changes for American families.

It's already a huge market. Some 10 million adults over the age of fifty are involved in the care of their aging parents.[2] That number is only going to grow. By 2030, the older population is projected to be twice as large as it was in 2000, growing to 72 million. The U.S. Census Bureau predicts that there could be as many as 19 million Americans over the age of eighty-five by 2050. Some researchers think that's a very *conservative* estimate.[3]

Alfredo is at the nexus of these two trends. He is spending more of his budget on health care (although insurance and his sister are picking up much of the cost), and he's also spending more of his *time* on health care. These are two factors that play into the kind of trade-offs he and his family have to make on decisions both small and large.

So far we've been spending our time talking about demographic trends of place, age, ethnicity, and family. In our remaining chapters we're going to look at three major industries and discuss how these trends are impacting them. As you can imagine, it's usually more than one trend at play. In the case of health care, the big factors are the aging population and changes to the middle class. Even for those with health insurance, costs can be prohibitive.[4] A significant disease like cancer can wind up costing well into six figures even for the insured.[5] Legislation is also now playing a role as the Affordable Care Act starts to take hold. Among other impacts of these new laws is a shift in the insurance market from a mostly business-to-business market to one that is now much more consumer focused.

In turn, health care and aging are driving changes in some household trends as elderly parents move in with their adult children and form more multigenerational households. This is exacerbating the middle-class income issues. One reason wages haven't been going up is that employees are costing employers more in other ways. If you look at overall compensation, which includes employer underwriting of benefits like health insurance, companies have indeed been "paying" more for employees even if that increase isn't going into their pockets, but into the health-care system.[6] It has now gotten to be too much for companies to keep bearing the brunt of the rising costs, so they've started passing a greater share of those costs on to employees, further squeezing their household budgets. Issues related to health-care access and affordability are important to look at. What we're seeing is that these are now issues impacting three generations at once. For marketers in this space, being able to communicate across and through generations simultaneously is paramount.

One reason: Half of online research about health care is done on behalf of someone else.[7] Often, that's a concerned family member like a parent or a child.

I could say that every generation is thinking about these issues, but it's probably more accurate to say that every generation is *worrying* about these issues.

Where you live plays a role, too, as it relates to both population makeup and lifestyle. Using some custom data analysis from GfK MRI, a leading producer of media and consumer research in the United States, we'll break down the geography of disease. We'll also take a necessary digression through the shifting definitions of "want" and "need" in today's marketplace. As people spend more on this very basic "need," they have to make some trade-offs. That leads to greater opportunities for some product categories than for others.

Once you're done with this chapter you will:

- See some trends in how different diseases are impacting different groups differently;

- Learn what categories might lose the most as consumers are forced into trade-offs;
- Consider what a shift from business-to-business to consumer marketing means for a brand like Blue Cross and Blue Shield (BCBS).

Why are we talking about diseases in a marketing book? In simplistic terms, it costs different amounts of money to care for people with different diseases. Different diseases also impact certain parts of the population at disproportionate rates and therefore impact certain geographies differently. As an example, let's take a quick look at one major disease: obesity.

In 2000 no state had an obesity prevalence of 30 percent. By 2010 twelve states had crossed that threshold. Colorado was until recently the only state that had under 20 percent of its residents qualifying as obese. Now all states are past that benchmark according to the U.S. Centers for Disease Control and Prevention. America doesn't seem to be getting healthier overall. This is just one reason to anticipate rising health-care costs.

As the American consumer gains weight, all sorts of changes occur that brands must consider. There are physical changes, like wider seats in restaurants and wider aisles in stores.

Then there are the reactions in the marketplace. New York mayor Michael Bloomberg decided to make an example of soft drinks and tried to enact a ban on large servings of sugary sodas at restaurants, for the same reason that New York City effectively eliminated smoking in all public areas—because it was killing us. In response, advertising giant Coca-Cola started airing spots touting the lower-calorie branches of its product tree.[8]

Marketers have generally been slow to address America's growing weight problem both in product offerings and in representing overweight consumers in creative advertising spots. In 2009 I spoke to a woman named Wendy Wimmer, who has contributed for years to the Big Fat Deal blog under the screen name Weetabix. She described the plus-size section of Target as the "fat-girl ghetto," located in the back corner of the store. To get there, she passed racks of "cute as a button" Liz Lange maternity wear with envy. "Someone is pregnant for nine months, but people are generally fat for their entire lives," she said.[9]

Obesity correlates with other sorts of diseases like heart disease, diabetes, and certain kinds of cancer. That's important when you consider two things. First, there's a 1 percent problem with health care, much as there's a 1 percent problem with income distribution in the U.S. In this case, 1 percent of Americans account for more than 20 percent of all health-care spending. Five percent account for half of all health-care costs.[10] Second, there's the insurance problem. Insurance rates, too, vary widely by geography for any number of reasons including economic considerations and levels of unemployment. In Norfolk County, Massachusetts, less than 4 percent of the population lacks insurance. On the other end of the spectrum, more than 40 percent of the residents of Hudspeth County, Texas, are uninsured.[11]

Thinking about how this would hit wallets in different ways led me to ask market researcher GfK MRI to run its survey data about disease prevalence through the Patchwork and Tapestry systems. In a post on the AdAgeStat blog, I created a map showing how the Patchwork segments skew in terms of the diseases they suffer from.[12]

Again, I realize that talking about disease might seem like a digression in a book about demographic and consumer trends. But data is most useful as it correlates to behaviors. So let's take a walk through one example of how to use a data set like this. I'm going to pick irritable bowel syndrome (IBS) as our sample disease. It afflicts more white Americans than black Americans. In addition, a study funded by GlaxoSmithKline and RTI Health Solutions found that those with lower education levels and lower income were more likely to be afflicted. East Baton Rouge Parish, our example county of the Patchwork Nation segment "Minority Central," certainly qualifies as lower income and lower education overall. That's where Sandra, our forty-something single mother of two girls lives. Areas such as this have a population with a skewed proportion of IBS sufferers.

According to the GfK MRI data, residents of areas like this are also much more likely to use a branded prescription medication than a generic version or a nonprescription remedy for this illness even though they mirror U.S. trends of generally feeling that generic medications are just as effective as branded ones.[13]

To layer in some data from other sources, a survey conducted exclusively for *Ad Age* by Ipsos Observer found that residents of areas like this are less likely than average to take their rising health-care costs into consideration while they are planning their household budgets. They also feel that their costs are going to increase in coming years.

In terms of care, they take a more old-school approach and are more likely to ask their doctor about symptoms and cures than to self-diagnose on the Internet.

So putting all of this together, we have a data-rich picture of a measurable phenomenon (disease prevalence) coupled with data about how consumers react and behave in terms of treatment solutions and how those decisions impact the rest of their budgetary decisions. It's a pretty holistic look, from a marketer perspective. Let's bring it to life with a little anecdotal information.

Sandra likes to self-diagnose first and then consult her doctor. If she's feeling symptomatic, she'll pop on the Internet to research further. Then she'll talk to her doctor, who she says is often exasperated by her tendency to try self-diagnosis.

"I do that with probably any ailment that I have," she says. "I research it first and then go into the doctor's office." When she presented her self-diagnosis hypothesis, her doctor could always tell she'd been researching on the Internet.

Big Data in Health Care

With just the pharmaceuticals sector of health-care marketing projected to become a $1.2 trillion industry worldwide soon, there's a lot at stake.[14]

Earlier I mentioned that one relationship that is hard for marketers to crack is the multigenerational care household. Marketing health-care products and services to the people who actually have the disease isn't always the best course. Sometimes it's more important to reach out to the people who are providing the care, such as a parent or an adult child. Having access to information about the medications they're taking, the treatment options, when they are supposed to come in for follow-ups, and ideas to further promote health would be valuable for consumers and marketers alike.

Scott Howe, the CEO of market data warehouse Acxiom, would love to see data being used effectively by marketers, thereby enabling companies to serve customers better. It's a win-win to him—as long as marketers can better articulate the value exchange. He and I talked about Alfredo's situation and how marketers can communicate messages across generations.

In Alfredo's case, he is caring for his mother, who has Alzheimer's disease, which he clearly doesn't suffer from himself. How do you target a message to him?

Mr. Howe said that privacy restrictions can make that hard for marketers, but he thought it would be valuable for consumers to have access to more relevant information. "We don't collect health-care information. We're not involved in insurance or credit decisions, but people think we are. We do marketing. If someone has had a number of conversations with their [doctor] and explicitly asked for information from folks who might have good information to give, that's incredibly helpful [for both consumers and marketers]."

There's a risk that a consumer would feel their privacy had been violated in such a case. "If you feel like 'someone's figured out that my mom has Alzheimer's and they're going to use that to take advantage of her . . .' that's incredibly scary. It comes back to permission, and choice. I'd like to see our business morph to helping individuals connect with marketers. I think that's where the industry has to go."

Spending Smarter/Spending More

It's not news that health-care costs are eating a bigger slice of our wallets. It's one of the fastest-growing costs we face—fuel costs being another. There are some natural balances.

So where are people cutting back and where are they likely to cut back?

A good place to start is by looking at the increased competition for share of wallet. In the last ten to twenty years, all sorts of new product categories have moved from non-existent to non-negotiable. These "new necessities" that consumers have to have can eat up a hefty chunk of a budget.

For instance, the percent of consumers who reported expenses on "computer information services"—including broadband and wireless Internet services—more than doubled in the last decade to 60 percent of households, according to unpublished data from the Bureau of Labor Statistics (BLS).[15] These services are an increasing must-have for people of all economic levels. The growth was even faster among the lowest 20 percent of earners, where three in ten now report spending in that category, up 300 percent from 2000. The figures kept growing right through the recession, showing the strength of the need. It's not a new expense that can be cut; it's a recession-proof cost that must be worked into today's household budgets. Mobile phone service grew even faster—and those figures weren't balanced out by the decline in the amount spent on landline-based phone service, which predictably dropped.[16]

What costs have dropped? In the last decade the BLS saw spending on apparel plummet 30 percent. Despite rising gas costs, transportation spending dropped 22 percent as people cut back on new-car purchases and, to some extent, on maintenance or on acquiring and upgrading second cars. But health care, a clear "need" and growing cost center for aging Americans especially, rose more than 22 percent to 6.6 percent of total spending, up from 5.4 percent in 2000.[17]

These decreases don't represent cutbacks for all people. In some cases, we're spending less for other reasons. Many are spending less on clothing, for instance, because a less formal dress code requires less expensive clothes. I'm far from the only one working in a coffee shop in a hoodie and cargo pants right now. Spending on food fell, partially due to consumers' cutting back on dining out, but also because production costs have steadily dropped on many kinds of groceries.

Until she switched jobs in 2012, Liz in Champaign County, Illinois, paid for all her health-care expenses herself because she didn't have insurance. Thankfully, she was basically healthy during that time and didn't rack up any life-changing expenses. But she was still making trade-offs. She found herself unable to save up for a laptop because she was spending all her discretionary dollars on other people's weddings—especially bridesmaid's dresses.

My point here is that when discretionary income gets squeezed to the breaking point, the trade-offs people make are increasingly across category. Laptop makers probably don't consider the wedding industrial complex as a competitive industry, yet in many real ways it is. It's helpful to think in the context of moving your product from a "want" to a "need" and further giving the consumer an excuse or justification for buying it.

Access and Cost

For people of all ages, two big concerns are on their minds: access and costs. As I mentioned earlier, people of all ages are worried not just about their own health but about that of other generations in their family.

Increasingly, it's not just a matter of concern for their loved ones, but a financial concern for themselves as well.

Liz in Champaign County had access issues. Like many Millennials, she was working full-time in a job that didn't offer health insurance. It was created as a "contract" position during the recession. By paying her as a non-salary employee, her employer was able to save money by not offering her benefits. She's responsible and a planner so she tried to get her own health insurance and was denied by three different companies. At a self-described 5'9" and 200 pounds, she was told that she needed to lose 45 pounds in order to qualify for private insurance. "To be defined as 'morbidly obese' is sort of a hard punch to the gut to take," she said.

That was a major consideration, which eventually led her to give up and switch jobs. Her new employer offers her full benefits. To some extent, she is perfectly happy paying for the benefits. "The feeling of wondering what you'll do if you get sick or get hurt is way worse than the feeling of having money taken out of your paycheck."

She worries a lot about her parents as well, and about her grand-mother. Her parents are in their mid-sixties, and her father has struggled with his weight throughout his life. He's also not a fan of doctors, which she realizes is a bad combination of factors.

Like Alfredo, Liz's parents are both taking care of one of their parents as well. Her grandmother has dementia and had to move in with one of her children. Liz at least is on her own so they aren't supporting both a generation above and below them. Still, it's not easy.

"That's taking a lot of their time, effort, energy, and sometimes fi-nances as well. My grandmother has her own coverage, but it doesn't pay for everything. I don't think it's completely depleting any kind of nest egg that they had, but it is something that I think is affecting their future. They keep telling me that I should put them in a nursing home if they ever become a burden.

"I don't think this is necessarily how they expected to spend their time after I flew the nest. But they're happy to do it, and I would be as well."

MICHAEL, WHO MAKES A PRETTY GOOD LIVING IN NEW YORK, WORRIES LESS about the costs of health care because he's always had insurance. But he still thinks about it and about how his aging parents and grandparents will impact his future.

His mom has insurance through her second husband (Michael's dad died when he was young), so he isn't too worried about her expenses just now. His father's mother is in her nineties and is active enough to still live on her own. She has a home health aide who visits from time to time. She had to cope emotionally and financially with taking care of Michael's grandfather, who died of Alzheimer's. She has the benefit of living near family, unlike his mother's parents. He thinks about how his mother isn't offering to have her aging parents move in with her. So when he thinks about his mom's care, he wonders, "How could I make this work? It seems like more hassle to me to try to take care of a parent from far away than to just be like, oh, forget it, they can just move in.

"I'm thinking about it from like a life-change type of perspective but not as far as how much that costs versus a retirement community versus something else."

In Leavenworth County, Kansas, Jay thinks a lot about his health-care costs, and it's a subject you shouldn't get him going on unless you have some time on your hands.

He recently entered his thirties and is in good health. He wrestled in college and coaches the sport now. Keeping in shape is a priority. As a teacher he gets insurance through his union school district. But he's not at all happy about it.

"I have the bare-bones worst plan you can get, and it's 200 bucks a month, which is ridiculous."

For all marketers, the skyrocketing costs of America's health-care system are an issue even if they're not related to their particular industry. It's a major cost-center for your consumers and they're making trade-offs in other product categories. It's also a time consideration. In 2011 the Bureau of Labor Statistics measured the time spent taking care of elders as part of its annual American Time Use Survey.[18] It found that every age group had at least 10 percent of the population involved in eldercare. More than 20 percent of Baby Boomers are taking care of an elder.

Focus on Consumers

Health care is a huge industry and is going through an interesting change. Due to changes in the employment climate such as the rise of self-employed and contract workers and changes in the legislative landscape, health insurers and others are having to focus their marketing efforts on consumers. In any number of industries, technology and big data are making it easier to reach what are essentially markets of one. As we'll discuss further in the next chapter, the ability to track consumers by their behavior and aggregate them in with others with similar habits—regardless of geography or demographics—can mean that it's possible to shift marketing from one-to-many to one-to-one. Watching an entire established, enormous industry like health insurance adapt its marketing practices can be a great lesson for marketers from all sectors.

Reaching out to individuals is basically a whole new ballgame for health insurers, but one they're scrambling to get up to speed on. Since various provisions of the Affordable Care Act mandate coverage for everyone, a raft of new consumers are entering the marketplace—often for the first time—and they're not coming in through their employers.

Among the steps that Blue Cross and Blue Shield, the nation's largest insurance network, took to prepare were bringing in a consumer marketing specialist and hiring a new agency. Cynthia Rolfe is now the vice president of Consumer Brand Strategy for the Blue Cross and Blue Shield Association (BCBSA). Her background is in ad agencies and consumer products—working for brands like Procter & Gamble, Alberto Culver, Revlon, and Enesco.

If you want to talk health care in America, there are few better places than the Chicago offices of the BCBSA, which is the national federation made up of the thirty-eight independent BCBS companies that collectively insure one in three Americans. I met with Ms. Rolfe and Maureen Sullivan, senior vice president and chief strategy officer for BCBSA. They're doing their best to stay ahead of a changing landscape in a disrupted marketplace.

"The industry is shifting but more importantly the consumer is sitting there at the other end of the change. Our goal is to make this category feel a whole lot more like other categories they shop. Health insurance should feel more like the experience of comparing other large purchases,"[19] Ms. Rolfe said.

"There are things that matter to people no matter what demographic, age, income level, or health state. They all want to be educated and to figure out what is the best plan for them.

"The other piece is transparency. If this particular item isn't covered in my plan, help me understand why and have a conversation with me about how this impacts my choice."

We talked about Dale in Teton County, Montana. The farming life can be rough on the body and, now in his fifties, Dale has had both hips replaced. Despite sitting on the board of the local hospital, when he has some serious doctoring (which is a verb in that part of the country) to do, he's likely to get on a plane. His daughter has seen specialists in Seattle. His hips were replaced at the Mayo Clinic. His local connections recommend specific doctors, and he goes to those they consider the best for whatever ails him or his family.

The Mayo Clinic is about as blue chip a brand as you'll find in health care. Brand is important for the insurer as well as for the hospital and even the doctor because people use it as a navigation tool. It helps people feel that they are taking some of the risk out of what can be a hugely critical decision.

Few "purchases" we make can literally be the difference between life and death. The stakes in health care are high, and marketers and consumers both realize that.

I asked if at some point we'll be able to sign up for health insurance online or from a mobile device. Ms. Rolfe likened it to car purchases. "It's a big choice. It's about my ability to take care of my family. Any attempt to commoditize that and trivialize it doesn't work very well." People will research online, but in the end, they want some sort of human interaction. To that end, BCBS companies are exploring retail presence in some markets, some even utilizing pop-up stores. Some BCBS companies have stores already.

That's something else that doesn't conform to big generational shifts. Even the all-digital Millennials want to discuss their options with real people. It's going to be a while before people are willing to deal with these decisions lightly.

Dale, too, is involved on a daily basis with his mother's health care. For tax purposes, she's now his dependent. He handles all her finances, including the bills for her assisted living facility, which costs thousands every month. That's on top of the $16,000 he spends each year for insurance for his family, plus other out-of-pocket expenses. Because the family's fortunes are directly tied to the farm, Dale has had to get smart about navigating the generational transfers of wealth and the tax issues. It's involved fire-walling his mother's finances from those of the farm. He told me that he watched his father pull out $400,000 from the farm proceeds—money that could have been spent growing and modernizing the operations—to pay for his own parents' care. Dale vowed to manage these arrangements better to take care of the older generations with an eye toward protecting the asset that will take care of the younger generations.

"The whole sandwich generation piece is interesting," said Ms. Rolfe. "We've found it really highlights the problem or the opportunity. These are people who, if they have health insurance, have likely been handheld or subsidized to some degree. Now they're in a place where they're really busy. Chances are they have kids and were looking forward to calming down their careers. Instead they're navigating a whole new world where they're caring for their aging parents."

BCBS is working to create products that are simpler and more tailored to specific "personas" of needs—a customer-centric and consumer-driven approach you likely wouldn't have heard from an insurance company even five years ago. During the meeting, Ms. Rolfe and Ms. Sullivan consistently caught themselves using an "alphabet soup" of acronyms: PPO, HMO, PCMH, and ACO. They recognize that they need to make the process easier to navigate for everyone, and that starts with simplifying the language with which they talk about their products.

"Plans are confusing," said Ms. Rolfe. "We need to completely clean up our language to be more a fourth-grade reading level. It's not about being patronizing, it's about making it easier and less time consuming."

Geography doesn't just play into disease prevalence; it plays into how people get treatment and how BCBS markets to them. BCBSA is a federation of local, independent BCBS companies, and each company tries to find the approach that works in that market. In some cases, it's paying for nurse's aides to be available at medical offices and hospitals to help patients work through the insurance system. In other regions, consumers are offered financial incentives to get regular check-ups and preventative care—services that might cost more up front but keep costs down over a patient's lifetime.

BCBS is working hard to hone the consumer persona and create products that work for all the various segments. "We're looking at what they functionally want from insurance." Customers who want to talk to people for information are different from those who want to get information from the website. Those who use the minute clinics that are often tied to pharmacies and are growing in popularity are different from those who want the flexibility to pick the best doctor in the nation for their care. So BCBS creates its segmentation based on functional needs and some attitudinal variables. In other words, while access to insurance is pretty key for everyone, access to coverage means different things for different consumers.

The amount of information they want from the insurer matters, too. In the age of content marketing, many brands try to be clearinghouses of information. Some people turn to BCBS for general health-care advice. Some just want to get their claims paid and otherwise be left alone.

Providing different messages for different types of customers is one problem. Providing them in all the different channels available now is another.

We've been talking about the fragmented media landscape throughout the book, but now let's turn our attention more fully to the new realities of information consumption. For that, we're going to take you back to New York County and Michael's apartment in Manhattan.

NINE

The Connected Consumer

How Screens Are Changing
the Targeting Game

MICHAEL IS THE EPITOME OF A YOUNG URBAN PROFESSIONAL. HE GREW UP outside Cleveland but he got his MBA in France and spent a year working in Jordan. While there, he learned how to use media in a multitude of ways, from information gathering to working to serving as his primary source of entertainment. A friend at school showed him some areas of the Internet that tend to be a little loose with their concepts of intellectual property. By the time he got back to the U.S., he knew how to access content for almost everything, from recently released movies to cable programming.

"I could access all of this content without actually paying for any of it."

And so he doesn't. He pays for Internet service, but not cable, and grabs most of his shows, often commercial free, through a variety of websites—authorized or not. That includes HBO shows like *True Blood* and *Curb Your Enthusiasm.* He consumes most of his media on a laptop and his partner's iPad.

"Mostly I watch shows from ABC, by virtue of the fact that I have the ABC app on my iPad. If I can watch these kinds of shows the easiest, then I'll watch these shows."

He watches *Modern Family* and *Happy Endings,* among others.

Every now and then, on a rainy Saturday, he'll text a friend to see if he can borrow her Netflix login.

Despite all the content he watches on it, he can't quite bring himself to buy his own iPad.

"If it was $300 or $200, I would get it, but it's just above that price point where I'd be willing to spend for it."

Michael consumes a lot of content. He uses his phone, the iPad, and a TV, although that's primarily for video games.

The content includes Facebook. He checks his partner's account more often than his partner does, and mutual friends know they can reach him that way. Some of his friends have connected with his partner to get to Michael. In many ways, Michael is a nightmare for marketers and media planners. He's a valuable target: he's black, urban, on the young end of his thirties, makes a decent living, and has plenty of discretionary income, which he likes to spend on entertainment. The problem is finding him. He is, in many ways, exhibiting all the frightening traits that keep media planners up at night.

IN THIS CHAPTER WE'LL TALK ABOUT THE FRAGMENTING MEDIA LANDSCAPE and some of the headaches that this creates for marketers. We'll also talk about some of the incredible opportunities it opens up. We're going to talk a little less about stats and more about trends because the actual numbers are moving so fast that they will basically be out of date by the time this book is available. To talk concrete percentages about digital habits in a paper book would likely be misleading and somewhat ironic. I could simply leave it at "we live in disruptive times," but let's focus on what those disruptions mean.

Your takeaways from this chapter will include:

- How the proliferation of screens is impacting the media landscape;
- How mobile is leading to new forms of marketing warfare;
- How big data is changing the way markets are defined;
- How marketers are dealing with the disruptions.

Let's start by surveying the landscape. In just the last couple of years, the proliferation of increasingly inexpensive tablet devices coupled with the continued rise of smartphones has led to a marketplace where consumers can be connected everywhere and all the time. They can access traditional media outlets through the Web and through streaming services. They're connected to brands through apps and ads and alerts. Perhaps most importantly, they're connected to each other through social media, e-mail, sharing sites like Instagram and Pinterest, and a whole host of technologies that didn't exist a decade or even a year ago.

As of 2013, Internet-connected devices outnumbered people on the planet.[1] Mobile users will surpass desktop traffic as soon as 2014.[2] In the developing world some would argue it's already happened.[3] It's like demographic tipping points, but for technology.

The level to which this is changing media, marketing, and especially the intersection of the two (aka advertising) is historic.

On the media side, we've raised a generation who are used to their content being free and increasingly available on-demand. This desire will only increase. Think about the kids growing up now. My daughter, born in 2008, will likely never have any understanding of scheduled programming. Everything she watches is on-demand, streamed, or an app. She can see any show she knows, any time. As a parent, I have to say that's awesome. There's age-appropriate programming when she wakes up on weekends and after she finishes her dinner on weekdays—no matter when that is. She will also never comprehend programming that can't be paused, started, and stopped at will. And frankly, why should she? It makes all the sense in the world for us to control our TV, not the other way around.

There are exceptions. As we touched on in chapter five, social media is actually making live viewing more fun for a lot of folks. The phenomenon is often called dual-screen or multiple-screen viewing. Basically you've got your TV on the wall and your tablet on your lap or your phone in your hand. Being able to interact with your social network is a virtual extension to "viewing parties" where we would gather in person to share the experience. "TV was always social," said Mark Ghuneim, founder and CEO of Trendrr, which measures real-time data for media and television.

Instead of waiting for the next morning to discuss plot points and calls by the referee that went against our home team around the office water cooler, we can now do this in real time. For actual viewing parties, people can use their second screens to have different experiences and consume the show or event differently. As Mr. Ghuneim pointed out, they can do this in a way that doesn't interfere with the primary experience. One person can watch and track along with his or her fantasy sports team, another can be looking up player biographies, and a third can be tweeting about the game without taking away from collectively watching the game and, even more importantly, without interrupting his or her friends. It can work for advertisers, too. If you see an ad, you can research or even buy the product in real time. "You can use the second screen to further engage with the advertiser and go deeper even while the show is on," said Mr. Ghuneim.

You see this with award shows, live sports, certain news events like the State of the Union address, and the Olympics—which really transcend "sports" and land in a category all their own. Social interactions around these events by both consumers and marketers continue to set new records with each passing event.

Part of the reason for this dual-screen interaction is also defensive. People will tune in to certain shows in real time because they know their social feeds will spoil it for them later if they don't. Content providers and marketers are increasingly taking note and even providing apps that facilitate and reward this. Fox lets users buy outfits worn by the casts of shows like *New Girl*.[4] USA Networks has second-screen simulcasts of some of its popular shows like *Suits* and *White Collar* that provide additional content as viewers watch along in real time.[5] Twitter hashtags have become ubiquitous on many shows like Fox's *Glee*, often changing during the show depending on what's happening in the plot.

Even politicians are getting in on it. If you tuned in to the 2013 State of the Union address, you could watch along with either party as they fact-checked and provided additional information and context for the president's remarks. The official White House "enhanced" site didn't have a social component, but it may be that we'll see that in version 2.0 with links to share the accompanying charts and graphics built right in.[6]

None of this is to say that old media or old media habits have all been replaced. Millennials still watch a lot of TV and learn about a lot of brands through commercials, product placement, branded content, etc.[7] Millennials still prefer a printlike experience of news consumption, even on their mobile devices.[8] The one thing they're not doing is reading newspapers in print, which Millennials have all but abandoned as a platform.[9]

"Mobile, Mobile, Mobile"

Consumers' interaction with mobile devices and another device like a TV is just one way that the proliferation of screens is reshaping the way we consume media. The mobile devices on their own are changing everything, too. Laura Desmond, CEO of the world's largest media-buying agency, Starcom MediaVest Group, said it simply: "Mobile, mobile, mobile. It's all about mobile."[10]

Mobile devices are changing how marketers reach us. That's partially due to the very helpful little geolocation devices embedded in most phones. As just one quick but powerful example, Ms. Desmond told me about a promotion they were able to run for Walmart on Black Friday 2012. Using a technology she referred to as "mobile conquesting," the retailer was able to target users of mobile devices in the parking lots of nearby competitors. It was able to deliver ads to mobile devices with specially designed messages that said essentially, "We see you're close to a Walmart. Come and save 20 percent," or "We see you're near one of our stores. Come inside and check out our deals on toys." Walmart saw a fourfold increase in store traffic based on those they served those ads to, according to Ms. Desmond. She said that Walmart is already testing similar technology in-store. Using a mobile app, customers can bring their own bags and scan their purchases on their phones as they shop. Initial tests went so well that the store is expanding the program.[11] It both saves customers the need to check out and allows a marketer to serve ads to people who are buying products that are complementary to—or even competitive with—its offerings.

The proliferation of screens is also disrupting how marketers reach us.

It would be one thing if people used only mobile devices. But they don't. Like Michael, they might be on their own phone and someone else's tablet, using a borrowed account for this and a shared account for that. Eight or more hours a day, Michael is also on a laptop owned by his employer. No matter which device he's using to access content and ads, he's the same person even though he's likely to show up in analysis as a different person on each device he uses. Marketers would like to track him consistently because he will eventually buy the same number of the same goods.

The Persistent Salesman

I once searched for a messenger bag on Zappos.com. For the next couple of weeks, as I traveled around the Internet, I would see ads for that specific bag. I eventually wound up buying it in a brick and mortar store because I wanted to try it out in person. But the ads kept coming. I wanted to click on them and tell Zappos I had bought the bag, and it could stop paying for the impressions. I also wanted to understand how Zappos knew where I was.

So I asked Darrin Shamo, director of direct online marketing for Zappos, and he walked me through the online advertising real-time marketplace.[12]

I'm going to oversimplify a little bit, but basically the process works like this: When someone visits a website, the publisher is often working with a real-time ad auction firm. That firm relays what it knows about the customer based on their browser history and other variables that it's been tracking through cookies placed on sites around the Internet. Advertisers then take that information and use their own big data piles of customer information, correlations of sites visited, purchase intent, and whatever else they can discern to determine that person's potential value as a customer and bid accordingly. The winner gets to serve the customer the ad of its choice. It all happens in fractions of a second.

As we learned from Obama for America's Harper Reed in chapter six, part of the so-called genius of the 2012 campaign came merely from applying tactics used by retailers in advertising to the political realm. Using voter rolls and other data, the campaign would assign someone a score based on the likelihood that they would vote for Obama. Zappos does the same thing and uses that score to determine how much it's worth to show you an ad.

Unlike some advertisers, Zappos uses mostly its own data. It doesn't try to round out the profile from your browsing history with third-party data, demographics, and consumer segmentation tools. Mr. Shamo thinks there really can be too much information. Zappos has also found through its own research and testing that some information is actually misleading. "We might know that a user is a female but that doesn't mean that we should recommend products for her. She may purchase for her husband 80 percent of the time. Spending a lot of money on inventory targeting her is not as effective as targeting information that's meant for her husband."

Mr. Shamo identified two problems with the tracking behavior like this: the "persistent salesman" phenomenon and creepiness.

Essentially what I noticed with my bag purchase was the persistent salesman problem. On every site I visited, Zappos would show up on the page with an ad unit urging me to buy exactly the same bag I had searched for and bought. This happened in 2010. Zappos has gotten smarter since then.

"We would follow a user around because in our scoring system we found that we could buy that user over and over and over again because that impression was so valuable to us relative to everyone else in the marketplace," Mr. Shamo said. Basically, because I'd searched Zappos' site, I'd signaled a very strong purchase intent. That meant a lot to Zappos, and it wanted to hit me with ads. I became much more valuable to the bag seller than to other advertisers. But I noticed all the ads and they didn't persuade me.

"We found a diminishing return in buying so many impressions. If you buy [ad] inventory across an [ad] network, you can control frequency caps. When you buy across multiple exchanges and networks, the count on frequency starts over so we had to build some technology that would allow us to see that user as they pass from publisher to publisher to publisher."

Then there was the creepiness factor. "Our research found that people would not be so creeped out by the process if they felt it was a happy coincidence." In one of the more ironic big data applications I've heard of, Zappos actually had to create an algorithm to dumb down what the marketer knew about you so that it wouldn't over-serve you with ads.

As long as the user stays on one device, this works with some degree of efficiency and reliability. Screen proliferation is really messing that up.

"If you just look back over the last fourteen months, our data suggests that [the frequency of people using more than one device] has more than doubled." Mr. Shamo explained that besides making it harder to follow people, it throws wrenches into benchmarked data like conversion rates. If a user shops on one device and buys on another, that user appears to have a 50 percent conversion rate instead of a 100 percent conversion rate. "A user may have spent thirty-eight minutes going through the site, but the average time on site has dropped to eighteen minutes because it's spread out among different device types. It would show as an increase in visits and decrease in time-on-site. It makes year-over-year and time-over-time tracking difficult."

These are the problems of 2013. They will be solved eventually, and new problems will emerge. All of this is what Starcom's Ms. Desmond would call a problem with distribution. It points to the next problem. "Big data has driven people to want to have the distribution conversation, but you have to have the content conversation. Once I know who you are, if I don't serve you the right message, I'm going to blow it. This is what I think creative agencies are really struggling over. Advertising is still a one-to-many model, but the content model is one-to-few."

Using big data, Zappos can make huge inroads just knowing about you and your behavior. Now imagine tying that to your social network.

The One-Billion-User Gorilla

Dale in rural northwestern Montana listens to a lot of talk radio. He spends his days in the cabin of his combine or tractor, riding in his pickup around his sprawling farm, or maintaining his fleet of farm equipment in his barn. The radio in his barn has been on and tuned to the same station for more than twenty years. When he moved into his house so many years ago, he didn't like leaving the barn unattended, and he thought the radio noise would scare off any trespassers, human or otherwise, so he left it on and hasn't seen fit to turn it off since.

You could say he's a pretty old-media guy. Where he lives is so remote that he doesn't even get mail service at his home every day. He will some-times have things sent to his "neighbor" a few miles away if he needs to get it in a hurry.

Besides the radio, there's one place marketers can still reach Dale every day: Facebook. Facebook is the most universally and evenly used site in the U.S. By that I don't merely mean popular, although it's that too. Of the thousands of websites tracked by comScore, Facebook's reach and time spent are spread evenly among demographics and geography. I discovered this somewhat accidentally.[13]

I had asked comScore to run its data through the Patchwork Nation and Esri's Tapestry segments and LifeMode Groups so I could study which ones over-indexed on which sites—in other words, which sites skewed most heavily to which areas of the country and the demographics they represent.

The results of that were certainly interesting. Among other findings, we saw that areas like Clark County, Nevada, where Chris lives, skews toward career services sites. Champaign County, Illinois, where Liz lives, and areas like college towns spend a lot of time at online auction sites. The wealthy suburban areas like Howard County, Maryland, where Rosemary lives, are above-average consumers of real estate sites.

What was even more interesting to me in the end was the opposite of what I had started off looking for. Facebook users in areas that are mostly rural or mostly urban, affluent or not-so-much, dominated by college towns or retirement communities, all use the site to essentially the same enormous degree.

Twitter has a higher percentage of black users and younger users. Pinterest skews slightly toward white users and heavily toward females. Almost no seniors use Twitter, Pinterest, or Instagram.[14] In contrast, the user base and demographics of Facebook look an awful lot like the overall universe of Internet users in America.[15]

Here's an absurd number for you. In the U.S. alone, Facebook sucked up 104,000 person years in just one typical month.[16] That's a desktop Web figure alone. It equates to more than six hours per user and an astounding 11 percent of all time spent on the Internet.

Now think of all that Facebook knows about you. It likely knows your name, your birthday and your age, where you live, who your friends and family are, which of those friends are close friends and which not-so-much. It knows which friends you went to school with and which you like to chat with. It knows what brands and shows you like. It knows what media you like to read and, more importantly, what kinds of content you want to share.

That's all within its own walls.

Finally, think about it this way. It's a platform that just about everyone on the Internet (in the U.S. and, increasingly, elsewhere) is on. So the potential audience is huge. And yet it has the ability to segment that down as far as you want based on a very wide array of demographics and behaviors.

It's about as big as big data gets. This enables a very detailed level of user targeting, and the more you know about your target, the more detailed you can get. I ran a little experiment once and, using readily available information, I targeted an ad to myself and to roughly twenty other pro-files. I had to hit "reload" a bunch, but in relatively little time I was able to get that ad to show up on my profile and essentially on no one else's. It cost me pennies to pull this off.

On the other end of the spectrum, Facebook can achieve scale the way almost no other site or platform can.

I spent some time with Carolyn Everson, Facebook's vice president, Global Marketing Solutions. Despite all the technology and all the big data, Ms. Everson takes a remarkably humanistic view of the platform—with good reason. Facebook, she says, is about replicating the offline experience.

"The biggest AHA! moment for me after getting to Facebook is that human behavior hasn't changed no matter how fancy all of this technol-ogy is. We still care deeply about what our friends think. Think about what Facebook is essentially doing, which is trying to mimic the offline world."[17]

Those relationships are a valuable tool for marketers; much as they tried to get into the middle of search behavior in the past, brands will increasingly try to get into the middle of the social conversation. That's especially true with mobile.

"As people are using their mobile devices, they're being exposed to brands in their news feeds. That has an influence on shopping. People are starting to ask for reviews and comments as they shop. We're really just getting started," Ms. Everson said.

Facebook can clearly be a targeted medium if you know your target.

Getting to know targets is where big data is coming into play more and more. It's all about connecting the dots between one behavior and another. For instance, when Ms. Everson and I spoke, a story was circulat-ing that suggested that Facebook knew when a woman was pregnant even if she hadn't posted specifically stating that fact. She said that individuals might unknowingly tip their hands by liking content, articles, brands, or products that are often liked by women who are expecting.

"If people update and talk about it . . . and often people do—they'll post the sonogram, they'll talk about things or they might connect to baby groups. In certain ways like that, yes, we can get at it. We don't know who's pregnant and who's not just as a blanket statement. There are some nu-ances to that."

As people are undergoing the kinds of demographic shifts that trigger shifts in consumer behavior, Facebook aims to help marketers get into the middle of that. In other words, big data is all about finding the individuals who are part of observed trends.

Facebook aims to do that without falling back on the traditional demographic models themselves. For instance, you can't target Hispanics as Hispanics. Instead, different marketers use different mixes of behaviors to talk to the Hispanic marketplace. According to Ms. Everson, "Facebook is going to allow you to find who you want to target and have a very specific message."

Again, the connections between people are key. As we heard earlier from Harper Reed, the Obama for America campaign was using Facebook to get people to motivate specific friends of theirs who met specific criteria.

Mr. Reed's use of friends influencing friends addresses one of the perceived weaknesses of Facebook: that it's an echo chamber. If your "news feed" is now dictated by your friends and if your friends are typically like-minded, it will become harder to be exposed to new ideas and new products.

Facebook's own research shows that's actually less true than you'd think.[18] Because the typical user has so many friends from so many parts of their lives, they are actually exposed to a lot of content they wouldn't see otherwise. That can be a great advantage for brands.

"If my friends were sharing information to me or recommending brands that I might not be aware of or offers that I might not know about, that's much more influential," Ms. Everson said.

Connecting All the Dots

At the end of 2012 and the beginning of 2013, Facebook announced partnerships that have the potential to be game changing. Working with Acxiom, Datalogix, and Epsilon, three giants in the consumer data space, the site will allow brands to match data from its loyalty programs to specific Facebook profiles.[19] Using the combined pile of big data, marketers will be able to target online ads based directly on offline behavior. The relationship will also help offline marketers track in-store purchases that were potentially influenced by online campaigns. Through another partnership, with BlueKai, Facebook will allow marketers to use their own data in their Facebook campaigns.

These partnerships are extensions of Facebook's custom audience tool.[20] This could really be the promised land, especially for consumer packaged goods whose products are readily tied to grocery and other loyalty-card data.

Facebook, which has often been the subject of consumer tirades about privacy, might have a tough sell to their users with this deal. When I talked to Acxiom's CEO Scott Howe before the deal was announced, he talked a lot about the need to pitch consumers on the value they get from marketing like this and how it was important to remind consumers that they get all of their Facebook services for free. Additionally, being presented with deals that are more applicable and useful can be beneficial and is likely to save customers some money. It's also going to require some new ways of measuring success.

"People who hold Facebook to direct marketing metrics are idiots," Mr. Howe said.

It's clear that big data is an integral part of the future of marketing. Privacy issues are its growing pains. As we work through those and work through the technology issues we've discussed, it's more and more possible not that we'll just see more ads everywhere, but that we'll see more applicable ads.

Partnerships like these bring offline world behavior into the online world. Other technologies are advancing to bring some of the online targeting into the offline world, too. In chapter six we saw Obama's campaign connecting voter rolls to TV viewing, which produced highly targeted and efficient ad buys on shows that were considered a bargain. Allstate has actually moved a step further and done a small campaign for renters' insurance that was directed at Dish Network and DirecTV subscribers who are renters.[21] Being able to connect big data to specific TV households is an innovation that's been dreamed of for years and is now becoming reality. How much longer will it be before your TV also knows which member of a household is watching it?

New Tech, New Habits

Delayed viewing of shows has been around to some extent since the popularization of the programmable VCR that you could set to record certain channels at certain times. But it had a number of downsides. You had to rewind the tape when you wanted to watch the show, and that took time. You had to know which shows were on which tapes. Tapes cost money, and they degraded if you reused them. Digital video recorders changed all that, allowing easy storage and fast access to shows you wanted to watch. DVRs also make it easy to fast-forward through commercials, skip boring parts of sports events, pause and restart, and so forth. They're also really easy to program and can record multiple streams of content at the same time. As a cohabiting couple I know once said, their DVR changed their lives more than officially getting married did.

Streaming services and DVD rentals like Netflix have changed the game, too, making it much simpler to get an entire season of a TV show at once. But that came with a price—the pressure to watch it quickly.

There are any number of new viewing habits that have cropped up because of DVRs and streaming, but I want to take a moment and touch on one: binge viewing. Being able to watch multiple episodes of a show in one sitting is a relatively new phenomenon. Netflix aired commercials with a tagline of "Watch Responsibly," which featured a group of guys stocking up on food and supplies as they prepared to watch seventy-eight episodes of a favorite show in one sitting.

Netflix truly capitalized on the trend by releasing the entire first season of its original show *House of Cards* at one time rather than rolling it out episode by episode. This was more than an attempt to play to one facet of its audience. The entire show was based on data-driven decisions. The company used its storehouse of user preferences and watching behavior to drive creative decisions about what show to produce and who should star in it.[22]

The plan certainly worked for Andrew in Hampden County, Massachusetts.

He was gearing up for a new season of AMC's *Mad Men* by bingeing on previous seasons. "I'm actually repeating a bunch of seasons because I'm so frustrated at how long it's been since I saw a new *Mad Men* episode."

Likewise, his viewing of the new Netflix show was exactly what the producers hoped for.

"I was a little crazy with *House of Cards*. I literally watched seven episodes in one night until 4:00 A.M. Netflix hit the nail on the head with figuring out what their consumers want. Waiting for a whole week for another episode is not normal in this age," he told me.

On-demand services like Xfinity's have enabled binge viewing, too. Some networks have chosen to have the ability to fast-forward through the commercials disabled during their on-demand shows. The frustration with that for consumers is that relatively few advertisers have jumped on board. So as you watch a series of episodes, you often see the same ad repeated over and over.

"I saw this ad introducing Savannah [Guthrie] on the *Today* show," complained an industry insider. "I hate her now and I've never even seen the *Today* show."

Binge viewing can also lead to a viewer habit that, at least anecdotally, seems to be increasing: waiting until a show gets picked up for a second season before watching the first season on DVD or a streaming service.[23]

"The kids in my office have a 'two-season rule' before they'll start watching," said Trendrr's Mr. Ghunheim. "I asked who was watching the last episode of *Homeland* and everyone under [age] twenty-four said, 'We were waiting for season two to close out so we could binge on it because we're tired of getting committed to something [that gets canceled].'"

Changes in Store for In-Store

It's difficult to imagine that such fundamental changes in the way we consume content will not also drastically alter the way we consume products. Shoppers now carry devices that connect them to friends, product information, and reviews. Barcode-scanning apps mean that checking prices at competitive outlets can be done in seconds instead of necessitating driving from store to store.

Starcom's Ms. Desmond discussed apps that allow people to take a picture of a clothing item in a store and "try it on" virtually using a pre-programmed digital version of themselves. Changing colors or patterns and sending a picture to friends for a quick consultation are all possible and all potential game changers for the way we shop. Shows like *Say Yes to the Dress* demonstrate the social side of buying big-ticket items like a wedding gown. The bride-to-be arrives at the store with an entourage, who discuss dress choices and help their friend find her perfect dress. Now consumers can take their friends with them virtually for even more mundane purchases.

The Speed of Disruption

Let's look at how social media is disrupting one of the biggest purchases people make: cars. No matter what the path-to-purchase, just about everyone ends their car-buying experience standing in a dealership. A Gallup survey found that fewer than 10 percent of consumers have a "very high or high" level of faith in the honesty and ethics of car dealers. That's lower than any other profession, including congressional leaders and advertising professionals.[24] Even with that lack of trust, consumers buy more than $30 billion of products from car dealers each year.[25]

Behavioral economist Daniel Kahneman coined the notion of "thinking fast" versus "thinking slow."[26] When we think "slow," we carefully consider all information, weigh pros and cons, and come to a fully informed decision. Thinking slow is like an AutoTrader.com approach with side-by-side model comparisons.

Conversely, we often think "fast" with brand decision making, especially in regard to durable goods. It's letting our instincts (which may be factually incorrect) and emotions play a large role. It works like this: We remember a decision we made in the past and assume it was a good one. We think "I bought this brand eight years ago and it worked fine. So I'll buy it again," without knowing anything about the quality of today's models. We believe in what could likely be bad data because our source is hugely trustworthy: ourselves.

Dealers tend to want to push everyone into fast thinking, but not necessarily in a good way. Here's how this experience has historically worked for consumers.

Andrew in Hampden County, Massachusetts, drove a used Chevy Malibu for several years. He bought it when he returned home after spending some time abroad. The dealer offered him a low rate on financing, but only if he purchased the car on the spot.

"I kind of rushed it. I got back from Honduras. I said, 'I need a car, I need a working car, I need a nice car.' I'm kind of disappointed in myself. I should have just waited and gotten something that, you know, was just more me. I liked it, and I just got it, and then I'm like, 'Oh, man, I can't wait to trade it in.'"

Basha, the empty-nesting senior citizen in chapter seven, was also given the hard sell by her dealer, but at least in that case, she ended up happy.

"I took [my previous car] in for service at this new dealership that opened up by us and of course all the salesmen come running up to you the minute you bring a car in for service. This very nice man came up to me and was talking to me and he says, 'I've got a beautiful car I want to show you.' I say, 'I'm really not interested in a new car.' And he says, 'Well, let me just show it to you.' He showed it to me and I fell in love." She still loves her Chrysler 300.

The Internet is proving to be a big equalizer for car consumers. The process starts before the dealership. Nearly 80 percent of new-vehicle shoppers check the Internet during their process.[27] Nearly one in three utilize social media to get recommendations from their friends and families.[28] Ms. Desmond says this is transformative and gives automakers a number of new points in the purchase process to make an impression on a shopper and insert themselves into the set of car brands being considered. For years, auto marketing has been all about search. The shift to social is the trend she sees continuing. "People want to talk about cars and car experiences and car recommendations even *before* they search," she said.

Once they have a car in mind, nearly one in three look at reviews before selecting the dealer, too.[29]

I spoke with Michael Sprague, executive vice president, Marketing and Communications, at Kia Motors America.[30] He goes so far as to say that the connected consumer now has the advantage in the purchase process. He says that a growing segment across all ages, but certainly the Millennials, are coming into the dealership with their cars specced out based on Internet searches.

"It's all in their mobile devices," said Mr. Sprague. "Customers walk in and say they are looking for a particular vehicle. They pull out their iPhones and say, 'This vehicle here is supposed to have X, Y, and Z. It says right here that it's at your dealership. Go find it.' They totally have the advantage."

He knew that the dealer experience had to pivot.

"We tell the dealers to elevate the customer experience and make them feel special. Empower them, give them what they want, and they will come back. That's where you'll make the sale."

Mr. Sprague told me that Kia encourages its dealers to recruit from AT&T stores and Best Buy to hire tech-savvy salespeople who can help customers learn how to use all the new in-car gizmos. Kia also recommends the use of big touch screens so that dealers can do virtual walkarounds of the eleven different models, changing colors and trim levels as they speak.

Because much of car shopping happens online, Kia, like many car makers, has "live chat" services available 24–7. "If someone is online at 2:00 A.M. researching car purchases, they're probably pretty serious."

Will They Stay Social?

Two questions loom large, and they both have to do with the Millennials. It's not surprising that much—though certainly not all—of the transformation of the media landscape is taking place in the younger generations. They've grown up with technology, are comfortable with its uses, and are driving innovation. But they're still young. As they age, how much of their behavior will they carry with them, and how much will they start to look more like older consumers? My bet would be that they'll wind up somewhere in the middle. Once they have families, they'll have other people's opinions to consider in terms of what and how much content they share about themselves. But they're unlikely to just turn their backs on all of their über-connected ways. There's also some evidence of what researchers are calling "Facebook fatigue."[31] People find themselves needing to take a break from social media, often for prolonged periods.

Liz, a Millennial in Champaign County, Illinois, feels that Facebook shaped the lives of people in her generation; she joined nearly ten years ago when she went to college and started the phase of her life outside her parents' home. "I think that we have come into our own and grown into our own and grown into our adulthood valuing odd things, sharing odd things, being very open. I hate using the word 'voyeuristic,' but we feel entitled to know every aspect of someone else's life as well, and so it's strange, and I think it's kind of molded us in a weird way. It's also changed how we communicate and how we view our lives and our friends and the social aspects of our lives."

She reached a point where she decided she was over-sharing and went back through her profile deleting status updates and photos that she didn't want to have as part of her permanent online record. She also unplugs to a large extent when she's home. She feels that she spends enough time on the computer during her workday and doesn't need to carry on doing that all night, too.

If Millennials do unplug even to some degree as they get older, how will that change this landscape? And how will the younger iGen, the oldest of whom are now well into their teens, behave differently from the Millennials? Only time will tell.

Technology has a role in our final trend, too. Trendrr's Mr. Ghunheim talked about how the increasing array of media options, or screens, and the proliferation of content options, gaming platforms, etc., means that competition for our time is fierce. Throughout the book we've talked about competition for our dwindling discretionary income. This has reinvented competition for our discretionary *time*.

One of the apparent losers in this battle is the great American love affair with the automobile. To talk about that in much greater depth, we're going to spend time with one more Millennial: Jay in Leavenworth County, Kansas. He's a high-school history teacher, but marketers, especially auto-related marketers, can learn a thing or two from him about their future.

TEN

The Car Culture Crash

How Cars Fit into Millennial Lives

JAY GREW UP POOR. THE REAL KIND OF POOR, WHERE YOU CAN ONLY AF-
ford to pay one bill each month so you choose whether to risk getting the
water or the electricity cut off. His family didn't have cable. They didn't
have a phone.

Jay's in his early thirties now and teaches high school in Leavenworth
County, Kansas, but his early years were tough for his family. His mom
never finished high school, wasn't married, and struggled financially as a
waitress and bartender. Jay talks about the year his mom spent in prison
and he spent bouncing around staying with friends and family.

There were periods when they couldn't afford a car, which was especially difficult where he lived. There weren't a lot of good options to get
around other than driving. Then things got a little better. His mother got
her GED, married, got a better job, and was able to send him to college
and scrape together enough to buy him a used car.

"My mom bought me a car with her tax return money. She spent
$1,000 on an old-school Oldsmobile with a fifth wheel on the back."

When he was growing up, owning a car was something he aspired to,
but it was out of reach financially. The Oldsmobile was transportation, but
just barely, and certainly not what he was looking for as he entered adulthood. After he graduated and got his first teaching job, he knew he had to
get his own wheels. It was all about demonstrating status.

"It was a silver, tinted windows, it had the disc changer CD, black leather seats. It was decked out. It was a Volkswagen Jetta and it was amazing. I thought I was the coolest person ever. And it was cool for a year."

Then reality set in. Cool came with a price, and it wasn't a price he wanted to pay. "The $450 car monthly payment was not cool. So after a couple of years, I realized this is idiotic that I'm paying this much for a car. You get older and smarter. So I traded that in and I got a Hyundai Elantra, which is almost paid off. And I can't wait. I'm going to just rock that thing until the wheels fall off because I do not want a car payment for a while."

Many marketers are probably reading this with mixed feelings. Since he's an apartment dweller, the car is the most expensive thing Jay owns. It's the kind of purchase that should confer some kind of status and should at the very least provide some sort of enjoyment. But Jay's not feeling it. On the other hand, at least he owns a car, which puts him at odds with one popular sentiment about Millennials: that they don't drive. If you read *The Atlantic* or the *New York Times* or the writings of urbanists like Richard Florida, you'll see both theories and hard data showing that Millennials, the oldest of whom are now entering their thirties, drive a lot less than previous generations did at their age. At the even younger end of the scale, fewer teenagers are getting their driver's licenses. Those who do are driving fewer and fewer miles each year.

Here's what the data looks like: those aged sixteen to thirty-four drove 23 percent fewer miles at the end of the last decade than they did at the start, according to the federal government's National Household Travel Survey. Looking back further, per capita mileage in the U.S. hasn't increased since 1996.[1]

Fewer than half of teenagers who could be driving are. That's down from nearly two-thirds of teenagers who had a license in 1998.[2]

The implications of these simple facts are far reaching. Certainly they're going to have a big impact on car makers and dealers. It's big for agencies and media, too. According to the *Ad Age* Datacenter, GM, Ford, Fiat's Chrysler Group, and Toyota are all among the top twenty advertisers in the U.S. Also, as people drive less, it plays into how and where they live and shop. For IKEA, for instance, this trend can account for part of the 40 percent rise in customers using the delivery services the furniture maker offers.[3]

There are parallels here to some of the cable cord-cutting trends we talked about in the previous chapter. While the overwhelming majority still have cable, some consumers are ditching it for streaming TV services like Netflix. When something goes from near universal to a trend reversal, industries take notice. The same can be said of driving. A big drop in the number of teenagers who have a driver's license is an important data point. I spoke with Pam El, vice president, Marketing and Advertising for insurance giant State Farm. She's been watching these driving trends and says, "There will never be a time when young adults are not driving cars. There's still a large population that wake up and rush to the DMV office when they're sixteen years old."[4] Still, the fall-off appears to be continuing and accelerating. A 2013 study by U.S. PIRG Education Fund and Frontier Group suggested that "the driving boom is over."

The study further stated: "A return to the steady growth in per-capita driving that characterized the Driving Boom years is unlikely given the aging of the Baby Boom generation, the projected continuation of high gas prices, anticipated reductions in the percentage of Americans in the labor force, and the peaking of demand for vehicles and driver's licenses and the amount of time Americans are willing to spend in travel."[5]

It's time to pay attention and study this.

The evidence is there that the car culture is crashing and side-cushion air bags aren't going to save it. This has a huge impact for businesses of all kinds.

In this chapter you will:

- Learn the four key reasons why kids are driving less;
- Learn what that's doing to their perception of cars;
- Learn what Madison Avenue and Motown can and cannot do about it.

So what's going on? There are really four things at play here: technology, the legal climate, the economy, and cultural differences between the Millennials and previous generations.

The first thing that is often cited is the rise of all the technologies we discussed in chapter nine. As teens and twenty-somethings are spending more and more time online and connected virtually to their friends and their networks, there's less incentive to get out and actually connect with people in the real world. Certainly there's strong evidence that Millennials are a hyperconnected generation deeply imbued with technology on an increasing array of portable screen sizes. This affects nearly all aspects of their lives, so it's not much of a stretch to assume that if they're spending all this time online, they're not spending it in other activities like driving and socializing in the real world. A 2013 study by car-sharing service Zipcar tried to move that connection from correlation to causal.[6] The results of the survey showed that nearly half of Millennials would rather spend time online with their friends than drive to see them. Now granted, one could argue that the survey comes from a source with an obvious stake in the results, but it makes sense.

Economic factors are also at play. It costs a lot of money to own a car. AAA estimates that the cost of ownership for a sedan is more than $9,000 per year and more than $11,000 for an SUV.[7]

In this climate, not buying a car for the teenager is a pretty logical cutback if you can get away with it. It's also an obvious cutback for a twenty-something with other transportation options. But once the economic situation changes, car buying can too. It's similar to the home-buying/life-stage arguments Trulia's Jed Kolko makes in chapter six but with some nuance. He said that you don't buy a house the day you get a new job, but sometimes you do buy a car the first day because you need it to get to that job. Or you buy a car because it requires a lot less of a down payment than a house does. Either way, it's an implied sign of financial stability and as the economy stabilizes, car buying might, too. But don't bet on it.

Because, let's also not forget gas prices. When gas prices hit a sustained $4.00 or even $5.00, different areas will suffer from those increased costs more greatly than others. As gas prices were spiking nationally in 2011, I conducted some research using consumer income and spending data from Esri and gas price data from Gasbuddy.com. It showed that if prices rose $1.00 from the current levels, nearly 70 million people would live in counties where an average of 15 percent or more of discretionary income would be spent on gas expenses, assuming driving patterns remained constant. When gas prices rise to $5.00 a gallon, nearly every county will be above 15 percent, with 78 million people living in counties where more than 20 percent of discretionary income is spent on gasoline.[8] These pains are felt fairly evenly across all Patchwork Nation types, meaning that urban, rural, and suburban areas will all be impacted.

The economic arguments can't explain the entire drop-off in the number of people driving, especially for the teenagers. For one thing, the number of miles driven in the U.S. began declining before the recession.[9] For another, mom and dad still have cars. On weekend nights, borrowing the keys is a well-ingrained ritual in pop culture and the reality it reflects. So the dip in kids getting their licenses hints strongly at something much more profound. It's one thing if kids can't afford to own a car. It's another thing entirely if they can't even drive one that's lent to them.

That leads us to one aspect of the equation that I think is often overlooked: the regulatory angle. For Boomers and really for Gen-Xers, too, cars symbolized freedom. Reaching driving age and getting your license meant that you could finally get out of the house under your own power. But the Boomers are a hugely protective lot. Parents are very rightly concerned with keeping their precious cargo out of harm's way while doing something as risky as riding in a car.

During the period from 1996 to 2006, all fifty states passed some sort of new driving restrictions for young drivers.[10] The restrictions take different forms in different states. In Alaska, for example, sixteen-year-olds can get a license after forty hours of supervised driving, at least ten hours of which must take place at night or in bad weather. Once they get their licenses, they can't drive at all between 1:00 A.M. and 5:00 A.M. and aren't allowed passengers for the first six months. Many states are more strict. Illinois starts its curfew at 10:00 P.M. on weeknights. Even South Dakota, with a traditionally low driving age due to the need to have kids work in the fields on their parents' farms, raised its driving age from fourteen to fourteen and a half and added more requirements and restrictions.[11]

Jay coaches his school's wrestling team. Overall he hasn't seen huge shifts in the number of his students driving. "We have hundreds of cars in the parking lot," he says, but he knows that they have to "jump through a ton more hoops" to get their driver's licenses than he did when he got his—just fifteen years ago. He was able to drive to school and back by age fifteen.

Generally, exceptions prove a rule, but what's important here is that there are starting to be exceptions at all to something that was nearly universal before. "A lot of my wrestlers don't have cars and don't care." The fact that he can identify a group of people who are perfectly OK not driving is new to him—especially since he lives in a very car-dependent city.

Over time a cohort of people has developed who reach adulthood without ever needing to drive. Even when they reach a point where a job or a life-stage change leads them to learn how to drive and buy a car of some sort, they're not going to look at it as a "freedom-providing" vehicle. It will be more like just another expense. You can see that evolution in Jay's thinking. First the car was aspirational, then the car was about status, but eventually the car was just another expense he had to pay in order to get to work and to Walmart. All the fun was gone.

There's some data to put behind the impact of the connected consumer on driving and the legislative climate. We can guess that these are two strong influences of the trend toward decreased license attainment, ownership, and miles driven.

What was missing was data looking at the emotional connection between Millennials and cars, how that is shifting from previous generations, and how marketers might still be able to rekindle the love affair between Americans and their cars.

Millennials Plus Cars Does Not Equal Emotion

I partnered with Carol Foley, Leo Burnett's executive vice president, director of knowledge, to research these issues. We fielded a large-scale survey of car owners with Ipsos Observer to look at perceptions of the automobile. We didn't want to focus narrowly on cars, but rather wanted to explore how cars fit into lives. To do that we looked at the broad category of things that help people's lives "move forward." That's literally and figuratively what cars represent. We had people rate a variety of products and activities on a wide range of attributes. Taking a broader look allowed us to ask about a lot of other brands and concepts like Facebook, air bags, insurance, getting a college degree, etc. We mapped the results in two-dimensional space. (See Appendix II for the maps, and a more detailed methodology.) The findings were fascinating. When we looked at the data for the entire survey sample (not just Millennials), we observed the following:

- Conclusion one: Cars are much more about creating memories and making enjoyable times stretch longer than they are about

setting goals, improving life, and sharpening skills. Regardless
of the type of car or the nature of the trip or accessory, cars are
perceived more as reward than as work. They're more about a
feeling of freeing than a feeling of containment.

- Conclusion two: All cars and car products are not created
equal. Some types of cars (like minivans) and car products
(like air bags) are more about defending your current situation
than about moving you forward in life. Others (SUVs and
car stereos) are more about change, accomplishment, and
aspiration. Those are about a future we imagine for ourselves
and are working toward.

- Conclusion three: No matter what the first car you drove
was as far as make/model/age, there was a strong emotional
attachment to it. You think of it more the way you think of the
car you aspire to or want to drive than the car you actually do
drive today.

What Did We Learn about Millennials?

We can focus in on the Millennials by looking at one key data point, "the car
you drive," and seeing how their response differs from other generations'.

Again, it doesn't matter what make, model, or style the car is or how
long the respondent has owned it. We were able to isolate a number of
economic factors as well. That left us to conclude that the above conclusions don't hold as true for Millennials.

For Millennials, the car is less about emotion and more about function.

That's striking because it moves the car farther away from the area oc-
cupied by all the things Millennials do care about—like Facebook, socializing, and music. So this is the opposite of what we presume the Boomers
and even the Gen-Xers looked like when they were younger.

In the heyday of the automobile, the coolest actors were associated
with the coolest cars. It's hard to imagine Steve McQueen touting the fuel
efficiency of a Mustang or Burt Reynolds talking about the air bags in his
Firebird. Think about the time machine in *Back to the Future*. It wasn't
some weird-looking device in a lab. It was a gull-winged DeLorean sports
car. Boomers and Gen-Xers grew up with some great cars and some great
car marketing.

Our research was also able to help us demonstrate that this movement from an emotional connection with cars to a functional one is a more profound difference than economic factors for Millennials. We were also able to show that the generational differences were independent of a number of variables including the age of the car, the style of the car, and whether it was domestic or imported.

One notable variable that did show some difference was whether the car was used for commuting. Regardless of generation, people who commuted with their cars had less of an emotional connection to their vehicles than those who didn't.

The Big Takeaway

Millennials just don't *love* their cars as much anymore and now we have a study that confirms it.

How can marketers use this data?

Marketers can't change the economy. They can't change the laws about graduated driver's licenses. They can't suddenly make teens and Millennials dislike spending time on their phones. What good marketing can help change is the emotional connection between consumers and the products they consume. At its heart, that's really what advertising is all about.

Millennials don't seem to be connecting cars with the freedom and social experiences that other generations seem to have associated them with automatically.

Emotion is often where habits are formed and where loyalty is forged between a consumer and a brand. Since today's consumers are likely to hold onto their cars longer, they will be in the market less often.[12] Over a lifetime that could translate into one or two fewer cars purchased per person. Since they're not in the market as often, you have to sell them once and be in the right place at the right time to sell them again when they might be starting fresh in their decision process.

Today, much of the messaging in this industry centers on fuel economy, safety features, and other practical aspects of the vehicle. To an extent, that plays to the practical and data-driven, spec-driven mindset and makes all the sense in the world. That's how consumers are looking at cars on all of the comparison websites like Autotrader.com and Cars.com. The other typical image you see in auto advertising is the glamour shot of the car in a setting unlike those most people drive in on a daily basis: closed test tracks, winding coastal roads, and wooded trails. In these cases, the car loses all of its social aspects. Either the locations are desolate, or the viewer is so far removed from the car that you can't see the occupants and the activities they're engaged in. The social aspect, which is so key for Millennials, is removed from the equation.

It's the Emotion, Stupid

James Carville is known for reminding politicians that in basically every political race, all that matters is the economy. It's one of those truisms that's helpful to be reminded of. This research is meant to have a similar impact. Today it feels as though features and product differences are based on fuel efficiency or integrated technology. Many logical choices can now enter into the car-buying process. It's as if advertising has moved away from the emotional appeal that defined the desired car for generations. For Millennials, many of the things they value are emotional, but the car isn't currently in that space. In analyzing our research, we see that the path to developing an emotional connection follows a clear line through sound systems and leather seating and toward social aspects like "dating sites," "going to parties," and "Facebook." Therefore, if marketers want to rekindle the love affair, they need to start working on the teenagers to bring back the excitement of the *first* car that still sits more in the emotional realm, even for Millennial drivers.

To get there, our research shows, play off of the tensions between working and rewards and between reinforcing and reinventing. Instead of Millennials seeing virtual social experiences and physical-driving-based experiences as an either/or, make the car more a centerpiece of social times. That is why the legal climate is such a big issue because many states place restrictions on who teenage drivers can have as passengers. In short, driving needs to seem more like Facebook, but not necessarily just by integrating Facebook functions into the car.

Emotion can help preempt the fully thought-through and attribute-based car search. It can get your brand into the consideration set or elevate it higher in the consideration set. Social relationships are increasingly important here.

Laura Desmond, CEO of Starcom MediaVest Group, the world's largest media-buying agency, told me that auto marketing has been focused on search engines for the last decade.[13] While not all Millennials are buying cars, her agency has produced research that shows the growing importance of social media for those who are. "People want to talk about cars and car experience and car recommendations even before they search."[14] Once they buy a car, they "want to declare it and post photos and comments in their social media world to validate and share what they believe is true."

Why Cars Might Be a Hard Sell

The study I conducted with Leo Burnett was of car owners and a small number of people who intended to buy a car. In the survey we saw the emotional disconnect of the younger consumers—who are already customers. Having a hard time creating product relationships with existing owners is one problem. Connecting with those who don't buy your product in the first place involves a whole different set of issues.

I spoke with someone who knows how tough selling cars to Millennials can be. She has made a movement out of renting them cars in bite-size increments. Robin Chase was the founder of car-sharing giant Zipcar, which allows people to rent cars by the hour. Instead of going to a rental location or airport, the vehicles are parked throughout the city in designated spots, say at your local grocery store or in a downtown parking deck. Ms. Chase now runs Buzzcar in Paris, which is a similar concept except that people can choose to rent out their own cars when they're not using them so Buzzcar itself has no fleet.

"I think that young people are uninterested in cars," she told me.[15] She brought up the 1990 film version of the iconic cartoon Jetson family. In the updated version, the patriarch George hops into a cute little jet car and instead of coasting through space immediately hits gridlock, even in the wide-open, 3-D landscape he should be able to move in freely. "That's what has happened over the last twenty years. The promise of cars as freedom and independence has met reality. So while car manufacturers try to sell me on the idea that you're driving on a [scenic] road in a canyon, the truth is that I'm not driving on that road, I'm driving on roads in a congested area. I think they're having a harder time selling that image."

For that growing share of Millennials who don't own cars and don't drive, they certainly seem to like it that way. We talked in chapter six about the movement of Millennials into downtown urban cores. These areas tend to have density, housing surrounded by shopping and amenities, public transportation, and more. The density means these areas can support sharing services like Zipcar. But Millennials aren't just sharing cars. They're sharing kitchen equipment, freecycling, kickstarting, crowdsourcing, and crowdfunding. It's all a more communal reflection of a mutually shared look at a sharing economy.

The data here is a little more ambiguous. It's the same situation we saw in chapter six. The raw numbers might be small but the impacts can be large. A neighborhood can be transformed by very few people if they make a drastic and visible enough change. If we look at census data, it appears that the overall percentage of workers commuting via public transportation is unchanged in the last decade. So is the share of people driving alone. If we look at the city level, we see increases in the raw numbers of bicycle commuters, and that's important here. Adding a few thousand bikers into a crowded downtown makes a noticeable difference because bikers are very visible.

It's impossible to ignore the increase in urban bike lanes in cities as large as New York and Chicago and as small as Decatur, Georgia.[16] It's also hard to ignore the emphasis being placed on walkable downtowns instead of driving-mandatory, less sustainable suburban sprawl.

Those trends are hard to see in the data today, but they're the ones to watch in the next decade.[17]

Today, the data would lead you to believe that Jay in Leavenworth is still the model. He doesn't have a lot of options. He needs his car to get to work, he needs it to get to the wrestling matches he coaches, and he uses it to shop. He runs quick errands in his town (which is a pretty quick drive from one end to the other) and for longer shopping trips to the big mall or outings to entertainment options in Kansas City.

Liz in Champaign County, Illinois, is in much the same boat, but at least she can take a bus to work—today. Despite her Millennial age, she loves her car and loves driving, but economic realities do set in. As she prepares to move in with her boyfriend, they're considering dropping one of their two cars, carpooling to work, and other changes. Having two cars when one or both of them would sit idle most of the time seems economically wasteful.

Who's Selling Well?

Earlier in the chapter we told of our discussion with State Farm's Pamela El about how young adults will always drive. State Farm, like a Boomer parent, worries a lot about these kids. Ms. El points to research that shows that the majority of accidents for young adults happen in the first year of driving. Reducing that keeps kids (and the bottom line) safe. She says that State Farm is also cognizant of wanting to promote driving by promoting *safe* driving. To that end, they've launched a teen driving site featuring a safe-driving app that help teens learn better driving habits and test themselves. Some of the programs even offer discounts to teens who demonstrate that they are good drivers. One of *Ad Age*'s one hundred most influential women in advertising, Ms. El understands the shifting place of cars among today's youngest drivers.[18] "Friends are first, communication is king. Driving is secondary, it really is. We showcase them in their own world."

State Farm's approach is to celebrate the achievement of getting a license with programs for teenage drivers. It helps promote the concept of driving, but she points out that it's not her job to sell cars.

Likewise, Toyota has a campaign that is clearly meant to appeal to "helicopter" parents and their Millennial or younger kids, the Toyota Mutual Driving Agreement. This program promotes safe driving for kids by encouraging their parents to take the pledge with them and model better behavior.[19]

In 2009, the Korean automaker Kia was in the midst of remaking itself. It was revamping its entire product line and building some models at new U.S.-based factories. As a less expensive brand overall than some of its competition, it saw the recessionary climate as a great opportunity. I talked to Michael Sprague, executive vice president, Marketing and Communications at Kia Motors America, about these trends and about how the company crafted its response.

He, too, sees that there are profound differences between the Boomer and Gen-X youth experience and that of the Millennials. "Driving is not as much of a priority as it was in the past," he said. "There are a lot more distractions and there are a lot more things to do than when I was growing up or even when my parents were growing up. The car was that source of freedom. Now the Internet is the source of freedom."

Kia created the hamster campaign featuring the rodents on their exercise wheel to represent boring, everyday cars. Then the "cool" hamsters appear in their Kia with fun music playing. It connects the young driver to their friends, to music, to social experience. To get there, Kia did some deep-dive research into Millennials. "We understood that they were passionate about music. They really didn't want to be spoken to [directly]. They were into graphical icons and things like that. So that's why in the hamsters campaign you never hear them talking. Everything is icons like you'd see on your iPhone or BlackBerry."

Further, there is some complexity to the social nature of Millennials that Kia wanted to address. "They wanted to stand out, but they didn't want to stand out *too* much from their core nucleus of friends. They travelled in packs. They were into gaming."

"The agency came to us with a couple of different concepts all under the umbrella of 'The new way to roll' because Gen-Y didn't want what their parents had, they wanted to express themselves differently."

Kia knew the music was important and produced four different spots with four different songs. It even did some testing to see which song had the best reaction ("Fort Knox" by Goldfish) and then used that song more frequently in later stages of the campaign.

Putting Social on Wheels

Knowing that online entertainment is a major draw outside the car, manufacturers are also working on bringing the virtual social world into the vehicle. Technologies like Bluetooth, Kia's UVO, or Ford's SYNC allow passengers to hook their mobile devices right into the car. This can reduce some of the perceived trade-off between tech and driving. Mr. Sprague spoke of how people, especially kids, now explore the world online rather than offline. They have a lot more options of things to do than hopping in their cars to socialize. The importance of that can't be overstated.

Amazingly, it's hard for the auto industry to see exactly what's working. For all the big data available in many sectors, the auto industry still relies on data collection that doesn't necessarily give them an accurate picture of their customer. "J. D. Power and [R. L. Polk & Co.] pull the information from the DMVs, and the registrations sometimes are put in the parent's name because they're underwriting the cost for the kids," said Mr. Sprague. That can effectively hide the principal driver. Signs point toward success for his brand. "Right now our [customers'] average age is forty-eight, which is down from fifty-five back in 2008. That is pretty significant for a brand to be able to lower their age that much." He said anecdotal evidence would suggest that the primary driver is getting younger and that this isn't somehow a change based solely on the registration data.

Having bad and possibly misleading data makes it much harder to spot trends, even those as big as the ones we've been discussing in this chapter.

The big x-factor that we keep coming back to is what happens when Millennials have kids and buy houses. That will impact everything. How will the sharing culture held by many of them adapt?

In some small ways, I think the "maker" movement is an extension of that. Once you have a home, some space, and some more permanent roots, making items yourself seems a logical next step from sharing them with others. In one (female-dominated) corner you have all the crafty do-it-yourself scarves, clothes, and picture frames we see sold by individuals on sites like etsy.com. In the other (male-dominated) corner you have 3-D printing technologies that are already getting better, faster, cheaper, and easier to use. People are making their own toys and clocks, watchbands, and more. This will be big. It's early to tell how big, but add this to your must-watch trend list.

What will happen to car sharing if Millennials move out of the transit-friendly downtowns and into car-heavy suburbs? Will the younger iGens move into their vacated lofts and condos and pick right up where the Millennials left off?

Having kids changes the equation of whether to own a car and what kind of car to own.

Let's go back to Rosemary in Howard County; she bought a Honda Element, which she considered a "family" car when she and her husband first wanted to start a family. By the time they had their daughter—years later—they felt the need to trade it in for a car with all the newly developed safety features.

Andrew in Hampden County decided to get his financial house in order when he found out his fiancée was expecting their first child. Part of that process involved re-evaluating car ownership. He traded in his Malibu for a Buick sedan and a lease because he no longer wanted to invest in an asset that lost value over time.

Ms. Chase told me that the demographic cutoff for car sharing is actually the *second* kid. Putting one car seat in a shared car is one thing, but two becomes more hassle than it's worth, based on what she hears from her customers.

Where Do We Go from Here?

If the trend toward decreased driving and car ownership in youth continues or accelerates, that could prove to be the most important trend in this book. Like many trends we've talked about, it will be shaped partially by the Boomers and even more by the Millennials. Arguably, it's also a trend that marketers can still hope to shape rather than just respond to.

Clearly, it could remake the auto industry, which also helps drive the media industry via its huge ad dollars. It could foster the drive toward urbanization we talked about in chapter six. It could potentially help with the bifurcation of the middle class. If some become less reliant on cars, that might free up some of the income increasingly tied up in transportation costs. If people are shopping without cars, that would mean more frequent trips to acquire fewer things—or more delivery and e-commerce. It's also hard to have a drive-through business with fewer people driving through.

What I hope you're seeing is that none of these trends exists in a vacuum. They're all part of the complicated demographic stew that is America—and we're just (a hugely spendy) 315 million of Earth's 7 billion consumers. Marketers have more tools available to them than ever to react to, respond to, and even predict trends through data big and small.

So where do we go next? What trends will emerge tomorrow? I think I've hinted at a few that merit more observation. More and more research is being pursued, and more and more big data is being collected. All the trends I've talked about in the book are still evolving. The digital landscape is certainly changing by the second, the economic recovery continues its uneven progress, and the Millennials get older each and every day. In this book we've been all over the physical U.S. from L.A. to New York to Florida and Montana and everywhere in between. Now I'd like you to join me for one last trip—into the digital realm. So I'd invite you to come and continue the conversation at Buyographics.com, like the book on Facebook at facebook.com/Buyographics, and follow me on twitter @buyographics. I'll be posting regular updates on these and other key trends impacting the media and the marketing world.

See you there.

Epilogue

Demographics, Data, and Democracy

WHEN A HIGH-PROFILE PRODUCT LAUNCH FAILS, BUSINESS REPORTERS AND pundits are quick to offer opinions on what went wrong. Blame gets assigned to the marketing, to the product development, to the packaging itself. All of this happens from the outside. The marketer itself might order an internal audit or postmortem of what failed and how it can be fixed next time around.

Rarely do we, the public, get to see a report like that.

As we said in chapter six, marketers can learn a lot from President Obama and the campaign he ran in 2012. Once the election was over, campaign officials were quick to talk about all the things the campaign did right. I talked to the campaign's CTO, Harper Reed, about some of the ways the campaign took the best lessons it could from marketing and applied them in politics—an area where such tactics were completely novel.

But then, in March 2013, a funny thing happened. The Republican National Committee came out with a 100-page document detailing all the ways it got trumped in the election. Who needs pundits when you can get it right from the elephant's mouth? It's a mostly spin-free document. In it, the GOP presents a harsh self-flagellation that zeroes in on the utter lack of ability to connect with young and minority voters. The Grand Old Party had decided it's too, well, old.

"Young voters are increasingly rolling their eyes at what the Party represents, and many minorities wrongly think that Republicans do not like them or want them in the country," the report says.[1] "When someone rolls their eyes at us, they are not likely to open their ears to us."

The GOP has seemingly recognized that it has two major shortcomings: a dearth of data and a demographic dissonance.

A considerable amount of the report is spent discussing how Mr. Obama's team outperformed the GOP's in the collection and utilization of data. One aspect in particular that stood out in the Obama for America campaign was the platforms built to share data among different parts of the campaign. The GOP thinks that was a competitive advantage. "Greater collaboration and sharing of information is critical," the report said. "Republicans do not do this very well."

The report also points to a need to heed the data that is available. "[There is an] immediate need for the RNC and Republicans to foster what has been referred to as an 'environment of intellectual curiosity' and a 'culture of data and learning.'"

The RNC had big data available to it in 2012. It had its own internal polling and it had access to all the polling Nate Silver read when he accurately predicted an Obama win as early as June and nailed the correct results in all fifty states. Yet the Republicans acted as if they knew something that everyone else didn't. This played out live in strategist Karl Rove's election-night meltdown on Fox News. There might have been a failure in the data, but there was also a failure in the human side of the analysis.

Sometimes data tells you things you don't want to hear. That doesn't mean the data is wrong. It means you might have an opportunity to fix the situation if you act quickly.

The second major focus of the report is on the demographic disconnect between the RNC and the electorate. The word "demographic" appears on one of every four pages of the report.

The surprising part of this is that the report reads as if no one in the party had paid any attention to the 2010 census, despite the report's being issued years after the census findings were released. Many of the trends revealed in the decennial census were foreshadowed in the now-annual American Community Survey. One might argue that this then presents a pretty clear argument for the GOP to quit trying to defund the ACS—because the GOP needs that data itself in order to adapt.[2] I'll step off that soapbox for now, but for anyone in marketing, the ACS is providing important data for you, and you should support it.

The GOP's report details several demographic groups (minorities, youth, single women) that are growing, tells how the GOP has failed to reach each of them, and explains how strongly President Obama carried each of their voting blocs.

I hope that by reading this book you've seen that big data is transforming the way marketers do business. Just as importantly, I hope you've also seen that big data and more traditional demographic data aren't an either/or trade-off. Each works best in combination with the other. All the big data in the world doesn't help you if you don't know the basics of what's going on in the population today and what markets are projected to grow, shrink, or stay the same.

The Obama for America team was able to utilize big data and technology in innovative ways and leverage the power of social media—not just the connections between people and the sharing of content and viral videos, but the power to connect all of that with offline behaviors that translate into the physical world. As we discussed in chapter nine, it's only the beginning.

That success was enabled by having the right messages (creative and policy) to reach the growing populations of the U.S.

Demographics drive purchases, as I've said, and big data can help you spot those trends and determine which behaviors are most important to the decision to purchase your specific product or service or tune into the content you're producing.

Demographics won't necessarily help you spot the up-and-coming big trends like the "culture of sharing" or the "maker movement" that we touched on in chapter ten. Demographics will tell you how big a market might take part in them and where those people are likely to be found.

The more data you have, from more sources, the more likely you are to succeed, especially if you listen and put it into context. So I hope you've noticed that I've been pulling in data and research from a lot of different disciplines—not just traditional consumer sources.

The story of American consumers isn't written in market research alone. It's written in technology. It's written in politics and economics and psychology and physiology. It's in actuarial tables as much as in what is put on the kitchen table, no matter what combination of people is sitting down to eat dinner. None of the trends in this book happen in a vacuum. There is a lot of interplay. Keeping an eye on the big picture helps you see those connections.

I hope you've also gained some insight from the families you've met throughout the book. When you think about health-care costs, think about how they're impacting Alfredo and how he is dealing with different circumstances than are Rosemary or Liz. When you stop to pick up groceries, think about how Michael's routine differs from Chris's or Andrew's. When you adjust your 401k, think about how Basha's life differs from how your parents or their parents aged and to what extent it's a model for the future.

Lastly, I hope *Buyographics* encourages you to get out of your office a little and talk to people. Each number on a spreadsheet or each dot on a chart has a story behind it. Go find some folks to tell you theirs.

Appendix I

Methods and Data

THIS BOOK FOLLOWS THE LIVES OF TEN REPRESENTATIVE FAMILIES IN TEN representative counties. How did I define "representative"?

I used two segmentation systems at the county geography level to determine representative counties. Segmentation systems are tools used primarily by marketers or businesses involved in real estate site selection that group people together based on a number of characteristics that can include demographics, spending patterns, media consumption habits, etc. For the book, I chose to do the segmentation at the county level. Why? There is more data available for counties than for some other geographies, and it's easier to do cross-year comparisons because counties don't change very often, unlike, for instance, zip codes.

The first segmentation I used was Esri's Tapestry Segmentation system. Esri, the world leader in geographic information software, has a vast storehouse of business-related data that can be provided for any geography. For years I've turned to the Esri media relations team to pull data for stories and other research projects. I had been aware of Tapestry through them, but this was the first time I really dove into the data.

Tapestry is what you'd consider a segmentation system. The sixty-five-segment Tapestry Segmentation system classifies U.S. neighborhoods based on their socioeconomic and demographic compositions. For a broader view of U.S. neighborhoods, the segments can be divided into summary groups. I used ten of the twelve LifeMode summary groups based on lifestyle and life stage to simplify the analysis a bit. People are characterized as fitting into one of those segments, which are given names like "High Society" to help marketers better understand that audience. Esri provided the dominant LifeMode group for each county in the U.S. for me, and that served as a starting point.

Then I brought in another segmentation system called the Patchwork Nation. The Patchwork Nation is a project created by journalist Dante Chinni and University of Maryland government professor James Gimpel and is now owned by the Jefferson Institute. Patchwork also provides twelve segments sliced at the county level. It was developed as a lens for reporting on elections, so the segments are based on demographics but coupled with more social data like voting patterns and religious views.

These two tools gave me a very complete set of data with which to study counties.

I looked at counties that matched up with a dominant LifeMode group and Patchwork segment. I wanted to find one county that fit nicely into both frameworks in a logical way. In many cases it was easy to find the match points. Patchwork's "Emptying Nests" correlated nicely with Esri's "Senior Styles" LifeMode group. Similarly "Monied 'Burbs" overlapped with "High Society." Finding the specific counties that aligned was a little more of a delicate dance. I complicated matters by wanting to get some geographic diversity. I also made the decision to focus on only ten of the segments in each system to keep the project somewhat more manageable.

It wasn't always an apples-to-apples comparison, so I consulted with Esri and Mr. Chinni to assist in the county selection. Where the counties didn't line up perfectly, I did the best I could, based on the demographic profiles of the segment. That led me to match Patchwork's "Industrial Metropolis" with Esri's "Solo Acts" LifeMode group, for instance. I was able to get incredibly close to a workable map for the project but in the end, I made one small compromise to get all the way there. Patchwork Nation lumps Los Angeles County in with the "Industrial Metropolis" segment, which is kind of a catchall for the large densely populated counties that are hard to classify more granularly. In looking over the original background scoring data Mr. Chinni provided, I found that Los Angeles also scored very high in the "Immigration Nation" segment and could just as easily have been classified as that. Since this was a project for an advertising and media audience, I wanted to include New York County (otherwise known as Manhattan) and Los Angeles County as the centers of those worlds. Bending the "rules" of the segmentations allowed me to do this with minimal friction. Since Los Angeles County's population is 35 percent foreign born and 48 percent Hispanic or Latino, it's not much of a stretch to call it an "Immigration Nation."[1] Esri classifies the county as the "Global Roots" LifeMode group, which lines up well.

As I talk about the segments, it's helpful to think of them partially as representative of certain types of places. Both of these frameworks have a strong geographic component to them. More importantly, it's good to think of the segments as representative of the kinds of people who live there. These two segmentation tools provided a starting place and a foundation on which to begin the discussion. There are any number of other ways I could have gone about a project like this, but this helped define a methodology to choose the counties and the families.

Having a county-level framework like this also proved useful for bringing in third-party data sources. I worked with comScore, GfK MRI, Experian Simmons, Ipsos Mendelsohn, Pew, and others to run their data through one or both of my frameworks. Even the Census Bureau's American Community Survey, which samples one in six households each year, doesn't have a large enough sample to provide data for every county. By clustering counties into types, it requires a much smaller sample to provide meaningful data for each type of county.

Once I had identified the ten representative counties within the ten representative segments, I needed to find a representative household in each of them to track for the year I was going to write this series. No problem. How hard could this be, right?

Finding ten needles in ten haystacks proved to be a months-long challenge. Communispace, which builds and manages customer communities for brands online, partnered with me to help find them. After weeks of searching, we had identified some of the families, but not all. I found the rest through a variety of channels but mostly by cold-calling county clerks, churches, landlords and realtors, chambers of commerce, business and social groups, and finally tapping my extended social networks. I was no closer than three degrees of separation from any of the families, as I'll detail later. In most cases, I had no connection whatsoever.

I was trying to balance a lot of different desires. Obviously, I wanted to get people who represented their respective segments. Beyond that, I wanted a mix of different demographics including age, race and ethnicity, income, education level, family status, household type, and so forth.

I started off by putting people in the same boxes that marketers do and made sure I could check off a lot of them. To take Michael in New York

County as an example, I quickly learned in chatting with him that he fit a lot of needed demographics (black, successful, Millennial, urban) and behavioral patterns (no cable subscription, gay, carless, with the bonus of being part of a cohabiting interracial couple with an extra roommate).

Then I had to get to know them. I spent a lot of time on the phone and was able to visit Alfredo, Basha, Chris, Dale, Michael, and Rosemary in their homes. I would love to have met all of them, but time and budget didn't stretch that far.

Another question I get asked is why the families would subject themselves to this. Here I'll note that they received a small stipend to do so. But that really never appeared to be a driver in any way. I'm honestly not sure why they agreed, and I never asked them, but I suspect they just wanted to tell their stories. It's one of the most human drives there is.

There are a couple of details I should note. In terms of timeline, I pitched the series of stories to my incredible and highly supportive editor, Abbey Klaassen, in December 2010. I started laying some of the groundwork and doing some of the research at that time. Finding the families proved harder and more time consuming than expected. That, coupled with a lighter publishing schedule in summer, had us looking at a fall launch. The natural place in the editorial calendar was an October special report called "The Consumer Issue." The series, which ran in *Ad Age* as the American Consumer Project, kicked off as the centerpiece of that issue.

I wrote monthly stories for *Ad Age,* supplemented by posts on adage.com until May 2012, at which point I left *Ad Age* to return to its sibling publication *Crain's Chicago Business*. I said my farewells to the families and prepared to move on, but I couldn't help feeling that there was still a bigger story to tell. In July 2012, I formally pitched the book idea through my excellent agent Cynthia Manson with the support of David Klein and *Ad Age,* who are co-publishing with Palgrave Macmillan. It was accepted and I was off again. I reached back out to the families and got the band back together, as they say. Thankfully, they agreed to keep going. I got really, really lucky with these folks.

The Families and the County Types

LIZ lives in Champaign County, Illinois, the home of the University of Illinois's main campus. She's a white Millennial in her twenties who is planning to move in with her boyfriend when their respective leases run out. I found her through a professor I know at the university. He put out a call through his connections there and was able to introduce me to Liz, a University of Illinois alumna. Champaign is a "Scholars and Patriots" area in Esri's Tapestry. Residents are young, with expected lower incomes, and live in atypical environments such as college towns or near military bases. Because of their transient lifestyle and life stage, homeownership rates are low. In the Patchwork Nation, it's classified as "Campus and Careers." These areas are cities and towns with young, educated populations who are more secular and more Democratic than other American communities.[2]

CHRIS lives in Clark County, Nevada. He's a white Baby Boomer in his early fifties who is the single divorced father of a teenage daughter. He has weekend custody, but she's a presence in his life and his home around the clock—even when she's staying across town with her mom. I found Chris through Communispace. In the Tapestry system, Clark County, home to Las Vegas and its suburbs, is classified as a "Family Portrait" area. Youth, family life, and the presence of children are the common characteristics across these counties. The group is also ethnically diverse: more than 30 percent of the residents are Hispanic. Most households include married couples with children who contribute to the group's large household size. In the Patchwork Nation, Clark County is a "Boom Town." In the run-up to the recession these areas were fast-growing communities with rapidly diversifying populations. Then they were among the hardest hit by the real estate crash.

SANDRA lives in East Baton Rouge Parish, Louisiana. She is a black Gen-Xer in her early forties with two daughters, one in college and the other in kindergarten. She's a single mom, working hard to make it all work for her family. I found Sandra through Communispace. Esri's Tapestry classifies East Baton Rouge as a "Metropolis" area. People in the "Metropolis" group segments live and work in America's cities. They live in older single-family homes, own fewer vehicles, and commute to service-related jobs. The segments in this group are diverse in terms of housing, age, and income. In the Patchwork Nation, it's a "Minority Central" area, home to large pockets of black residents but a below-average percentage of Hispanics and Asians.

ANDREW lives in Hampden County, Massachusetts. He's a Hispanic Millennial in his mid-twenties living with his white Jewish fiancée. When we began this project, she had finished grad school. Now they've had a daughter and they're planning their wedding. I found Andrew by calling the local

Latino Chamber of Commerce where he worked at the time. I described the characteristics of the family I was looking for, and Andrew pitched me on using himself. He's a born politician. Tapestry classifies Hampden County in the "Traditional Living" LifeMode group, which conveys the perception of real middle America—hardworking, settled families. The group's higher median age (thirty-eight) also conveys their life stage—a number of older residents who are still taking care of children while anticipating retirement. In the Patchwork Nation, Hampden is classified as a "Service Worker Center" characterized by midsize and small towns with economies fueled by hotels, stores, and restaurants and lower-than-average median household income by county.

ROSEMARY lives in Howard County, Maryland. She and her husband are Korean Americans in their early forties. Her husband's family immigrated from Korea shortly after he was born; Rosemary was born here. They have a young daughter and a dog and lead what appears to be a quintessential middle-class suburban life. It just takes a lot more income to get them there. I found Rosemary through a college friend of mine who knew someone who worked for their local newspaper, who in turn knew them. The dominant Tapestry LifeMode group is "High Society." Residents are affluent and well educated. Their employment in high-paying positions such as professional or managerial occupations is a primary reason for their affluence. Most households are married-couple families. In the Patchwork Nation, this area is considered a "Monied 'Burb" characterized by wealthier, highly educated communities with a median household income of $15,000 above the national county average.

BASHA lives in Lake County, Florida. She's a white, married empty nester in her mid-seventies. She and her husband are still quite active; both work part-time and enjoy the programming and sports at their retirement community. I found Basha through Dante Chinni, who knew someone at the South Lake County Chamber of Commerce who, in turn, knew Basha. Illustrating the diversity among today's seniors, Tapestry's nine senior segments comprise "Senior Styles," the dominant LifeMode group for Lake County. Younger, more affluent empty nesters are traveling and relocating to warmer climates. Settled seniors are looking forward to retirement and remaining in their homes. Their lifestyles can be as diverse as their circumstances. In the Patchwork Nation, this area is considered an "Emptying Nest." These areas are home to many retirees and aging Baby Boomer populations and are less diverse than the nation at large.

JAY lives in Leavenworth County, Kansas. He is a white high-school teacher and wrestling coach in his early thirties, just on the older end of the Millennials. When we met, he was single and subsisting largely on salsa. Now he's engaged and eating much better. I found Jay through a college friend whose cousin knew a city commissioner in Leavenworth who knew Jay's family. The dominant Tapestry LifeMode group is "Upscale Avenues." Prosperity is the overriding attribute shared by counties in "Upscale Avenues." Residents have earned their success by years of hard work. They invest in their homes, including landscaping and remodeling projects. Renters buy new furnishings and appliances. They also save and invest. Leavenworth is home to a large military base and a prison as well as a number of other federal institutions. The officers and retirees help make up this part of the population. In the Patchwork Nation, this is considered a "Military Bastion," an area with high employment in the military or related to the presence of the military and large veteran populations who are likely to vote Republican.

ALFREDO lives in Los Angeles County, California. He is a Cuban immigrant in his late forties, which puts him on the young end of the Baby Boom. He lives with his wife and they have a daughter graduating from high school and a son in middle school. His mother, who suffers from dementia, lives in the apartment next door. I found Alfredo through Communispace. Tapestry identifies the dominant LifeMode group for this county as "Global Roots." Ethnic diversity is the common thread among the segments in "Global Roots." As new households, these residents are young, earn modest incomes, and tend to rent in multi-unit buildings. Reflecting recent immigration trends, half of all households have immigrated within ten years. In the Patchwork Nation, this county could be considered an "Immigration Nation." These areas consist of communities with large Hispanic populations and lower-than-average incomes, typically clustered in the South and Southwest.

MICHAEL lives in New York County, which is otherwise known as Manhattan. He's in his early thirties, on the cusp of the Millennials and Gen-Xers. He is black and lives with his Hispanic partner and a roommate. He has big-city issues (tight space, no car) but both discretion and discretionary income to manage them. I found Michael through an e-mail mailing list I'm on. Someone on the list has a sister who knew a friend of Michael's. The dominant Tapestry LifeMode group is "Solo Acts," which is made up of singles who prefer big-city life. Many are young, just starting out in more densely populated U.S. neighborhoods; others are well-established renters with no kids. They tend to be well-educated working professionals with considerable discretionary income. In the Patchwork Nation, this county is an "Industrial Metropolis." These counties are the largest and most densely populated in the U.S. They are highly diverse urban centers; incomes trend higher than the national average and voters lean Democratic.

DALE lives in Teton County, Montana. He's a white farmer in his mid-forties, which puts him on the younger end of the Baby Boomer generation. He lives with his wife and has three daughters. The oldest lives and works nearby, having graduated from a nearby college that his middle daughter still attends. His youngest is still in high school. I found Dale through Paula, the county clerk and recorder in Teton County. She passed me to one of the county commissioners who knew Dale. The dominant Tapestry LifeMode group for Teton County is "Factories and Farms." These counties represent rural life—from small towns and villages to farms. Employment in manufacturing and agricultural industries is typical in these areas. Population change is nominal. In the Patchwork Nation, this county is "Tractor Country," made up of mostly rural and remote smaller towns with older populations and large agricultural sectors.

Appendix II

The Millennial Disconnect

A Study of the Role of the Automobile
in Today's American Culture

IN CHAPTER TEN I PRESENTED A SUMMARY OF A RESEARCH PROJECT I *conducted with the Chicago-based ad agency Leo Burnett. This appendix is a much more detailed look at the methodology and findings.*

Carol Foley's corner office at Leo Burnett is filled with books, knickknacks, photos, and whiteboards. The center is a large glass working table, often covered with more books. The main distraction, however, is the view as it overlooks the Chicago River, pointed out toward Lake Michigan with a number of wonderfully architected Chicago buildings in the foreground.

I spent a lot of time at that table as Ms. Foley and I conducted a research study seeking to identify the role of the automobile for today's American driver.

The auto industry is a broad subject. We were especially interested in getting at generational differences in perception. To explore the issue, we settled on a process the agency had worked on while developing a number of campaigns called "What-if" mapping.

Rather than study the auto industry in isolation, we decided to reimagine it as a much broader product category. We thought we'd learn more by stepping back and looking at a bigger picture than by trying to discern brand preferences and the like. We called our reimagined universe the category of "moving forward in life"—which, after all, is literally and figuratively what cars do for people.

By re-framing cars this way, we could imagine a broader universe with both literal car-related items and things that were aligned metaphorically with "moving forward." In an ideation session, we dreamed up seventy-seven brands, products, and activities (which I'm just going to refer to as "items") like safety features, other types of transportation like flying or taking the bus, and even things that have nothing to do with transportation, but that definitely move you forward in life—like graduating from college, having a family, or starting a business.

Next, we needed a set of attributes on which people could rate the seventy-seven items. Functional vehicle attributes about styling and performance and price no longer work when many have nothing to do with those things. This meant we had to create entirely new attributes that revolved around the higher-level emotional rewards and benefits of the various items. The process is called a "laddering-up exercise," meant to get at the emotional essence of an item and its place in a consumer's life.

Taking "getting a college degree" as an example, we'd ask ourselves what it accomplished in terms of moving a person ahead in life. Each time we came up with an answer, we asked ourselves, "Why is that important?" and then came up with another answer. At a certain point you "ladder up" so far that you can go no farther. You write it down. We did this for all of the items and then narrowed that down to fifty-five attributes in total.

Our list included items about fulfillment, meaning being on top of things, achieving freedom, realizing possibility, gaining competence, growing, discovering, self-actualizing, and much more. With these attributes in hand, we were ready to survey people and find out which ones best described each of the seventy-seven items and uncover, as a result, what insights this revealed for cars.

We turned to our survey partner, Ipsos Observer. The survey giant was given some difficult marching orders. We wanted to be able to look at the data not just by the typical demographic slices of age or gender but also by Patchwork Nation segments (which are detailed in Appendix I). The Patchwork Nation consists of a series of county types based on demographic and other factors including voting patterns and religion. The county types, such as "Emptying Nests," "Immigration Nation," and "Industrial Metropolis," are comprised of hundreds of America's 3,141 counties. Therefore, we needed a large enough sample in each of those combined geographies. We aimed for 200 completed interviews in each of those segments. The survey was conducted in May 2012 with more than 3,000 completed interviews. The majority were car owners with a small portion (roughly 3 percent) of people who intended to purchase a car in the next twelve months.

Each of our respondents was asked about "the car they drive" plus one other item. "The car you drive" was a generic term. It didn't matter for us what the make, model, or year of the vehicle was, simply how they viewed their current car. Similarly, we also asked some respondents about their "first car" and the car they would like to drive. Additionally, in another portion of the survey, we did ask specifics about the car they currently drive. We were able to use this to confirm or rule out certain theories we'll talk about in a minute.

Using statistical techniques like factor analysis and correspondence analysis, we were able to produce a two-dimensional map that arrays the seventy-seven items in space, based upon how they were rated on the fifty-five attributes by our sample.

Since everyone answered the question about the car they drove, we could also segment attitudes about that question with a high degree of granularity because we had a large enough representative sample.

Look at the map of the seventy-seven items on the next page. Let's first take a look at how things organize generally around the map and then we'll get into the car-specific takeaways, and in particular, the takeaways about Millennials. For now, we'll look at the map as it is laid out for all respondents.

Attributes that were more about goal setting and attempts at improvement pulled to the left, while those that were more about relaxation, rejuvenation, and enjoyment of the richness of life pulled to the right. We're going to call this the "work–reward" axis. For example, on the far left side of the map we saw attributes like "helps you plan and formulate goals" or "helps you to improve, become more skilled or competent." That's the hard but needed stuff. So you see that specific items that relate to those feelings and goals fall into this space, too. "A strong work ethic" or "a polished résumé" will help you formulate and meet goals.

On the right side, we saw attributes that were the payoff like "helps make the good moments in life last longer" and "allows you to renew, recharge, or rejuvenate." The items that correlate to those attitudes and goals are things

REINVENT — REWARD

WORK — REINFORCE

Space travel

Dating sites like match.com

A great sound system in your vehicle

Going to a party or social gathering

An airline mileage or hotel rewards program

Flying

Pursuing a hobby or interest

The vehicle you wish you could drive

A good wardrobe

A luxury car

Your own blog or Twitter feed

The very best vehicle you ever owned

Private club membership

Buying a house

An SUV

Facebook

Custom car interior or exterior features/detailing

A group of close friends

The vehicle you drive

A hybrid car

A pickup truck

An American car or truck

LinkedIn

Having a family

Accessories/features that make your vehicle more versatile

Working out/getting physical exercise

A team-building seminar or experience

An imported car or truck

A Rotary club or business club

A college or graduate school alumni network

Accessories and features that make your vehicle function better

A life coach

A network of extended friends and acquaintances

Getting married/being in a committed relationship

Text messaging

Establishing family traditions

Your local government

Minivan

Taking public transportation

Air bags

Car alarm system

Your religion or faith

Onstar

Your doctor

Vehicle insurance

Life insurance

Lawyer

Moving out of your parents' place and into your own place

Starting your own business

Retraining for a job

Winning an award/being recognized for an accomplishment

Getting a promotion at work

Getting a good education

The Internet

A polished résumé

Being competitive

Having ambition and determination

Being a good communicator

A strong work ethic

Having good leadership skills

Career counseling

A smartphone

E-mail

A personal computer

Attending a conference on a work-related-subject

Having a strong set of values

Being a good listener

A financial planner

A therapist or counselor

Cooperation

Multitasking

Self-discipline

Things that help you stay organized

Staying on top of the news

Office supplies

like "going to a party or social gathering," "an airline mileage or hotel rewards program," or "establishing family traditions."

The up-down dimension involved two more constructs. At the top of the map were attributes that were all about moving forward on offense. For example, "helps you realize a dream" or "gives you status or recognition—showcases your accomplishments." The items we see in this space are things like "a good wardrobe," "dating sites," and "moving out of your parents' home." Each of these items is about dreaming, moving forward to new life stages, or at least looking the part.

By contrast, the bottom of the map was anchored by attributes related to holding your own, preventing, recovering, repairing, and consolidating. For example, "removes obstacles and dangers from your path" or "helps you consolidate and protect what you've already achieved." Lawyers, vehicle insurance, doctors, and even office supplies can all help you with this "reinforcing" of what you have.

So we're calling this the "reinforce–reinvent" axis.

Looking at the seventy-seven items on the map, clear themes emerge in each quadrant. The items that fall in the lower left quadrant are simultaneously about improving and goal setting but in a protective and cautious way. It includes things like staying on top of the news, having a strong work ethic, or attending a work-related conference. The upper left is also about improvement and goal setting, but in a much less defensive, more forward-moving way. It includes things that are very accomplishment oriented such as getting a college education, starting your own business, or getting a promotion at work.

Moving diagonally across the map, the lower right quadrant is simultaneously about relaxing, rejuvenating, and enjoying life, but in a more traditional and grounded way. It includes things like establishing family traditions, your religion or faith, or an extended network of friends and acquaintances. Finally, the upper right quadrant is also about rewards, but in a more forward-moving, fun, and indulgent way. It includes things like going to a party, pursuing a hobby, or going on Facebook.

What Does This Tell Us about Cars?

First, did you notice that everything that has to do with cars falls onto the right side of the map? That tells us that when it comes to looking through the broad lens of things that move you ahead in life, cars are much more about enjoying life than they are about goal setting and improving and sharpening skills. Regardless of the type of car or the nature of the trip or accessory, cars are more reward than work. They're about freeing rather than constraining. Cars and car accessories in general live more in the land of friends, family, and fun technology as opposed to the land of work, education, and résumés. No matter how challenging or serious life has grown or how goal oriented our society has become, cars still sit on the summer side of the map, where we seek to create memories and make enjoyable times stretch longer.

Second, although cars and car products gravitate toward the right, they don't cluster at all on the reinvent–reinforce spectrum on the map. This means that some types of cars and car products are about defense and consolidation—highly practical and meant to keep things from falling apart. Others are more about change, accomplishment, and aspiration. On this basis we see the minivan as vastly separated from the SUV or the luxury car, just as air bags are more or less the antithesis of a great sound system. The cars and features that live up on the map are all about what we want to do. They're about a future that we imagine for ourselves and that we are working toward. Those that are down on the map are all about what we should do but in a very specific way. They're about protecting what we have.

Third, the "first vehicle you ever owned" as well as the "vehicle you wish you could drive" are both much more accomplishment- and aspiration-oriented than "the vehicle you drive right now." This suggests that people view themselves as more constrained and more practically forced into their current vehicle than they either were in their youth or will be in what they hope might be their future. Again, these questions were not about the specific car, but rather about what the car represents to the respondent.

That shows the importance of reconnecting with and re-sparking the feeling of freedom and imagination that the first car conveyed. It also shows the path to do that. Making the car you drive right now more like the car you first owned or the car you want to own more exciting means shifting that message and that experience more into the realm of "reward/reinvent." The tricky part is that nostalgia doesn't seem to be the right way to do this. Tradition and anything tied to the past are all on the "work" side of the attribute map—exactly where you don't want to be, given that everything car related is on the "reward" side.

Fourth, taking public transportation is clearly not going to be capturing the hearts of most Americans any time soon. Far down on the bottom right of the map, it couldn't be much farther away from "the car you wish you could drive" or even "the car you actually drive." Those two cars are closer to flying and almost closer to space travel than they are to public transportation. We talked a little about public transportation and even walkability in chapters six and seven. Cities (even Detroit) are investing in more options for moving people around.[1] Having more transit options can truly be seen as a boon for urban areas. The subway or light rail might convey Americans from one place to another more pleasantly and more efficiently than sitting in traffic, but that doesn't mean it conveys an image of freedom or victory.

In a similar vein, the ongoing resistance to hybrid vehicles is explained on the map. Though heavily marketed and quite practical, they are drifting toward the lower right quadrant, home of the minivan and taking public transportation—making them much more of a "should do" than a "want to do." Depending on a raft of things ranging from fuel prices to sticker price to environmental consciousness, hybrids will likely continue to grow, but for practical reasons, not emotional ones. They are not really where most people's hearts are.

Fifth and finally, when viewed through the lens of moving through life, distinctions between American cars and imports are minimal. While we know there are segments of buyers who still strongly gravitate toward one or the other, in this broader view, the type of car is the bigger discriminator.

With those overall findings providing some context, what did we learn about Millennials? On the next page, you can see how the different age groups view "the vehicle they drive."

As you can see, there's a definite progression or perhaps regression as we look at the different generations. From the late Millennials (25–34) to the Gen-Xers (35–44) to the early Boomers (45–54) to the older Boomers (55–64), there is a steady move toward the "reward" side of the axis and generally drifting up to the "reinvent" side. The data hiccups a little during the peak "driving your family around" years. The younger Millennials (18–24) are significantly off by themselves at the far end of the "reward" axis, almost drifting into "work."

The younger the driver, the less having a car is about emotion, escapism, and reward, and the more it becomes a rational and thought-out functional decision on the left side of the map. This is the opposite of what we presume the Boomers and even the Gen-Xers would have looked like when they were younger.

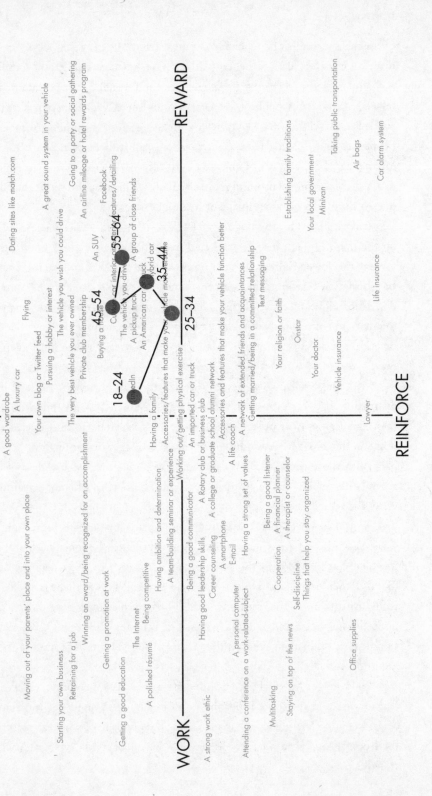

Several explanations for the shift come to mind; by layering in responses to other questions in the survey, we're able to rule out all but one. First, is this all just a factor of the recession? With Millennials getting squeezed economically, maybe the car is viewed as more of a necessary albatross than a freeing eagle.

There are two ways to disprove that.

For one thing, as we've been saying throughout this book, the recession hit every age group to at least some extent. So while we might expect movement if we looked at this before and after the recession, there's no reason to expect that one age group would move a lot more than others. As we move through the age groups in our data, we see a nice continuum of movement in terms of where the "your car" brand plots on our two axes. It's unlikely that Millennial attitudes would shift dramatically further than other generations once the recession abated.

Also, when we looked at the Patchwork segments, which take socioeconomic status into account, there was a clear bifurcation. Three of the least affluent segments ("Immigration Nation," "Service Worker Centers," and "Minority Bastions") were located left and up in our grid toward rational and even toward flat-out functional. All of the other segments clustered not all that far from the average plot point on the map.[2] Looking at other questions on the survey, we see that these segments, like the pool as a whole, didn't have a lot of variation in average tenure of car ownership and type of car owned. These groups do tend to over-index on pickup ownership, a trait that is highly correlated to education or, specifically, the lack thereof. Therefore, the differentiation comes from other demographic and socioeconomic factors, not just age. Two of the segments with the most skewed age ranges—"Campuses and Careers" and "Emptying Nests"—both plotted in pretty much the same place with the lower cluster. That means that those who are struggling most are even more skewed than the younger age range of the entire pool and that the others are showing no real difference.

The one outlier was the relatively low-income, small-town "Evangelical Epicenters." According to our survey, they own substantially older cars—but that tracks with our unexpected finding that older cars draw a more emotional relationship than newer ones. The second way to dismiss this notion that Millennials' economic situation is causing them to view cars more functionally than do other age cohorts would be to look at the cars that Millennials are driving. Given the economy, they probably drive older, smaller, cheaper cars than Gen-X or Boomer drivers who have traded up to their nice cushy sedans and their midlife-crisis mobiles. Therefore, it would make sense that they wouldn't feel the same way as Boomers do about their rides, right?

Well, no. That's not it at all. We asked our entire sample to report what types of cars they drive. There was relatively little variation across age groups on the size and style of the car, on its classification as domestic or imported, on whether it's leased or owned, or in terms of the age of the car that would explain the trajectory we see in the data.

This led us on a bit of an interesting tangent. We looked at the age of the vehicle to see if people who drove newer cars had different impressions than those who drove older cars. We broke the sample into three segments. The first segment was people who have owned their cars longer than ten years, roughly the average length of time people are hanging on to cars these days. We also split out the people who drive cars from the two most recent model years to give us a look at what are essentially owners of "new" cars. The third segment was everyone in between.

What we found here was especially unexpected. Newer cars are more to the left of the graph than older cars. Why is that? It could be that people who bought cars in the last couple of years did so for pragmatic reasons. They might have had to make trade-offs with other products (like a vacation) to afford the car. They might have had to sacrifice more in terms of features than they wanted to. They might not have wanted to get a new car at all, but had to due to demographic changes or to their previous vehicle giving out. Maybe they didn't buy the car they wanted but bought the car they could afford.

As we've said, there was little variation in the age, size, and style of the cars across the age groups we tested. One aspect of the driving demographic that does show variation across age groups was the percentage of people who use their car to drive to work. That decreases as the sample gets older, probably because there are fewer of them in the workforce. If they don't drive to work, that means they use their car for other things like vacation and leisure and shopping. Maybe that creates a more emotional connection.

So we reran the data looking at those who drive to work and those who don't. Sample size precluded our overlaying every specific age cohort on this cut, but we were able to look at eighteen- to thirty-four-year-olds and those thirty-five and older. Even here we found no variation in the opinions of the car they drove and how it fit into their lives.

Now we can rule that out, too.

That leaves us with one big conclusion.

Younger drivers have a different relationship with their cars than older drivers do. It's not a factor of the age or the style of the car itself. It's not a factor of what they use the car for. It's a factor of how Millennials interact with cars and how those cars are generally marketed to them. Other factors are likely at play, too. Perhaps the increasingly complex nature of cars that makes them essentially impossible to tinker with on your own comes into play. As behavioral economist Dan Ariely points out, there's an "IKEA effect" whereby we have more emotional attachment to things we build (and can fix) than things we just buy.[3]

In case you jumped here without reading all of chapter ten, we gave more detail there about our findings and provided some specifics about how marketers could use this data to interact with Millennials. We also talked about how this relational shift is emerging in the data about driving, car ownership, and even the number of teenagers getting their driver's licenses. If these trends continue, and if Millennials continue to eschew the car, which has quite literally driven much of consumer behavior, the economy, and the very way we build our towns and our homes, then we will see a greatly changed America in the coming decades.

Notes

Introduction

1. Matt Carmichael, "Twin-conomics: 10 (Times Two!) Stats about How Fertility Is Creating a New Market," *Advertising Age,* January 25, 2011.
2. Gregory Trotter, "Wilmette's Highcrest Middle School Sets Record for Twins," chicagotribune.com, May 23, 2013.
3. Constance L. Hays, "What Walmart Knows about Customers' Habits," nytimes.com, November 14, 2004.
4. "Daniel Kahneman," Woodrow Wilson School of Public and International Affairs, Princeton University, http://www.princeton.edu/~kahneman/.
5. Daniel Kahneman, *Thinking, Fast and Slow* (New York: Farrar, Straus and Giroux, 2011).
6. These will be discussed further as we talk about each county over the course of the book. They are also detailed in Appendix I. For more information, please visit patchworknation.org and esri.com/tapestry.

Chapter 1

1. Ben Woolsey and Emily Starbuck Gerson, "The History of Credit Cards," Creditcards.com.
2. Pew Research Social & Demographic Trends, "The Lost Decade of the Middle Class: Fewer, Poorer, Gloomier," August 22, 2012.
3. Throughout *Buyographics* I will be including information about and quotes from the ten families I tracked during this research. Interviews were conducted by phone and in person between July 2011 and March 2013. In addition, several online surveys of these families were conducted in 2011 and 2012. Some of this material appeared in *Advertising Age* and on adage.com as part of the American Consumer Project, upon which this book is initially based. That material is reprinted here with permission of *Advertising Age*; copyright Crain Communications Inc. Many of the quotes and narratives are previously unpublished. As any given paragraph might contain both published and unpublished information collected over the course of several interviews, these will not be referenced separately. Throughout the work I will use only the first names of the individuals and occasionally their spouses to preserve their privacy. At the end of the project, the families were given a small stipend for their participation. For more on the families and the counties they represent, please see Appendix I.

4. Matt Carmichael, "What's Left of the Middle Class Is More Diverse, Harder Working—and Still Shrinking," *Advertising Age,* October 17, 2011.

5. Matt Carmichael and Peter Francese, "The Redistribution of Wealth? It Already Happened," adage.com, February 24, 2011.

6. John Edwards, Marion Crain, and Arne L. Kalleberg, *Fragile Families: The Vanishing Middle Class* (New York: The New Press, 2007).

7. U.S. Census Bureau, Current Population Survey, Annual Social and Economic Supplements, 2011.

8. Experian Simmons 2011 Discretionary Spend Report.

9. Elizabeth Warren and Amelia Warren Tyagi, *The Two-Income Trap: Why Middle-Class Mothers and Fathers Are Going Broke* (New York: Basic Books, 2004).

10. Michael I. Norton and Dan Ariely, "Building a Better America—One Wealth Quintile at a Time," *Perspectives on Psychological Science* 8, no. 1 (January 2011): 9–12.

11. Dave Gilson and Carolyn Perot, "It's the Inequality, Stupid," *Mother Jones,* March/April 2011.

12. Board of Governors of the Federal Reserve System, Statistical Release, 2013.

13. Jane Kim, "Banks Get Picky in Doling Out Credit Cards," WSJ.com, August 5, 2009.

14. "How Hard Is It to Get a Credit Card with Bad Credit," Credit.com, March 22, 2012.

15. Kelly Dilworth, "Reversing Course Again, Consumer Credit Card Balances Fall in June," FoxBusiness.com, August 9, 2012.

16. E. J. Dionne et al., "America's Endangered Middle Class: Exploring Progressive and Conservative Remedies," Panel Discussion Transcript, February 24, 2011.

17. Jesse Bricker et al., "Changes in U.S. Family Finances from 2007 to 2010: Evidence from the Survey of Consumer Finances," *Federal Reserve Bulletin* 98, no. 2 (June 2012).

18. Alfred Gottschalck and Marina Vornovytskyy, "Changes in Household Net Worth from 2005 to 2010," U.S. Census Bureau's Random Samplings Blog, June 18, 2012.

19. Ibid.

20. Pew Research Social & Demographic Trends, "The Lost Decade of the Middle Class," August 22, 2012.

21. Interview with the author, October 19, 2012.

22. "Trends in the Distribution of Income," Congressional Budget Office blog post, October 25, 2011.

23. "Table 694: Share of Aggregate Income Received by Each Fifth and the Top 5 Percent of Households: 1970 to 2009," U.S. Census Bureau, Statistical Abstract of the United States: 2012.

24. Richard Fry and Paul Taylor, "A Rise in Wealth for the Wealthy; Declines for the Lower 93%," Pew Research Social & Demographic Trends, April 23, 2013.

25. Steven Rattner, "The Rich Get Even Richer," *New York Times,* March 25, 2012.

26. Ibid.

27. Michael Lind, "Who Won the Great Recession: The Ultra Rich," *Foreign Policy,* November 2012.

28. Ben Paynter, "Suds for Drugs," *New York,* January 6, 2013.

29. Data provided to the author by IRI. Includes total U.S. Supermarkets, Drugstores, and Mass Merchandise Outlets (excluding Walmart), Latest 52 Weeks Ending July 8, 2012.

30. The Associated Press, "Procter & Gamble's Quarterly Profits Rise on Sale of Snack Unit," *New York Times,* August 3, 2012.

31. Stephanie Strom, "Frito-Lay Takes New Tack on Snacks," *New York Times,* June 12, 2012.

32. PepsiCo's Second Quarter 2012 Earnings Call Transcript, http://www.pepsico.com/Download/PEP_Q212Transcript.pdf.

33. U.S. Bureau of Labor Statistics, Consumer Expenditure Survey, 2011.

34. David Court and Laxman Narasimhan, "Capturing the World's Emerging Middle Class," *McKinsey Quarterly,* July 2010.

35. Joshua E. Keating, "Who Won the Great Recession? These Seven Countries," *Foreign Policy,* November 2012.

36. Chrystia Freeland, "The Rise of the New Global Elite," *The Atlantic,* January/February 2011.

37. Interview with the author, October 16, 2012.

38. Target Corporation Second Quarter 2012 Earnings Call Transcript, http://seekingalpha.com/article/809321-target-management-discusses-q2-2012-results-earnings-call-transcript.

39. Data provided to the author by the Las Vegas Convention and Visitors Authority.

40. Interview with the author, September 19, 2012.

41. Interview with the author, September 11, 2012.

42. Acxiom Corporation filings with the United States Securities and Exchange Commission, accessed at sec.gov.

Chapter 2

1. U.S. Census Bureau, American Community Survey, 2011. Much of the research in this book is based on data from the U.S. Census Bureau, especially the annual American Community Survey releases. The ACS is an invaluable public resource that can be accessed for free via the Census Bureau's website, www.factfinder2.census.gov. This data is a fantastic example of your tax dollars at work and you should urge your congressional leaders to maintain its funding.

2. "The Mendelsohn Affluent Survey," http://www.ipsos-na.com/products-tools/media-content-technology/syndicated-studies/mendelsohn-affluent-survey.aspx.

3. "Ellicott City Station," http://www.borail.org/Ellicott-City-Station.aspx.

4. U.S. Bureau of Labor Statistics, Consumer Expenditure Survey, 2011, www.bls.gov/cex. Political commentary from note 1 applies here, too.

5. Compare Cost of Living tool, Sperling's BestPlaces, www.bestplaces.net.

6. Amy O'Leary, "What Is Middle Class in Manhattan?" *New York Times,* January 18, 2013.

7. Jesse Bricker et al., "Changes in U.S. Family Finances from 2007 to 2010: Evidence from the Survey of Consumer Finances," *Federal Reserve Bulletin* 98, no. 2 (June 2012).

8. Data cited is from the Mendelsohn Affluent Survey, an annual nationally representative study of more than 13,000 adults aged 18+ living in households with at least $100,000 in annual household income.

9. David Hirschman, "The New Wave of Affluence," *Advertising Age,* Trend Report, May 2011.

10. Data provided to the author from Experian Marketing Services, Simmons LOCAL Spring 2011, an annual survey of U.S. adults conducted through June 2011. Sample sizes vary by DMA, with an average in-tab of 25,000.

11. Interview with the author, November 5, 2012.

12. Experian Marketing Services, SimmonsLOCAL Spring 2011.

13. Matt Carmichael, "More Cash for Marketers to Chase as Savings Rate Drops," *Advertising Age,* December 5, 2011.

14. Mendelsohn Affluent Survey.

15. Lee Barney, "34% of Americans Have No Retirement Savings," Financial Planning.com, February 3, 2011.

16. BlackRock Inc., "Volatility Propels Emotional Investing," BlackRock; Bloomberg; Informa Investment Solutions, Dalbar, December 3, 2012, https://www2 .blackrock.com/us/financial-professionals/market-insight/chart-of-the-week /volatility-propels-emotional-investing.

17. Interview with the author, September 13, 2012.

18. Interview with the author, January 11, 2013.

19. Data provided to the author from The Shullman Luxury and Affluence Monthly Pulse.

20. Interview with the author, November 16, 2012.

21. "Cinépolis Luxury Cinemas," http://www.cinepolisusa.com/.

22. U.S. Census Bureau, American Community Survey, 2009–2011.

Chapter 3

1. U.S. Census Bureau, 2011 American Community Survey.

2. Eric Savitz, "The Path to Becoming a Fortune 500 CEO," *Forbes,* December 5, 2011.

3. "Female Fortune 500 CEOs at Record High," Huffington Post, October 26, 2011.

4. U.S. Census Bureau, "Households, Families, Marital Status and Living Arrangements," March 2012.

5. U.S. Census Bureau, American Community Survey, 2011.

6. U.S. Census Bureau, Current Population Survey, 2011.

7. U.S. Census Bureau, Current Population Survey and Annual Social and Economic Supplements.

8. U.S. Census Bureau, American Community Survey, 2011.

9. D'Vera Cohn, "Marriage Rate Declines and Marriage Age Rises," Pew Research Social & Demographic Trends, December 14, 2011.

10. Derek Thompson, "The Death (and Life) of Marriage in America," *The Atlantic,* February 7, 2012.

11. American Student Assistance, Student Loan Debt Statistics, http://www.asa .org/policy/resources/stats/default.aspx.

12. U.S. Census Bureau, American Community Survey, 2011.

13. Eric Klinenberg, *Going Solo: The Extraordinary Rise and Surprising Appeal of Living Alone* (New York: Penguin Press, 2012).

14. Suzanne Macartney and Laryssa Mykyta, "Poverty and Shared Households by State: 2011," U.S. Census Bureau, American Community Survey Briefs, November 2012.

15. Frank Hobbs and John F. Long, "Examining American Household Composition: 1990 and 2000," U.S. Census Bureau, Census 2000 Special Reports, August 2005.

16. Daphne A. Lofquist, "Multigenerational Households: 2009–2011," U.S. Census Bureau, American Community Survey Briefs, October 2012.

17. Christopher Palmeri and Frank Bass, "Grandma Bunks with Jobless Kids as Multigenerational Homes Surge," Bloomberg News, August 29, 2011.

18. U.S. Census Bureau, American Community Survey, 2011.
19. U.S. Census Bureau, Current Population Survey, 1960 to 2011 Annual Social and Economic Supplements.
20. U.S. Bureau of Labor Statistics, Consumer Expenditure Survey, 2011.
21. U.S Bureau of Labor Statistics, American Time Use Survey, 2003 and 2012.
22. Greg Clary and Athena Jones, "Baby Boomer Divorce Rate Doubles," CNN.com, June 27, 2012.
23. U.S. Census Bureau, Current Population Survey/Housing Vacancy Survey, 2012.
24. U.S. Census Bureau, American Community Survey, 2011.
25. U.S. Census Bureau, "Median and Average Square Feet of Floor Area in New Single-Family Houses Completed by Location," 2011.
26. U.S. Census Bureau, "Highlights of Annual 2011 Characteristics of New Housing," 2012.
27. U.S. Census Bureau, American Community Survey, 2011.
28. Klinenberg, *Going Solo*.
29. Interview with the author, September 17, 2012.

Chapter 4

1. U.S. Census Bureau, Decennial Census, 2010.
2. Zach Rosenberg, "Bad Dadvertising: Hyundai Azera," 8BitDad.com, March 9, 2012.
3. U.S. Bureau of Labor Statistics, Consumer Expenditure Survey, 2012.
4. U.S. Census Bureau, "Who's Minding the Kids? Child Care Arrangements: Spring 2010," December 2011.
5. Kim Parker and Wendy Wang, "Modern Parenthood: Roles of Moms and Dads Converge as They Balance Work and Family," Pew Research Social & Demographic Trends, 2013.
6. U.S. Census Bureau, "America's Families and Living Arrangements: 2012."
7. Julia Overturf Johnson et al., "Changes in the Lives of Children: 1990–2000," U.S. Census Bureau, Population Division Working Paper No. 78, November 2005.
8. Wendy Wang, Kim Parker, and Paul Taylor, "Breadwinner Moms," Pew Research Social & Demographic Trends, May 29, 2013.
9. U.S. Census Bureau, "Who's Minding the Kids? Child Care Arrangements: Spring 2010," December 2011.
10. Bonnie Rochman, "Stay-at-Home Dads: No More Angst. These Guys Love What They Do," *Time*, June 15, 2012.
11. Alex Williams, "Just Wait until Your Mother Gets Home," *New York Times*, August 10, 2012.
12. U.S. Census Bureau, "America's Families and Living Arrangements: 2012."
13. U.S. Census Bureau, Current Population Survey, and Annual Social and Economic Supplements.
14. Erica Scharrer, "From Wise to Foolish: The Portrayal of the Sitcom Father, 1950s–1990s," *Journal of Broadcasting & Electronic Media* 45, no. 1 (Winter 2001).
15. Tvtropes.org.
16. Jack Neff, "Time to Rethink Your Message: Now the Cart Belongs to Daddy," *Advertising Age*, January 17, 2011.
17. Jack Neff, "Dove Gives Guys a Break in Men+Care Push," *Advertising Age*, March 12, 2013.

18. Lisa Terry, "Dudes to Dads: U.S. Men's Attitudes Toward Life, Family, Work," *Ad Age,* Trend Report, 2012.
19. "We're Dads, Huggies. Not Dummies," Change.org, http://www.change.org /petitions/we-re-dads-huggies-not-dummies.
20. Deborah Pike Olsen, "The Real Cost of Raising a Baby," BabyCenter.com, July 2011.
21. David Sterrett, "Jewel Thins Out Selection as Grocery Competition from Walmart Intensifies," chicagobusiness.com, July 5, 2010.
22. Jill Cataldo, "What Is SuperValu Doing to Jewel-Osco," JillCataldo.com, July 29, 2010.
23. Michael Learmonth, "CES's Biggest Miss: Marketing That Just Doesn't Get Women," *Advertising Age,* January 8, 2013.
24. Amy Chozick, "A New Generation of TV Wimps," *Wall Street Journal,* June 10, 2011.
25. U.S. Department of Labor, Women's Bureau, "Facts on Working Women," December 1993.
26. Lorraine Woellert, "American Men Dominate Job Gains Taking 88% of Spots: Economy," Bloomberg.com, April 3, 2012.
27. Interview with the author, September 21, 2012.
28. Tierney Bricker, "*Whitney, Guys with Kids, Up All Night* Canceled by NBC," eonline.com, May 9, 2013.
29. Interview with the author, September 11, 2012.
30. Brad Harrington, Fred Van Deusen, and Beth Humberd, "The New Dad: Caring, Committed and Conflicted," Boston College Center for Work and Family, 2011.
31. Child Trends DataBank, http://www.childtrendsdatabank.org/?q=node/231.
32. Child Trends DataBank, http://www.childtrendsdatabank.org/?q=node/196.
33. U.S. Census Bureau, American Community Survey, 2011.
34. Child Trends DataBank, http://www.childtrendsdatabank.org/?q=node/196.
35. Michael Cohen, *Live from the Campaign Trail: The Greatest Presidential Campaign Speeches of the Twentieth Century and How They Shaped Modern America* (New York: Walker & Co., 2008).
36. Stephanie Clifford, "More Dads Buy the Toys, So Barbie, and Stores, Get Makeovers," *New York Times,* December 3, 2012.
37. Interview with the author, September 17, 2012.
38. Francine Kopun, "IKEA Sets up Playpen for Men," *Toronto Star,* September 23, 2011.

Chapter 5

1. To be specific, he finished in a virtual tie but was appointed to the position when someone else dropped out.
2. U.S. Census Bureau, Population Division.
3. U.S. Census Bureau, Decennial Census, 2010.
4. Campbell Gibson and Kay Jung, "Historical Census Statistics on Population Totals by Race, 1790 to 1990, and by Hispanic Origin, 1970 to 1990," U.S. Census Bureau Working Paper Series No. 56, September 2002.
5. "An Older and More Diverse Nation by Midcentury," U.S. Census Bureau news release, August 14, 2008.
6. U.S. Census Bureau, "Intercensal Estimates of the Resident Population by Sex, Race, and Hispanic Origin for the United States: April 1, 2000 to July 1, 2010."

7. U.S. Census Bureau, "Percent Distribution of the Projected Population by Race and Hispanic Origin for the United States: 2015 to 2060."

8. Seth Motel and Eileen Patten, "Characteristics of the 60 Largest Metropolitan Areas by Hispanic Population," Pew Research Hispanic Center, September 19, 2012.

9. Matt Carmichael and Peter Francese, "Five Surprising Facts Marketers Should Know about 2010 Census Stats," *Advertising Age,* April 4, 2011.

10. Thomas Gryn and Christine Gambino, "The Foreign Born from Asia: 2011," American Community Survey Briefs, October 2012, https://www.census.gov/prod/2012pubs/acsbr11-06.pdf

11. Paul Overberg, "A County-by-County Look at Diversity," *USA Today,* July 14, 2010.

12. Carmichael and Francese, "Five Surprising Facts Marketers Should Know about 2010 Census Stats."

13. U.S. Census Bureau, American Community Survey, 2011.

14. U.S. Bureau of Labor Statistics, "Education Pays," Infographic, January 28, 2013.

15. Motel and Patten, "Characteristics of the 60 Largest Metropolitan Areas by Hispanic Population."

16. U.S. Bureau of Labor Statistics, Consumer Expenditure Survey, 2011.

17. Richard Alba, "Language Assimilation Today: Bilingualism Persists More Than in the Past, But English Still Dominates," Lewis Mumford Center for Comparative Urban and Regional Research at the University of Albany, December 2004.

18. Carmichael and Francese, "Five Surprising Facts Marketers Should Know about 2010 Census Stats."

19. U.S. Census Bureau, "The Two or More Races Population: 2010," 2010 Census Briefs, September 2012.

20. U.S. Census Bureau, Decennial Census, 2010.

21. Sam Roberts and Peter Baker, "Asked to Declare His Race, Obama Checks 'Black,'" *New York Times,* April 2, 2010.

22. "Millennials: A Portrait of Generation Next," Pew Research Center, February 24, 2010.

23. Episode 2138 (11/2/2006), Summary, nofactzone.net.

24. Carlos E. Garcia, "Tipping the (Survey) Scales: How to Set the Multicultural Record Straight," *Quirk's Marketing Research Media,* January 29, 2013.

25. Natalie Zmuda, "Five Questions with Shawn Gensch, Target's Senior-VP Marketing," *Advertising Age,* September 19, 2012.

26. Interview with the author, September 17, 2012.

27. Aronté Bennett, "Minorities Differ Much from Each Other, but Not When Reacting to Ads," adage.com.

28. Cynthia Rodriguez Cano and David J. Ortinau, "Digging for 'Spanish Gold': How to Connect with Hispanic Consumers," *Journal of Advertising Research* 52, no. 3 (September 2012): 322–332.

29. Interview with the author, March 4, 2013.

30. Dominic Patten, "NBC to Finish 5th in Sweeps for First Time; Network Falls behind Univision," Deadline.com, February 21, 2013.

31. Brian Steinberg, "NBC's 44% Plunge Reveals: Football Has Become TV's Addiction," *Advertising Age,* February 18, 2013.

32. Michael McCarthy, "Women's Top-Watched Show Is Not What You Think," *Advertising Age,* September 24, 2012.

33. Interview with the author, September 17, 2012.

34. Interview with the author, October 3, 2012.

Chapter 6

1. Steven G. Wilson, David A. Plane, Paul J. Mackun, et al., "Patterns of Metropolitan and Micropolitan Population Change: 2000 to 2010, U.S. Census Bureau, September 2012.

2. Greg Hinz, "The Hottest Urban Center in the U.S.—Chicago's Mega-Loop," *Crain's Chicago Business,* March 4, 2013.

3. Laurie Volk and Todd Zimmerman, "America's Two Largest Generations Are Headed Downtown," http://www.cnunext.org/icharrette/documents/DemographicImperative.pdf.

4. Matt Carmichael, "Jeff Speck on Walkability: The Livability Interview," March 5, 2013.

5. Matt Carmichael, "The City as a Developer, an Interview with Elizabeth Plater-Zyberk," Livability.com, April 1, 2013.

6. Matt Carmichael, "Real Estate Trends or Home Buying Myths? Trulia's Jed Kolko Has Answers," Livability.com, June 4, 2013.

7. Joel Kotkin and Wendell Cox, "Cities and the Census: Cities Neither Booming nor Withering," Newgeography.com, April 7, 2011.

8. Matt Carmichael, "The City Has Triumphed. Have Your Customers?" adage .com, April 4, 2011.

9. "The Affordability Index: A New Tool for Measuring the True Affordability of a Housing Choice," prepared by the Center for Transit Oriented Development and the Center for Neighborhood Technology as part of the Brookings Institution's Urban Markets Initiative, January 2006.

10. U.S. Census Bureau, 2010 Decennial Census.

11. Kotkin and Cox, "Cities and the Census."

12. "Urban Boom, More and Bigger Cities than Ever," Trendwatching.com, February 2011; and the Central Intelligence Agency WorldFactBook, 2010.

13. Richard Florida, *The Rise of the Creative Class, Revisited* (New York: Basic Books, 2012).

14. Lacey Plache, "Who's Not Buying Cars?" Edmunds.com, June 18, 2012.

15. Joan Naymark, "Target and the American Community Survey," http://www.you tube.com/watch?v=jgsdQxTv5kY.

16. Barbara J. Lipman, "A Heavy Load: The Combined Housing and Transportation Burdens of Working Families," The Center for Housing Policy and the Center for Neighborhood Technology, October 2006.

17. Robert Hickey, Jeffrey Lubell, Peter Haas, and Stephanie Morse, "Losing Ground: The Struggle of Moderate-Income Households to Afford the Rising Costs of Housing and Transportation," The Center for Housing Policy and the Center for Neighborhood Technology, October 2012.

18. Robin Marantz Henig, "What Is It about 20-somethings" *New York Times Magazine,* August 22, 2010.

19. Matt Carmichael, "Joel Kotkin: The Livability Q&A," Livability.com, February 11, 2013.

20. Jonathan Rothwell, "Housing Costs, Zoning, and Access to High-Scoring Schools," Brookings Institution, April 19, 2012.

21. Claudio E. Cabrera, "Study Claims Income Causes More Segregation Than Race," *Black Enterprise,* March 17, 2013.

22. U.S. Bureau of Labor Statistics, "Education Pays," January 28, 2013, http://www .bls.gov/emp/ep_chart_001.htm.

23. Charles Murray, *Coming Apart: The State of White America, 1960–2010* (New York: Crown Forum, 2012).

24. Matt Carmichael, "Behold—Now We Present: The iGen," *Advertising Age,* October 17, 2011.

25. Jason Oliva, "Aging in Place—or Stuck? Boomers May Cause Next Housing Crash," SeniorHousingNews.com, March 18, 2013.

26. David Wasserman, The Cook Political Report, 2012, as cited in http://common cts.blogspot.com/2012/11/final-2012-presidential-election.html.

27. Randy A. Simes, "Cities Won the 2012 Election for President Obama," UrbanCincy.com, November 12, 2012.

28. Ted Marzilli, "Top Red and Blue Brands," YouGov Brand Index, October 23, 2012.

29. Experian Marketing Services, SimmonsLOCAL Spring 2012, an annual survey of U.S. adults conducted through June 2012. Sample sizes vary by DMA, with an average in-tab of 29,000.

30. Interview with the author, December 14, 2012.

31. Ashley Parker, "Romney Blames Loss on Obama's 'Gifts' to Minorities and Young Voters," *New York Times Caucus Blog,* November 14, 2012.

32. CNN Exit Polls, http://www.cnn.com/election/2012/results/race/president.

33. Matt Carmichael, "Nate Silver on Life as a Political Piñata and Pop-Culture Meme," chicagobusiness.com, November 12, 2012 (unpublished excerpts).

34. Joshua Green, "Obama Campaign's Chummy E-Mails Reveal Science in Fund-raising," *BloombergBusinessweek,* November 29, 2012.

35. Michael Scherer, "Inside the Secret World of the Data Crunchers Who Helped Obama Win," Time.com's *Swampland* blog, November 7, 2012.

36. Sasha Issenberg, "How President Obama's Campaign Used Big Data to Rally Individual Voters," *MIT Technology Review,* December 19, 2012.

37. Ibid.

38. Kirsten Dirksen, "Manhattan Shoebox Apartment: A 78-Square-Foot Mini Studio," faircompanies.com, 2012.

Chapter 7

1. U.S. Bureau of Labor Statistics, Consumer Expenditure Survey, 2011.

2. U.S. Census Bureau, Current Population Survey, Annual Social and Economic Supplements, 1960–2012, http://www.census.gov/hhes/families/files/graphics /HH-3.pdf.

3. Haya El Nasser, "Poll: Life's Just Good for Most Older Americans," *USA Today,* August 8, 2012.

4. Jesse Bricker, Arthur B. Kennickell, Kevin B. Moore, and John Sabelhaus, "Changes in U.S. Family Finances from 2007 to 2010: Evidence from the Survey of Consumer Finances," *Federal Reserve Bulletin,* June 2012.

5. U.S. Bureau of Labor Statistics, "Spotlight on Statistics: Older Workers," July 2008.

6. Mark Thompson, "Millions Expect to Outlive Retirement Savings," CNNMoney .com, February 19, 2013.

7. Bureau of Labor Statistics, Consumer Expenditure Survey, 2011.

8. Portions of this chapter originally appeared as part of the American Consumer Project in *Advertising Age* under the headline "Welcome to the Marketing Waste-land," May 28, 2012. Reprinted by permission.

9. U.S. Census Bureau, American Community Survey, 2011.

10. Paul Mackun and Steven Wilson, "Population Distribution and Changes: 2000 to 2010," Census Brief issued March 2011.

11. Tamara Draut and Robert Hiltonsmith, "Social Security: Built to Last for Generations to Come," Demos.

12. Matt Carmichael, "Jeff Speck on Walkability: The Livability Interview," March 5, 2013, Livability.com (unpublished excerpts).

13. Patricia Reaney, "Older Americans Upbeat about Aging, Future: Survey," chicagotribune.com, August 7, 2012.

14. Interview with the author, March 21, 2013.

15. U.S. Census Bureau, Current Population Survey Data on Geographical Mobility/Migration, 2012.

16. David K. Ihrke and Carol S. Faber, "Geographical Mobility: 2005 to 2010," U.S. Census Bureau briefing, December 2012.

17. "Special Report: The World's Oldest Populations," Euromonitor International, September 13, 2011.

18. "China's Population: Only and Lonely," *The Economist*, June 12, 2011.

Chapter 8

1. World Bank, accessed via Google Public Data.

2. "The MetLife Study of Caregiving Costs to Working Caregivers: Double Jeopardy for Baby Boomers Caring for Their Parents," June 2011.

3. David Hirschman, "Cross-Generational Healthcare: How to Communicate with Boomers, Gen-X, and Gen-Y about Their Healthcare Choices," *Advertising Age*, Trend Report, March 25, 2012.

4. Jennifer E. DeVoe et al., "Insurance Plus Access Does Not Equal Health Care: Typology of Barriers to Health Care Access for Low-Income Families," *Annals of Family Medicine* 5, no. 6 (2007): 511–518.

5. Steven Brill, "Bitter Pill: Why Medical Bills Are Killing Us," *Time*, March 4, 2013.

6. Sean Williams, "5 Reasons U.S. Wages Aren't Rising," *The Motley Fool*, November 6, 2012.

7. Susannah Fox, Pew Internet: Health, February 20, 2013.

8. Natalie Zmuda, "Coca-Cola Addresses Obesity Head-on in New Ads," *Advertising Age*, January 14, 2013.

9. Matt Carmichael, "Product Offerings Are Pretty Slim for Obese Consumers: As Americans Grow Larger, Most Marketers Outside Clothing Are Content to Ignore the Demographic," *Advertising Age*, September 20, 2010.

10. Kelly Kennedy, "5% of Patients Account for Half of Health Care Spending," *USA Today*, January 12, 2012.

11. U.S. Census Bureau, Small Area Health Insurance Estimates, 2010.

12. Matt Carmichael, "The Demographics of Health Care: How Do Consumers Budget for Its Costs, and How Do They React When They Get Sick?" *Advertising Age*, April 9, 2012.

13. Based on a custom analysis of the 2011 Spring GfK MRI survey (weighted to population). Data was aggregated at the county-type level using the Patchwork Nation and the Esri's Tapestry segmentations.

14. "IMS Study Forecasts Rebound in Global Spending on Medicines, Reaching Nearly $1.2 Trillion by 2016," IMS Institute for Healthcare Informatics press release, July 12, 2012.

15. U.S. Bureau of Labor Statistics, Consumer Expenditure Survey, Prepublication Interviews, 2005, 2010.

16. Matt Carmichael, "The New Necessities: What Products and Services Can Consumers Not Live Without," *Advertising Age,* November 14, 2011.

17. U.S. Bureau of Labor Statistics, Consumer Expenditure Survey, 2000, 2010.

18. U.S. Bureau of Labor Statistics, "Eldercare in 2011," American Time Use Survey Factsheet.

19. Interview with the author, October 31, 2012.

Chapter 9

1. "Cisco Visual Networking Index: Global Mobile Data Traffic Forecast Update, 2012–2017," Cisco.com, February 6, 2013.

2. Charlie Minato, "ComScore: Mobile Will Force Desktop into Its Twilight in 2014," businessinsider.com, June 14, 2012.

3. Steven Musil, "Mobile Internet Traffic Gaining Fast on Desktop Internet Traffic," CNet.com, December 3, 2012.

4. Annlee Ellingson, "Gotta Have Zooey Deschanel's Bracelet? Fox Has an App for That," *L.A. Biz,* November 14, 2012.

5. "USA SYNC," USA Network, http://mcdn.usanetwork.com/page/syncSuits White.m.htm.

6. The 2013 State of the Union Address (Enhanced Version), WhiteHouse.gov video, 1:00:05, February 1, 2013, http://www.whitehouse.gov/photos-and-video /video/2013/02/12/2013-state-union-address.

7. Matt Carmichael, "When Marketing to Millennials, It's Not All about Digital: The Hovered-Over Generation Likes to Do the Hovering, Too," adage.com, April 11, 2011.

8. "The Demographics of Mobile News," Pew Research Center's Project for Excellence in Journalism, December 11, 2012.

9. "In Changing New Landscape, Even Television Is Vulnerable: Trends in News Consumption: 1991–2012," Pew Research Center for the People & the Press, September 27, 2012.

10. Interview with the author, March 4, 2013.

11. "Wal-Mart Expands iPhone-based Checkout," Chicagotribune.com, March 20, 2013.

12. Interview with the author, November 15, 2012.

13. Matt Carmichael, "They Might Not Get Mail Every Day, but They're Sure to Be on Facebook," *Advertising Age,* March 5, 2012.

14. "Demographics Vary across Social Networks," eMarketer.com, March 11, 2013.

15. Matt Carmichael, "The Demographics of Social Media," adage.com, May 16, 2011.

16. comScore Media Metrix, U.S., December 2012.

17. Interview with the author, September 11, 2012.

18. Eytan Bakshy, "Rethinking Information Diversity in Networks," Facebook.com research, January 17, 2012.

19. Cotton Delo, "Facebook to Partner with Acxiom, Epsilon to Match Store Purchases with User Profiles," *Advertising Age,* February 22, 2013.

20. "New Ways to Reach the Right Audience," Facebook.com release, February 27, 2013.

21. Brian Steinberg, "Addressable TV Ads Might—Finally—Be Ready for Prime Time," *Advertising Age,* September 3, 2012.

22. Andrew Leonard, "How Netflix Is Turning Viewers into Puppets," Salon.com, February 1, 2013.

23. "How Binge Viewing Is Changing the TV Industry," WallStreetJournal.com video blog, July 12, 2012.

24. Frank Newport, "Congress Retains Low Honesty Rating," Gallup.com, December 3, 2012.

25. National Automobile Dealer Association State-of-the-Industry Report, 2012.

26. Daniel Kahneman, *Thinking, Fast and Slow* (New York: Farrar, Straus and Giroux, 2011).

27. J. D. Power and Associates, 2012 U.S. Sales Satisfaction Index Study, November 28, 2012.

28. "The New Automotive Purchase Journey," Starcom MediaVest Group, 2013.

29. J. D. Power and Associates, 2012 U.S. Sales Satisfaction Index Study.

30. Interview with the author, October 3, 2012.

31. Lee Rainie, Aaron Smith, and Maeve Duggan, "Comings and Goings on Facebook," Pew Internet & American Life Project, February 5, 2013.

Chapter 10

1. Tony Dutzik and Phineas Baxandall, "A New Direction, Our Changing Relationship with Driving and the Implications for America's Future," U.S. PIRG Education Fund and Frontier Group, 2013.

2. Amy Chozick, "As Young Lose Interest in Cars, G.M. Turns to MTV for Help," *New York Times*, March 22, 2012.

3. Information provided by IKEA via e-mail.

4. Interview with the author, November 19, 2012.

5. Dutzik and Baxandall, "A New Direction."

6. "Zipcar Survey Reveals Millennials Are More Dependent on Mobile Phones than Cars," Press Release, zipcar.com, February 28, 2013.

7. "Cost of Owning and Operating Vehicle in U.S. Increased Nearly Two Percent According to AAA's 2013 'Your Driving Costs' Study,' Press Release, AAA.com, April 16, 2013.

8. Matt Carmichael, "Pain at the Pump: Running on Empty, Americans Cut Spending," *Advertising Age*, March 29, 2011.

9. Brad Plumer, "Why Aren't Younger Americans Driving Anymore?" washington post.com, April 25, 2013.

10. Benjamin Davis, Tony Dutzik, and Phineas Baxandall, "Transportation and the New Generation," U.S. PIRG Education Fund and Frontier Group, 2012.

11. "Effective Dates of Graduated Licensing Laws," spreadsheet provided to the author, prepared by the Insurance Institute for Highway Safety.

12. Brad Tuttle, "Jalopy Nation? The Average Car on the Road Has Never Been Older," *Time*, January 18, 2012.

13. Bradley Johnson, Kevin Brown, et al., "The Agency Report," *Advertising Age*, April 30, 2012.

14. Interview with the author, March 4, 2013.

15. Matt Carmichael, "Zipcar's Founder Robin Chase: The Livability Interview," Livability.com and unpublished excerpts, February 26, 2013.

16. Mitchell Klein, "More Cities See the Attraction of Bike Lanes," Livability.com, February 15, 2013.

17. Matt Carmichael, "Should Cities Invest in Biking? Why Small Growth Matters," Livability.com, March 11, 2013.

18. "Women in Advertising: The Power Players," *Advertising Age,* September 24, 2012.

19. "Toyota and Teens—Helping Our Newest Drivers Hit the Road Safely," Video on Toyota.com, 2:22, http://www.toyotainaction.com/story/toyota-and-teens -helping-our-newest-drivers-hit-the-road-safely.

Epilogue

1. "Growth & Opportunity Project," Report prepared by the Republican National Committee, 2013, http://growthopp.gop.com.

2. Michael McAuliff, "House Votes to Cut Census Survey Done since Thomas Jefferson," Huffington Post, May 9, 2012.

Appendix I

1. U.S. Census Bureau, American Community Survey, 2011.

2. The county descriptions are reprinted with permission from "Meet Our Families," which was published on adage.com as part of the American Consumer Project, adage.com/consumer.

Appendix II

1. Ryan Felton, "A 12th Stop Might Be in M1 Rail's Future, Pending Federal Approval," *Crain's Detroit Business,* February 14, 2013.

2. We didn't have enough sample size to segment out the heavily rural "Tractor Country" type.

3. Matt Carmichael, "Making the Most of Our Irrationality," adage.com, September 21, 2010.

Index